SOUTHERN ARIZONA
Nature Almanac

SOUTHERN ARIZONA

Nature Almanac

A Seasonal Guide to Pima County and Beyond

ROSEANN BEGGY HANSON

&

JONATHAN HANSON

Illustrations by Jonathan Hanson

The University of Arizona Press Tucson

The University of Arizona Press

First University of Arizona Press paperbound edition 2003

∞ This book is printed on acid-free, archival-quality paper.

Manufactured in the United States of America

08 07 06 05 04 03 6 5 4 3 2 1

Library of Congress Cataloging-in-Publication Data

Hanson, Roseann Beggy.
Southern Arizona nature almanac : a seasonal guide to Pima county and beyond / Roseann Beggy Hanson & Jonathan Hanson ; illustrations by Jonathan Hanson.
p. cm.
Originally published: Boulder, Colo. : Pruett, 1996.
Includes bibliographical references (p.) and index.
ISBN 0-8165-2305-3 (pbk. : alk. paper)
1. Natural history—Arizona—Pima County—Guidebooks. 2. Natural history—Arizona—Guidebooks. 3. Seasons—Arizona—Pima County—Guidebooks. 4. Pima County (Ariz.)—Guidebooks. I. Hanson, Jonathan. II. Title.

QH105.A65 H36 2003
508.791′77—dc21

2002073297

British Library Cataloguing-in-Publication Data
A catalogue record for this book is available from the British Library.

All photographs by the authors

Contents

PREFACE

A natural history must be a vast collection of reliable facts—plus a personality. The facts herein are the best available. Whether the personal touch they bear is acceptable remains to be seen.

—*Ernest Thompson Seton* (1928)

What kind of bird is that? Is that an Emory oak or a white oak? When do hummingbirds arrive for summer? Perhaps—like many of us—you wander the wilds of southern Arizona and idly wonder about such things and ask many questions about the workings of the natural world.

But although you have an interest in natural things, you may be unsure how to tackle bird or plant field guides because they're usually organized in systematic (scientific) order by genus and species. If you can't tell a warbler from a waxwing, you have no idea where to start. Identifying plants can be just as difficult; most guides are organized by flower color, and because most flowering periods are quite short, chances of easy identification are as rare as a Tumamoc globe-berry.

The Southern Arizona Nature Almanac *is a broad-based guide, which we hope will help you identify, learn about, and enjoy the natural history of the region. Each chapter is filled with a month's worth of natural happenings you're likely to experience during that time. As often as possible we distinguish plant communities, such as desertscrub or oak woodland, so that if you know roughly where you are, you can be reasonably sure what you might see. We use the terms plant communities, communities, and habitat interchangeably. And we tried to organize the information to be useful to newcomers to the area, but we hope that old hands and natives will also find it of interest.*

Although the book is focused on Pima County, it can be considered a guide to most of southern Arizona. Pima County is an ideal template and convenient boundary, because its 9,000 square miles contain every life zone from desertscrub to spruce-fir forest—the equivalent of a drive from Mexico to Canada—all within picnic distance of Tucson. This diversity is echoed throughout the southern half of Arizona. Thus, the information presented for the pine forests of the Santa Catalina Mountains should be generally applicable to the same habitat in the Chiricahua or Pinaleno mountains, and many of the species found in Saguaro National Park can also be seen in the Superstition Wilderness near Phoenix; these are just a few examples (though of course there are exceptions to this generality).

In the chapter sections titled Places to Visit, we list specific places you might see the plants, animals, or natural phenomena we've discussed in that chapter. We consciously avoided making these sections "giveaways" to Little-Known-and-Hidden-Spots, believing those places are best discovered personally. Like Pima County itself, our Places to Visit suggestions are intended as examples and starting points for individual exploration. After two half-lifetimes of discovery, we still find new spots every year and have no fear of running out soon. And although both of us were born in Tucson and have studied and written about nature subjects for decades, we were amazed—and quite humbled—to realize how much natural history we still had to learn to compile this guide, which of course but scratches the surface of the diversity of our home.

In each month's chapter essay, we include one of the traditional O'odham names for that month. The Tohono O'odham are the Desert People, longtime dwellers of the Sonoran Desert region that is the heart of Pima County; the Akimel O'odham, the River People, are their close cousins. These names—there can be more than one for each month—reflect the people's close ties to the land, since for most of their history they were hunter-gatherers of the desert's bounties. We offer them our apologies if we have poorly represented their language, for it has only recently been put to paper.

One of the pitfalls of writing a nature guide is the mercurial nature of Nature, and when one multiplies that uncertainty by four or five plant communities, it becomes hazardous to write in stone about blooming dates, migration times, species ranges, and the like. An early spring, a late winter, light rains, or heavy frosts can warp those averages in either direction. And trying to offer reliable weather information is really tempting the gods. We hope the reader will keep in mind that this is a guide, not a bible, and accept the inherent variation in such things.

As the human population of Pima County grows, our wildlands and wildlife, whether in wilderness or in the heart of a city, will become ever more precious. We hope this book contributes in a small way to helping people see those areas with greater appreciation, that they might find their own small way to help preserve the wildness that makes southern Arizona one of the most special places on Earth. To this end, we recall for our readers the words of the great ecologist Edward O. Wilson, who wrote in his seminal 1984 book, Biophilia: *"The more we know of other forms of life, the more we enjoy and respect ourselves. Humanity is exalted not because we are so far above the other living creatures, but because knowing them well elevates the very concept of life."*

—J.H.
—R.B.H.

Acknowledgments

There is an old saying: If you steal information from one person, it's plagiarism; if you steal from two or more, it's research. In writing this book, we've researched the work of innumerable authorities. And although many people helped us with information, and we used many sources, we take full responsibility for any errata.

We owe a tremendous debt to Ruth Carol Cushman, Stephen R. Jones, and Jim Knopf, authors of the Boulder County Nature Almanac, *on whose format this book is based. Their natural history expertise and dedication provided a special inspiration. We would like to offer our deepest thanks to ecologist Mark Dimmitt of the Arizona–Sonora Desert Museum who reviewed the final draft. Truly one of our region's best naturalists, he did a spectacular and thorough job.*

Steve Prchl of Sonoran Arthropod Studies, Yar Petryczyn and Steve Russell of the University of Arizona, and Howard Lawler of the Arizona–Sonora Desert Museum also corrected drafts of sections, and we are indebted to them for their invaluable help.

Gary Paul Nabhan provided much-needed encouragement and inspiration. Jim Harsha and Cassandra Leoncini helped get the whole ball rolling, and we owe them greatly. Many moons ago, Steve and Ruth Russell helped forge the basis for our natural history education; today they continue to be our greatest inspiration for observing, recording, and preserving the wonders of nature.

To those—there are too many to name here—who accompanied us on countless desert and mountain forays, birding and botanizing, rock hounding and herping, we wish to thank you all. And we especially want to thank our parents, Charlie and Terry Beggy and Patricia Mauler, for giving us unheard-of freedom to range widely (perhaps they never knew how *widely) in the desert, canyon, and mountain landscapes around our homes.*

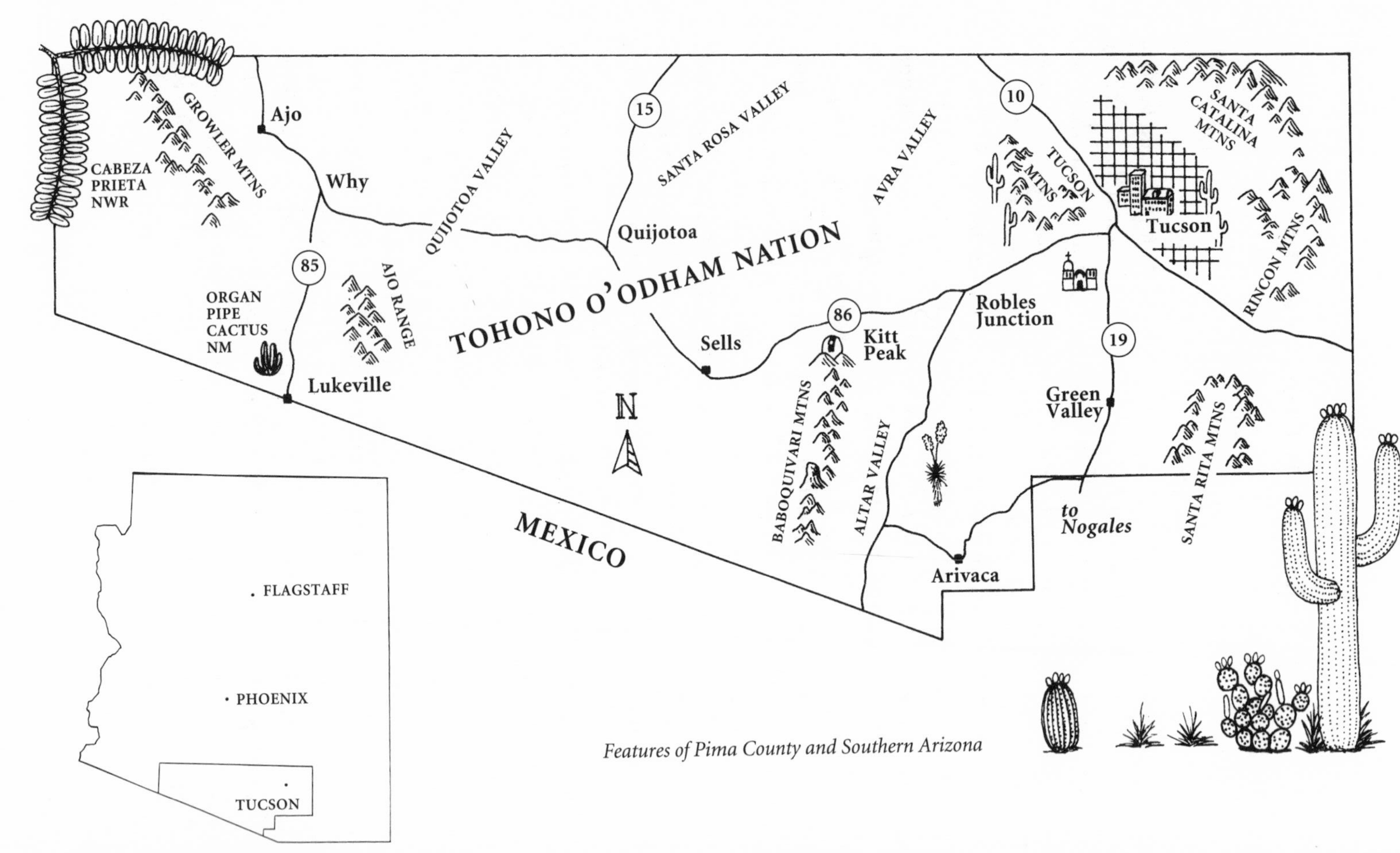

Features of Pima County and Southern Arizona

Exploring the Nature of Pima County and Southern Arizona

It is just after sunrise on a July day in Pima County.

You are in a rocky desert canyon in the Cabeza Prieta National Wildlife Refuge, 125 miles west of Tucson. This desert—one of the driest in North America—sits about 1,000 feet above sea level, at the far western edge of Pima County. The sky is clear, bleached blue, and already it is 80°F in this desertscrub community. Vegetation is sparse and spiny. The earth is dry, dusty. Framed by the mouth of the canyon, jagged cordillera rise several thousand feet from the flat-pan plains; the widely spaced dots are small shrubs and clump grasses. As you crouch behind a blind near a precious pool of water, a desert bighorn sheep cautiously approaches for a drink. Slowly it kneels down and takes its fill, distending its belly with more than five gallons of water—enough to last it nearly a week.

Assuming you could travel as the raven flies, you leave the Cabeza Prieta and head east about 75 miles. Now you are in the middle of Pima County. The land has risen steadily to 3,000 feet above sea level, near the Quijotoa Mountains on the Tohono O'odham Indian Reservation. The desertscrub is noticeably more lush than in the far western deserts, with large mesquite and ironwood trees, saguaro cactuses, grasses, thorn bushes, and many perennial and annual shrubs strewn across the rocky ground; this type of habitat is often called an arboreal desert. The terrain mimics the pattern in the west: nearly flat plains interrupted by mountains—like corrugated cardboard. Scientists use the term basin and range to describe this topography. It is still early morning, and the sun is coaxing the thermometer up to 85°. Though you haven't seen him, nearby on the ground under a dense mesquite tree, a well-camouflaged coyote curls up comfortably to doze through the heat of the day. High overhead, three Harris' hawks circle lazily, scanning the brush for a jackrabbit or cottontail, which they will hunt cooperatively and then share.

Before you continue heading east toward Tucson, you take a slight detour south, near Robles Junction, where arboreal desert gives way to grassland habitat in the Buenos Aires National Wildlife Refuge. Here in south-central Pima County, the elevation is 3,500 feet and the temperature is slightly cooler than in the desertscrub. Lovegrasses and cottontops wash around you in a rolling, golden sea, interrupted by reef-like clumps of stunted mesquites or yuccas. West and east of you, tall mountains, 6,000 or 7,000 feet high, run down toward Mexico, hemming in the grass plains. Suddenly a flash of movement catches your eye and you turn in time to see a small herd of pronghorn antelope coursing across the grassland sea; at 30 miles an hour, these graceful animals are barely exerting themselves. In the blink of an eye they are but specks on the southern horizon.

You continue your journey, passing over the desertscrub plain of Tucson, whose urban fingers spread across the northeastern corner of Pima County. The Santa Catalina Mountains are a dark blue wall enclosing the city's northern edge and you begin to climb their southern flanks, stopping in Molino Basin. At 4,400 feet you are well over 3,000 feet above the desert of Cabeza Prieta. As you breathe deeply, your nostrils take in the verdant moisture of oak woodland: three species of oak trees, red manzanita shrubs, silk-tassel trees, yuccas, grasses, and a burbling creek. At your feet a black-necked garter snake slithers into the creek in search of frogs. Just up the canyon, a troop of raccoon-like coatimundis dozes in a shallow rock cave. Occasionally their long noses twitch as they inspect the breeze, and their long, ringed tails curl comfortably around their rust-colored bodies. By now it is late morning, and cumulus clouds build in the hot convective air currents over the mountains.

You move up the mountain, to 6,000 feet at upper Bear Canyon. It is 10° cooler than it was in the oak woodland. The oaks here are larger and more numerous, so the forest is dark and dense, with huge ponderosa pine trees and bright green walnut and ash trees. You are now in pine-oak woodland. A pine twig full of needles drops to the ground next to you; high above in the ponderosa pine, an Abert's squirrel finishes eating the bark of a small branch it just trimmed. Acorn woodpeckers, flashing unexpected red, dart among the trees. Suddenly sunlight disappears as clouds close in. Thunder rolls up the canyon.

Now you hurry to the very top of the mountain, at 9,000 feet. You've gone from mixed woodland to more sparse-looking coniferous forest, where there is less understory and many tall trees like ponderosa and white pines, corkbark and Douglas firs. Bracken ferns and columbines grow in the gloom of the forest floor. You need a sweater now, because the temperature is 65°. You hear a loud wooden crash over the next rise: a black bear has overturned a log to look for grubs. In the white pine tree across the meadow a brown creeper climbs the trunk in a spiral pattern as if following the red stripe on a barber pole, as it hunts for insects in the bark. When the tiny bird reaches the top, it flies to the base of the next tree to repeat the process. Thunder claps loudly. It begins to rain hard, and you run for cover from the pelting drops and nearby lightning.

In less than half a day, between breakfast and lunch, you have traveled the equivalent of 2,200 miles across the continent, from Mexico to southern Canada. But you never left Pima County.

Such is the varied and unique nature of Pima County, a 9,000-square-mile chunk of Sonoran Desert that takes up almost three-quarters of southern Arizona. The county stretches from nearly the

Colorado River in the west to the San Pedro River in the east and from the Mexican border in the south to a few miles north of Tucson.

Although the region is called the Sonoran Desert, it is hardly a desert in the classic Anglo-Saxon definition of the word. Naturalist Ruth Kirk wrote that the first known outsiders to experience the North American deserts, the Spanish, called the Sonoran and Chihuahuan deserts altiplanos, *or* desiertos, *interchangeably; they found the regions (which were hot in summer, cold in winter) similar to their homelands and described them without emotion. It was the Yankees, the "cultural progeny of Britain's damp greenness," who translated the American southwest's* desierto *into* desert, *a word that for them was synonymous with deserted, wasteland, lifeless. To many people,* desert *still conjures images of hostile, blistering landscapes of sand dunes, snakes, scorpions, and cactus. Although there are dunes and snakes and scorpions and cactus within the Sonoran Desert region, there is also a surprising diversity of plant and animal life that attracts scientists and tourists from the four corners of the earth. From low, indeed harsh deserts to damp, dark montane forests, southern Arizona is one of the most topographically and ecologically diverse places in the world.*

The fact that this area is a desert and not a tropical rainforest is due to a few complex global phenomena. Look at a globe; run your finger along the 30th parallel north of the equator and then along the 30th parallel south of the equator. Your finger will pass through the major deserts of the world, including the Sahara and Kalahari deserts in Africa, the Atacama in South America, the Saudi Arabian, Iranian, and Australian deserts—and the Sonoran Desert in North America. As it spins around its axis, the earth generates surface speeds of about 25,000 miles per hour at the equator and nearly zero at the poles. This huge difference in speeds creates atmospheric circulation patterns that affect world climate; one of the patterns includes two bands of dry and hot descending air over the 30th parallels north and south.

Other circumstances also create deserts. Rainshadow deserts, such as the Great Basin, lie leeward of great ranges of mountains, which steal all the moisture from storms as they travel across the land; and inland deserts, such as the Gobi, are just too far from the coasts to benefit from their moisture. The Sonoran Desert exhibits characteristics of all three world desert types. It slices diagonally from the southwest quarter of Arizona down the Sea of Cortez coast of Sonora, Mexico, to the Rio Yaqui, butts up to the Sierra Madre in the east, and extends west over parts of Baja and up into the lower southeast corner of California.

On a more local level, the great diversity of southern Arizona's plants and animals evolved partly because of distinct regional climate patterns and variations in landforms, such as the surprising mountains that pop up on the desert plains. True desert communities exist from roughly sea level to about 4,000 feet, but what about on those mountains? For every 1,000 feet gained in elevation, the average temperature drops about 4°, and rainfall increases about 4 inches. So while the deserts around Tucson are baking at 110°F on a dry June midday, the mountain peaks are a comfortable and damp 85°F, thus allowing species to thrive that would die if you plucked the hapless creatures off the mountains and deposited them in the desert. The elevational break in heat and additional moisture are the keys to life for the plants and animals that survive in the Sonoran Desert region on mountain ranges surrounded by seas of desert and grassland. This mountain-as-island phenomenon is the origin of the romantic term "sky islands" now popularly used to describe the 42 or so such ranges in the deserts of southern Arizona and northern Mexico.

In *Saguaro: A View of Saguaro National Monument and the Tucson Basin*, botanist Gary Paul Nabhan describes a climb to the top of the Rincon Mountains east of Tucson, where the plants are the same as those found on mountaintops across southern Arizona: "You're surprised how familiar rather than how foreign the peak's plants are to you. You have landed on another island in an archipelago in which each isle is a minor variant of the others, but all are within the same current." The "current" is known botanically as the "Apachian floristic element," after the old Spanish name for this land, *Apachería (land of the Apaches), and includes plants found only in the Southwest. Certain species of yucca, catclaw, cactus, wild bean, and acacia are among those plants that find their way around the mountains of southern Arizona as a current among a greater sea of plants common to the Sierra Madre of Mexico and the U.S. and Canadian Rockies. Plants and animals from the Rocky Mountains (which end at the Mogollon Rim in central Arizona) pop up on southern Arizona mountains, where they meet up with their counterparts from the Mexican Sierra Madre (which end in northern Mexico). Pima County marks a "tension zone," according to Nabhan, where the edges of the two biological fabrics meet, sometimes overlapping, sometimes not. Mexican Apache pine trees are found in the Santa Rita Mountains south of Tucson but not in the nearby Rincons or Santa Catalinas. Species of Rocky Mountain alpine firs are found in the Santa Catalinas but not in the Rincons, and likewise common Rocky Mountain birds such as golden-crowned kinglets and orange-crowned warblers reside in the Catalinas but have ventured no farther south.*

Thus, in Pima County, the natural histories of North America converge and we can say a drive from Tucson to the top of the Santa Catalina Mountains equals one from Mexico to Canada, biologically speaking. You might say that Mother Nature was practicing free trade long before the signing of the North American Free Trade Agreement. ❧ ❧ ❧

CLIMATE

Arizona experiences a bi-seasonal weather regime comprising two seasons of rain and two of drought. To further clarify important life cycles for southern Arizona desert plants and animals, some naturalists have taken to adding another season to our Sonoran Desert year, creating a year that starts with spring (February, March, and April), moves into a severe fore-summer drought (May and June), then summer and our period of greatest rain (July, August and the first half of September), followed by fall and our second and less severe time of drought (late September through early November), and finally winter and our second period of rain (late November through January).

Summer rains, normally a little over half the area's total annual rainfall and incorrectly dubbed "monsoons" (monsoon describes a seasonal wind of the Indian Ocean that blows from the southeast), come from the south. In early summer, the end of June through the middle of August, the storms typically come from the Tropical Atlantic air mass, pulling moisture from the Atlantic Ocean and Gulf of Mexico. These storms are primarily small—less than 3 miles in diameter—intense and convectional in nature, the result of moist tropical air moving over strongly heated and mountainous terrain in northern Mexico and southern Arizona. When the air mass hits the highlands, it rises rapidly, cools, and condenses. This process creates spectacular thunderheads that tower 20,000 feet into the atmosphere. Usually these rains begin with a bang in late June or July, cutting the intense dry heat of May and June as surely as a knife. The

Seasons of the Sonoran Desert

Newcomers to the Sonoran Desert region often bemoan the lack of seasons in the desert. But natives know that the desert is seasonally rich. The Arizona–Sonora Desert Museum describes five seasons:

SPRING: *From February through April, the desert blooms and reproduces after gentle rains that begin in fall and early winter and may continue through March. Temperatures are mild.*

FORESUMMER OR DRY-SUMMER: *May and June are hot and dry, the longest and most severe time of drought for the desert. Temperatures soar into the 100°s and rain is just a memory.*

SUMMER MONSOON: *July through mid-September bring blessed rains and lower temperatures for the desert and a second growing and breeding season for many plants and animals.*

FALL: *Mid-September through early or mid-November marks a second season of drought in the desert, though less severe than May and June. Temperatures drop steadily, as we slide gently into winter.*

WINTER: *Late November through January are chilly in the desert, though warm days pop up now and then. The second rainy season arrives, an important event for the early spring-blooming annual wildflowers, which need moisture during their winter germination period.*

relief to all life-forms is apparent as plants burst forth with new leaves, desiccated amphibians come out of their temporary dry tombs to mate, and humans adopt more pleasant moods. Historically, the Tohono O'odham people, long accustomed to the ways of the Sonoran Desert, began their new year on June 24 with ceremonies to bless their crop seeds and welcome the summer rains, *las aguas,* which water their farm fields. The crops are adapted from tropical crops—squash and corn—and wild desert plants—including tepary beans—that have evolved to grow with a short summer rainy season, and their yield helped sustain the O'odham the rest of the year.

In late summer, the end of August through September, the storms often come from the Tropical Pacific air mass, drawing their moisture from the Pacific Ocean and Gulf of California. These storms are usually larger than those of Atlantic origin and may be fringes of Mexican west coast hurricanes.

The most rainfall ever reported in the state of Arizona occurred in Tucson, July 11, 1878, when two storms converged over the tiny town from opposite directions. More than 5 inches of rain fell in less than two hours. The *Arizona Star* reported the "streets of Tucson leading to the bottom lands were a roaring sea of water . . . [and there was] a vast ocean between Main Street and the mountains on the opposite side of the bottom."

October through early November is usually dry, though on rare occasion there can be unusually wet periods, characterized by days on end of gentle rain. These wet spells are the result of El Niño, a phenomenon affecting world weather patterns that occurs when warm Pacific Ocean currents off South America move farther north than normal, sending out-of-season tropical storms north. When this condition persists for days or weeks at a time, spectacular flooding causing millions of dollars of damage can result.

In winter, a second, less intense season of rain occurs. Westerlies bring Polar Pacific air moisture onto the continent through Washington and Oregon and occasionally central California. Depending on the location of the jet stream, these storms may pass into Arizona. Other storms may originate off Pacific Baja and enter Arizona from the southwest; these generally bring a lot more rain than the storms from the northwest. Because thermal heating is much less intense in the winter, upslope air movement is slow, the clouds are widespread, and the rain is gentle and covers broad areas. But winter rains are much less dependable than summer rains; it is not uncommon for southern Arizona to receive negligible winter precipitation. Our early, pre-December winter rains, *los equipatos* to the native oldtimers, determine the successful germination of spring annual wildflowers.

Although rains may have more effect on native species' evolution and distribution, southern Arizona's most famous weather trait is its infamous fore-summer heat. From May through June, the rest of the country watches while places like Yuma (just west of the Pima County border) rack up 115°+ days with minimal humidity, or Tucson goes for a record of 100 consecutive days of temperatures over 100°. The high temperatures are caused by prolonged periods of cloudless days, which build up the mercury like interest in a savings account. The process is called insolation. Most animals, even reptiles, cope by just ceasing activity during the hottest part of the day.

In June, when the heat builds like a shimmering wall, you'll hear people say, "Yeah, but at least it's a *dry* heat." We say this because our humidity is very low, so body sweat can perform evaporative cooling. When humidity and heat are high, evaporation is slowed and one feels damp and hot—"muggy," we say. Fortunately, we don't experience the latter too often in the desert.

For the purposes of this almanac, we chose three weather station sites to illustrate average and extreme weather patterns for each month at progressively higher elevations. Ajo, in the far western reaches of Pima County, lies at just 1,800 feet elevation and is flanked by some of the hottest, driest desert in North America. The weather data for Tucson was compiled from the station at Tucson International Airport, at an elevation of 2,584 feet; the habitat there is creosote-dominated desertscrub. This site was chosen over other sites in more arboreal desertscrub because its data was the most complete of the numerous Tucson weather station sites. The final station is at 8,800 feet on top of the Santa Catalina Mountains, near the Mount Lemmon summit. Throughout Pima County the weather values for similar elevations should roughly resemble those of our selected stations.

The weather data was compiled from *Arizona Climate: The First Hundred Years* (Sellers, Hill, and Sanderson-Rae, 1985). The data for Ajo includes readings from 1914 through 1982; Tucson International Airport, from 1948 through 1982; and Mount Lemmon, from 1958 through 1982.

COMMUNITIES OF PIMA COUNTY

Scientists have long been classifying "zones" of specific habitat as a means of describing and comparing what they study—desert grassland, oak woodland, coniferous forest, to name a few. In 1890 C. Hart Merriam and his associates published the first list of elevationally arranged zones of plant life for Arizona, mapping and naming communities from 3,000 feet to 13,000 feet on the San Francisco Peaks near Flagstaff. They compared the vertical layering of species on the mountain with a horizontal trip from Arizona to Canada. During the next century, these initial zones were developed by Merriam and others into a system of life zones and corresponding biotic communities for Arizona still in use and being refined today.

For the *Southern Arizona Nature Almanac* we define and describe six communities. Desertscrub is a community of the Lower Sonoran life zone; desert grassland and oak woodland are communities of the Upper Sonoran life zone; pine-oak woodland is in the Transition life zone; and mixed coniferous forest is a community of the Canadian life zone. We also use riparian woodland to describe communities of broadleaf deciduous plants along perennial water courses in both Lower and Upper Sonoran life zones. Each community is named for the plants that best characterize and thus define the myriad components that make a habitat: moisture, soil, temperature, sun exposure, elevation, and so on. Plants, not animals, are used as defining elements because they are most "stuck" with the environmental factors dealt out by Nature, whereas animals can more easily adapt to changing environments by moving out of town, so to speak.

By referring to the communities as often as possible in the text, we hope to make it easier for all readers—particularly beginner naturalists—to identify the plants and animals in the landscape. If you can identify the community you are in, then you can use the information in the almanac to determine what it is you're likely to be seeing at a particular time of year. For example, it is December, a warm, clear day, and you're hiking through lovely oak woodland; ahead of you a flock of 10 or 15 small birds flits in and out of shrubs, always just out of clear sight but tinkling like little bells. Because you know you are in oak woodland, you can be reasonably sure they are black-chinned sparrows; if, however, you are hiking through desert grassland, the birds are probably rufous-winged sparrows. It is just a matter of matching proper habitat and season.

The following community descriptions are very broad and are intended to be a starting point for recognizing community types. The communities are characteristic of southern Arizona habitats. Elevations and plants will vary with the slope exposure; for example, a habitat on a south-facing slope will extend higher up the mountain than on a north-facing slope because of increased sun exposure. The animals listed are common residents (present all year or at least most of the year); all species listed are only examples, and the lists should not be considered thorough. At the end of each description, we list a specific site of that community type along the Catalina Highway, which climbs from the northeast side of Tucson 26 miles and 6,000 feet to the top of the Santa Catalina Mountains, a journey described at the beginning of this chapter.

Desertscrub

(Approximate elevation:
100 feet to 4,000 feet)

Pima County desertscrub is mostly the variety known as Arizona Upland,* a rich mixture of trees and shrubby understory, large columnar cactuses, short or bushy cactuses, grasses, and annuals.

PREDOMINANT PLANTS: In most dry situations, foothill palo verde, ironwood, saguaro, and chainfruit cholla are common large trees and shrubs; in moister situations, blue palo verde, mesquite, catclaw, desert willow, and desert hackberry are common. Smaller shrub understories are commonly dominated by a single species such as triangle-leaf bursage, creosote, jojoba, or brittlebush. Smaller cactuses include barrel, prickly pear, hedgehog, and pincushion.

COMMON RESIDENT BIRDS: Gambel's quail, mourning dove, greater roadrunner, black-throated sparrow, Gila woodpecker, northern (gilded) flicker, cactus wren, Harris' hawk, curve-billed thrasher, phainopepla, northern cardinal, and pyrrhuloxia.

---

*Scientists recognize six subdivisions of desert communities in the Sonoran Desert: Lower Colorado River Valley, Arizona Upland, Plains of Sonora, Central Gulf Coast, Vizcaíno, and Magdalena. Only Arizona Upland and Lower Colorado River Valley are found in Pima County and in the United States, and the latter community is limited to the far western reaches of the county west of Ajo. We refer to this area as the "west deserts." There is a small patch of Lower Colorado River Valley desert in Avra Valley, close to Tucson.

Other common resident animals: Mojave rattlesnake, western diamondback rattlesnake, common kingsnake, gopher snake, zebra-tailed lizard, desert spiny lizard, desert horned lizard (horny toad), coyote, antelope and black-tailed jackrabbits, desert cottontail rabbit, Harris' antelope squirrel and round-tailed ground squirrel, Merriam's kangaroo rat, rock and Bailey's pocket mice, cactus mouse, white-throated wood (pack) rat, kit fox, and javelina.

Example of desertscrub community along the Catalina Highway: Milepost marker 0; 2,900 feet elevation; park in the small pullout on the west side of the highway.

Desert grassland

(Approximate elevation:
3,500 feet to 5,000 feet)

Grasslands vary with elevation and soil types, from nearly pure grass slopes to rolling hills where yuccas and cactuses share space with the grasses, runty mesquite trees, and other shrubs.

Predominant plants: Where soil is deep and erosion limited, grass species such as the gramas (black, blue, sideoats, slender, and hairy), plains lovegrass, cottongrass, and three-awn dominate. On rocky foothill slopes, however, competition from other species is greater and grasses such as red three-awn and fluff grass are interspersed with ocotillo, sotol (desert spoon), shindagger, Engelmann prickly pear, mesquite (shrub form), and cane cholla.

Common resident birds: Grasshopper sparrow, vesper sparrow, lark sparrow, house finch, American kestrel, and horned lark.

Other common resident animals: Mule deer, Mojave rattlesnake, western diamondback rattlesnake, common kingsnake, gopher snake, coachwhip snake, antelope and black-tailed jackrabbits, banner-tailed kangaroo rat, desert cottontail rabbit, Harris' antelope squirrel and round-tailed ground squirrel, silky and desert pocket mice, southern grasshopper mouse, western box turtle, coyote, and javelina.

Example of desert grassland community along the Catalina Highway: Milepost marker 4.5; 4,300 feet elevation; park at the Molino Canyon overlook parking area; the grasslands are across the road to the west.

Riparian woodland

(Approximate elevation:
2,000 feet to 6,000 feet)

Riparian means "of, pertaining to, or situated on the bank of a river," but when the word is used to describe a community its definition is a little more broad. A riparian community is dependent on the existence of perennial, intermittent, or ephemeral surface or subsurface water, often characterized by broad-leaved deciduous trees and a shrubby understory. Desert washes, lined with mesquite, palo verde and ironwood trees and thornshrubs, can also be considered riparian communities, although when we speak of "riparian woodlands" we are generally referring to broad-leaved deciduous plant communities.

PREDOMINANT PLANTS: The "big five" riparian trees in southern Arizona include species of cottonwood, willow, sycamore, ash, and walnut. In upper elevations: narrowleaf cottonwood, Texas mulberry, Arizona alder, southwestern chokecherry, boxelder, and Rocky Mountain maple. In lower elevations, Frémont cottonwood, Arizona sycamore, western soapberry, velvet ash, and netleaf hackberry.

COMMON RESIDENT BIRDS: Black phoebe, acorn woodpecker, ladder-backed woodpecker, Abert's towhee, canyon wren, black-tailed gnatcatcher, and vermilion flycatcher.

OTHER COMMON RESIDENT ANIMALS: In the water, whirligig beetle, predaceous diving beetle, water strider, and Sonoran mud turtle; around the water, dragonfly, damselfly, canyon treefrog, red-spotted toad, and black-necked garter snake. Other animals common to riparian corridors include raccoon, coatimundi, rock squirrel, and striped skunk.

EXAMPLE OF RIPARIAN WOODLAND COMMUNITY ALONG THE CATALINA HIGHWAY: Milepost marker 4.5; 4,000 feet elevation; stop at the Molino Canyon overlook parking area.

Oak woodland

(Approximate elevation:
4,000 feet to 6,000 feet)

Dominated by a confusing array of oak species, this habitat is usually an open woodland interspersed with grasses, shrubs, succulents, and cactuses.

PREDOMINANT PLANTS: Emory oak is often the most dominant tree, along with Mexican blue and Arizona white oaks, alligator juniper, and border piñon; mountain yucca, manzanita, wait-a-minute bush, sotol, and bunchgrass are common shrub and grass species.

COMMON RESIDENT BIRDS: Dark-eyed junco, acorn woodpecker, rock wren, gray-breasted jay, bridled titmouse, and bushtit.

OTHER COMMON RESIDENT ANIMALS: White-tailed deer, western diamondback rattlesnake, gopher snake, Sonoran mountain kingsnake, mountain short-horned lizard, cliff chipmunk, gray squirrel, rock squirrel, and porcupine.

EXAMPLE OF OAK WOODLANDS COMMUNITY ALONG THE CATALINA HIGHWAY: Milepost marker 5.5; 4,370 feet elevation; park in the lot near the restrooms at Molino Basin campgrounds.

Pine-oak woodland

(Approximate elevation: 6,000 feet to 7,000 feet)

The principal identifiers of pine-oak woodland are mid-elevation large pines and several species of oaks and junipers. An understory of deciduous species as well as succulents and cactuses is common.

PREDOMINANT PLANTS: Mexican blue oak, silverleaf oak, Arizona oak, Emory oak, Gambel oak, Arizona madrone, ponderosa pine, Chihuahua pine, Arizona walnut, alligator juniper, buckbrush, locust, mountain yucca, woodland sumac, bunchgrass, and blue grama grass.

COMMON RESIDENT BIRDS: Bridled titmouse, acorn woodpecker, hermit thrush, pygmy nuthatch, gray-breasted jay, and rufous-sided towhee.

OTHER COMMON RESIDENT ANIMALS: Cliff chipmunk, gray squirrel, rock squirrel, gopher snake, Sonoran mountain kingsnake, Madrean alligator lizard, mountain short-horned lizard, striped skunk, and black bear.

EXAMPLE OF PINE-OAK WOODLAND COMMUNITY ALONG THE CATALINA HIGHWAY: Milepost marker 12; 6,000 feet elevation; park in the General Hitchcock campground lot.

Mixed coniferous forests

(Approximate elevation: 7,000 feet to 10,000 feet)

Stands of mixed-species tall conifers (cone-bearing plants) indicate this habitat. There is less understory than in the lower-elevation pine-oak woodlands. At slightly lower elevations ponderosa pine forests are common in our mountain ranges, dominated largely by the one species. To simplify matters, we do not break out this community from coniferous forests, as most of the animal species are the same for mixed coniferous forests and ponderosa pine forests.

PREDOMINANT PLANTS: Dominated by Douglas fir and white fir, southwestern white pine, golden aspen, corkbark fir, ponderosa pine; in moist areas, bigtooth maple, Rocky Mountain maple, box elder, bracken fern, red-osier dogwood, snowberry, and columbine.

Common resident birds: Mountain chickadee, hermit thrush, yellow-eyed junco, white-breasted nuthatch, Steller's jay, and northern (red-shafted) flicker.

Other common resident animals: Abert's squirrel, cliff chipmunk, mountain short-horned lizard, and black bear.

Example of mixed coniferous forest community along the Catalina Highway: Milepost marker 26; 9,000 feet elevation; except when ice or snow covers the top of the mountain, you should be able to drive to the top. In the winter, you can park at the ski area and walk the road beyond the locked gate.

INCREASING YOUR SEEING POWER

Arizona is home to 137 species of mammals, 434 different birds, 48 snakes, 41 lizards, 22 amphibians, and thousands of arthropods. The addition of a stunning 3,370 species of plants gives us many lifetimes of discovery. If you want to augment your wild explorations with more formal education, at all times of the year you'll find natural history workshops, classes, trips, and volunteer opportunities that pertain to everything from bugs to whole ecosystems. Appendix 6 lists some helpful local resources. Also in Appendix 6 you'll find listings for conservation groups and land management agencies, including nongovernment organizations, sources for nature-watching equipment, and suggested periodicals and books.

Although spring wildflower "chasing" and casual plant identification are popular pastimes among those of us who walk the wildlands, trying to catch more than a flash of an animal's hind end is very difficult, to say the least. Here are some tips that may increase your chances of quality wildlife encounters, be they with birds, reptiles, or mammals.

When: Dawn and dusk are the best times to "hunt" wildlife. Nocturnal (animals active primarily at night, such as bats), diurnal (animals active in the daytime, such as most birds), and crepuscular (animals active primarily around dawn and sunset, such as deer) are all more likely to be seen at the beginning and end of a day. Most animals rest at midday.

Where: Situate yourself on the edge of open areas, so that viewing opportunities are increased (dense habitats such as streamside thickets or mountain chaparral are good hiding places for animals, thus they make for difficult clear viewing). Another opportunity-enhancer is to choose a site where two habitats converge, such as a grassland near a riparian corridor. The convergence of habitat increases the numbers of species likely to be passing your observation point.

How: Most modern humans have a compulsion to go somewhere. But we miss so much when we zoom along a hiking trail toward a pre-chosen goal; our powers of observation diminish and animals can easily hear us and quickly hide or leave. Choose a suitable site and stay put with a pair of binoculars. Wear natural-colored, dull, and quiet clothing—birds have excellent color vision. Avoid wearing scents such as aftershave, perfume, even bug repellent or sunscreen (wear a hat, long-sleeved shirts, and pants)—most mammals have keen senses of smell. With that in mind, stay downwind of your chosen observation area. Here are some tips for using your binoculars to the best advantage: a tripod mount is a terrific tool; slowly scan an area methodically (left to right, top to bottom), looking over the entire field of view for something that stands out as irregular among the vegetation (an ear, a straight line, a glossy coat, a tail); move your eyes around in the binocular field rather than the binoculars. Be patient. A few minutes won't do it; many successful deer hunters report using such techniques and spotting 20 or more deer in a day.

Do not: Bait animals for viewing or feed them to keep them around for pictures or to try to "pet" them. Each year more than a dozen Arizona black bears are killed by "human kindness." Deer in Grand Canyon National Park must be killed when they eat too much nondigestible human material, which settles in their stomachs and causes them to slowly starve. Close encounters with humans and human food are nearly always detrimental to animals. Never touch or remain near baby animals; never harass any animal.

TREADING LIGHTLY

A thing is right when it tends to preserve the integrity, stability, and beauty of the biotic community. It is wrong when it tends otherwise.

—Aldo Leopold (1949)

One of the great conundrums faced by naturalists is the impact we make even as we seek out those things we love. It's tempting to think that as individuals, our impact is not significant in the grand scheme of things. But one set of

Africanized Bees

Everyone who explores the nature of Pima County should be aware that Africanized honey bees have colonized southern Arizona and do pose a slight risk; several people and animals have been killed by Africanized swarms. Experts offer these tips: (1) Avoid wild bee hives—if you happen too close to one, move away slowly, *and don't swing at any bees that approach you. (2) Avoid wearing scents but do wear light-colored clothing. (3) Keep dogs with you because they can bring angry bees to your position. (4) If all precautions fail and you are attacked, by all means run, covering your head as much as possible. Adults can run faster and farther than bees will fly. If you are stung, remove the stingers by scraping them off with a blade or fingernail; stingers have poison sacs attached to them and will pump more venom, especially if squeezed. Report any suspected Africanized bee attacks to the Arizona Department of Agriculture. Although bees are most active in spring and summer, in Pima County they may be active throughout the year.*

footprints might lead another explorer over the same path, and another, and another, until a trail is born; erosion sets in and a gully is born; and so on. The Wyoming-based National Outdoor Leadership School led the way decades ago with its Leave No Trace set of outdoor ethics. Gentle reminders teach us the best ways to walk the land and leave nary a trace of our passing.

Plan Ahead and Prepare: Knowing the "lay of the land" will help you choose the best trails and campsites. Call the proper land agencies for information before you leave home.

Make sure you have the equipment you need to take care of yourself if something goes wrong; a hiker who lacks proper clothing to stay warm in an unexpected storm, for example, will probably build a fire, which leaves scars and destroys resources.

Concentrate Use in Resistant Areas: In desert areas, try to concentrate your heaviest use on resistant surfaces such as sand or rock. If possible, camp in already established sites.

Try not to trample delicate desert vegetation; plants rebound less quickly in arid environments. Never move rocks and vegetation litter to "make" a campsite.

On existing trails, walk single file inside the use zone. Shortcutting causes erosion. When traveling off-trail, stick to durable surfaces; groups of two or more should spread out, taking different paths to avoid creating a permanent "trail" others might follow.

Avoid Places Where Impact Is Just Beginning:, Avoid lightly impacted trails or areas where others have freshly camped.

Protect and Conserve Water Resources: Water is a finite resource no matter where we are in southern Arizona; carry as much as you'll need if possible.

Camp at least 200 feet (70 adult paces) from water.

Avoid polluting water sources with dishes or bodies (body oils, sunscreens, and lotions contaminate limited water supplies).

Pack It In—Pack It Out: Pack out all inorganic as well as organic waste from cooking.

Properly Dispose of What You Can't Pack Out: Shallow catholes are the preferred method for solid human waste disposal in the desert. Choose a site that gets maximum sun exposure (to help kill pathogens, many of which can survive up to a year in buried human waste) at least 200 feet from water (70 adult steps). The cathole should be re-covered with soil. Use toilet paper sparingly (white, non-perfumed) and if possible pack it out. Do not burn (too much fire danger). Consider leaves (just not poison ivy!) instead.

Leave What You Find: Allow others the same sense of discovery you enjoyed by leaving archaeological artifacts, rocks, plants, and other natural objects as you find them. Consider taking up photography or sketching to record your finds.

Use Fire Responsibly: It's always best not to build a campfire in the desert where wood is scarce and scars are permanent. If you must build a fire, do not use rocks to make a fire ring; instead, make the fire on a mound of mineral soil that you have built up on a tarp or fire pan (to keep the heat from sterilizing the soil). When you are ready to leave, crush and widely scatter the cold ashes with your hands. Pack out anything that can't be crushed and scattered.

Keep the Wilderness Wild: Wear natural-colored clothing and equipment to avoid visual "noise."

Avoid speaking loudly and making loud noises.

Keep pets quiet and on leashes or leave them at home with a bone.

For more information or to order the excellent booklets of the National Outdoor Leadership School (NOL) "Leave No Trace Outdoor Skills & Ethics: Desert & Canyon Country," and the bilingual "Minimum-Impact Camping Techniques for Desert & Coastal Mexico," call (800) 332-4100 (other Leave No Trace Skills & Ethics booklets include "Rocky Mountains," "Southeastern States," "Backcountry Horse Use," "Western River Corridors," "Temperate Coastal Zones and Pacific Northwest"). See appendixes for other resources, including land agencies, conservation groups, publications, equipment sources, tips on keeping field notebooks, additional species lists and tables, and a glossary.

Snow caps the upper Molino Basin in the Santa Catalina Mountains

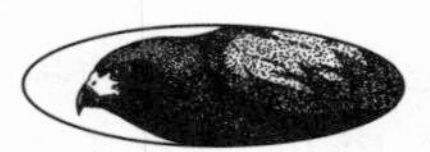

january

LIT BY A *lazy sun and visited semiregularly by weepy, lead-colored clouds that shuffle in from the west like pensioners to church, January seems like such a mellow month. When we were kids, we thought January dragged by. It seemed so boring. Short days meant less time to explore our desert and canyon haunts, plants seemed leafless and dead, and the exciting animals (at least to eight-year-old males) like reptiles were tucked away in burrows and rock crevices, unavailable for our amusement.*

Decades later, we now find that January is actually a very busy month in the wilds, though much of the activity is either hidden or very subtle. In the desertscrub and grasslands, spring is just around the corner, and although we humans might have lost our ability to sense its arrival, the plants and animals are well aware. Far from "dead," the landscape fairly vibrates with the energy of impending spring.

Take a close look at a saguaro during the month of January. Its body language will clearly tell you what it's up to: its accordion outer skin will expand, as its insides bulge with as much winter rain as it can suck up; some saguaros actually gain a spare tire partway up the trunk in very wet years. All the succulents guzzle water this month. Woody plants, the trees and shrubs like mesquites and catclaw, are surreptitiously using winter moisture to aid in extending their roots and preparing to set new leaves or flower buds. In lower desert riparian areas we've seen Frémont cottonwoods send out their first tender leaves and blossoms by mid-January. The River People, the Akimel O'odham, call January Auppa Heosig Mashath, *"moon of the cottonwood blooming."*

If you're lucky enough to witness a wintertime flash flood in one of the dry washes (a common but short-lived occurrence when hard rains melt a great deal of snow in the high country), you'll see yet another important event for desert life. From the surrounding desert, floodwaters carry rich nutrients and seeds, which are then deposited along the sides of the washes. Flash floods in temperate seasons (mainly summer but also mild winters) are important for many desert plants. Their seeds depend on abrasion of the hard seed coats to aid in germination. They are carried along in the roiling rock and sand of hundreds of flooding little arroyos, become scarified, and as the floodwaters recede, are conveniently deposited in moist banks where their new roots can take advantage of the rich soil and moisture.

But perhaps the biggest event of this month is silent. All across the desertscrub millions of vibrant green annual wildflower and grass seedlings, which germinated in November and December and have been "idling" until now, are thrusting their cotyledons skyward and gulping as much sun and water as they can. In about a month they will begin splashing the landscape with shades of crimson, gold, violet, white, and azure.

The high mountains are still locked in winter, but they contribute greatly to the desert winterscape: a foot or more of snowpack weeps gently into the gullies and streams, the clear, cold water dancing down the rock canyons and out onto the grasslands and desertscrub. Throughout January, the desert rings with the song of water tinkling past mesquites and saguaros, a gift from the mountains. Tanque Verde Creek, fed by the Rincon Mountains, often runs many miles into the desert before it sinks into the warm sand. The Catalina Mountains give us Bear and Sabino creeks, which merge and might run through the heart of Tucson before the water recedes; and Sutherland Wash in Catalina State Park, which feeds an unusually low-elevation oak woodland in addition to a mesquite grove known as a bosque, adds its bounty to Cañada del Oro Wash.

Along these ribbons of mountain water you'll find some mountain refugees. Many bird species that breed in summer among the conifers and mixed woodlands of the sky islands spend their winters foraging and stoking up on the plant and insect bounty of lowland streamsides. Tiny sage-colored birds with white partial eye rings, two white wing bars, and a little red cap are ruby-crowned kinglets. Sparrow-sized gray birds with a bright rufous back and dark eyes are gray-headed juncos, a southern Rockies race of the dark-eyed junco. Yellow-rumped warblers are black, white, and yellow; they forage conspicuously in the outer canopies of the deciduous trees. You might also see lark sparrows scratching on the ground; they have rust, white, and black racing stripes on their heads. They summer in high grasslands and woodlands.

Breeding begins in earnest for many desert dwellers in January. Harris' hawks, dark brown and copper raptors with conspicuous white bars on their rumps and tails, mate during this month. Ubiquitous desert packrats (white-throated woodrats) are beginning their long breeding season, which will last through August. And curve-billed thrashers, members of the mimic thrush family, are conspicuously singing their melodious territory songs as they prepare to nest later in the month, continuing through March.

In the oak woodlands and grasslands Coues' white-tailed deer are mating, and tucked away in their mountain dens black bears begin bearing an average of two cubs this month and next. The tiny creatures, which will emerge as rowdy cubs in early spring, weigh only half a pound and will nurse and grow as the mother continues her winter semihibernation.

Although the stirrings of spring charge the air, don't be surprised if January throws a curveball: within one week in January, we lounged in a mid-town Tucson cafe watching snow flurries pour

JANUARY WEATHER

	Sunrise	Sunset	Avg. Relative Humidity/Tucson
January 1	7:25 MST	5:30 MST	5 a.m. 62%
January 30	7:18 MST	5:56 MST	5 p.m. 32%

Stations	Ajo	Tucson	Mt. Lemmon
Station Elevation	(1,800 ft.)	(2,584 ft.)	(8,800 ft.)
January Averages			
Max. temperature	64°F	63.7°F	49.5°F
Min. temperature	41.2°F	38.1°F	20.9°F
Precipitation	.75 in.	.86 in.	4.43 in.
Snow	.02 in.	.31 in.	10.5 in.
# days 100° & over	0	0	0
# days 32° & under	2	6	31
# days precip.>.01"	3	5	5
January Extremes			
Max. Temperature	85°F (1971)	87°F (1953)	65°F (1959)
Min. Temperature	17°F (1937)	16°F (1949)	-4°F (1960)
Max. Snow/month	1.0 in. (1937)	4.7 in. (1949)	19.0 in. (1962)
Max. Snow/1 day	1.0 in. (1937)	3.5 in. (1949)	12.0 in. (1960)
Max. Precip./month	2.9 in. (1949)	2.94 in. (1979)	8.11 in. (1982)
Max. Precip./1 day	1.83 in. (1979)	1.08 in. (1960)	2.96 in. (1962)

January Notes

In one week in a recent January, snow flurries poured from the sky; the following weekend, the mercury climbed to 80°F. In January, you never know what you're going to get. You can count on some cold rainshowers for about two to five days in the deserts, and snow in the mountains. It will freeze every night up in the mountains, and only about six nights in the deserts. Extremes are the norm if anything can be considered normal for January: in 1913, low-lying areas in the Tucson valley reported unofficial temperatures of 0°F, while in 1971 the weather station at the University of Arizona reported a high of 90°F. And sometimes in January unusually heavy rains in the deserts or warm rains in the mountains (melting snowpack) can also precipitate serious flooding.

For information about data sources for these listings, see the Climate section of the chapter Exploring the Nature of Pima County and Southern Arizona.

from a lead-colored sky and swirl in drifts on the windshields of parked cars; two days later we hiked a desert trail under a sun as warm as a bakery.

We celebrate January with as many desert hikes as possible, such as along Tanque Verde Creek, but we don't hesitate to head up the mountains to enjoy "real" winter, as it is called by our New England friends. Because midwinter is the best time for astronomical viewing, we try to visit Kitt Peak National Observatory in the Quinlan Mountains on a public viewing evening. And a special treat awaits those who travel to the southeastern corner of Arizona to see the spectacular flocks of sandhill cranes, Canada geese, and snow geese on their wintering grounds around the great shallow Willcox Playa.

FLORA

Creosote: A Ground-Zero Xerophyte

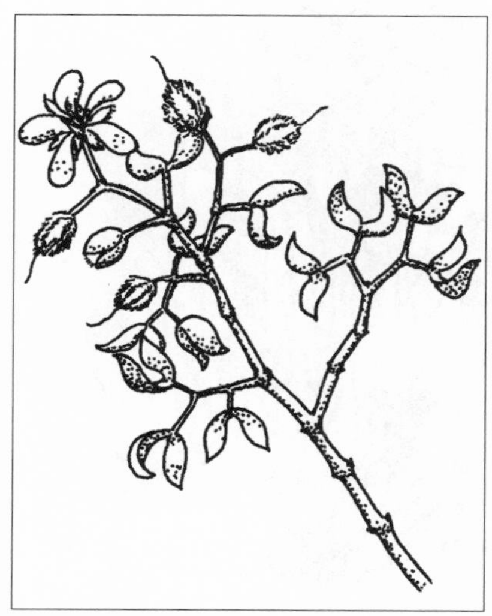

It grows where nothing else will—great broad valleys full, carpeting the baked intermountain pans of the Cabeza Prieta National Wildlife Refuge and the lower Colorado River Valley in western Arizona. Scientists once thought creosote bushes exuded some sort of toxin that prevented the growth of other shrubs. Nope. *Larrea tridentata* is simply the only perennial plant willing to endure the most hostile stretches of North America's four deserts—the lowest and driest and hottest.

At the Yucca Flats proving ground in Nevada, where numerous aboveground nuclear tests were performed in the 1950s and 1960s, creosote was the first plant to grow back through the blasted crust of the soil, astounding radiation-suited scientists whose clicking Geiger counters had convinced them no such regeneration would happen for years. Apparently, shrugging off a few million roentgens of radioactivity was no problem for a plant adapted to decade-long droughts and 160° ground temperatures in the summer.

Creosote is a wonderfully successful and utterly unloved resident of millions of acres in the Southwest. Noxious resins secreted by its

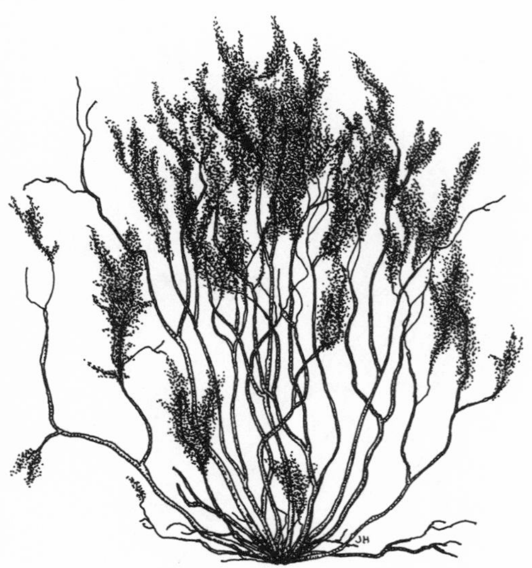

leaves render the plant worthless as cattle browse; removal of this coating can turn the plant into a nutritious feed, but the process is economically impractical. Even hard-core desert rats spend little time exploring the unarguably monotonous habitat that seems to host creosote and little else.

Many desert plants boast specialized adaptations for life in an arid land: they have trunks and stems that contain chlorophyll and can photosynthesize, thus saving water that would be lost through large leaves; or they drop all their leaves during periods of drought, standing dormant through the dry months. Creosote appears to possess none of these features, although the resins that coat its leaves do inhibit evaporation—in hotter conditions, the plant produces more resin. If conditions get tough, creosote will drop some leaves, or if times are extremely hostile, say after a year or so without water, they will drop all their leaves; but we've never seen a creosote without most of its foliage, though it may be dulled and brown from dust and drought.

Creosote is not only tough; it is durable. Although it bears flowers, the shrub often reproduces by sending out cloned (genetically identical to the parent) shoots, a process called vegetative reproduction. Because these shoots radiate from the plant, the result is a ring-shaped creosote. Parts of several huge rings in the Mojave Desert have been estimated by carbon dating to be more than 10,000 years old. These plants represent the

Above, *Creosote bush: a tough and durable plant*

original "pioneers" that settled the newly formed desert areas after the last ice age.

Of course, *L. tridentata* is not completely asocial—it mixes with many other species in the more benign parts of its range. It can be found well into the lush desert-scrub of the foothills, looking fat and happy under a full 12 inches of annual rainfall. Also, although four-footed herbivores may find it distasteful, creosote supports a variety of smaller animals. One species of grasshopper and a walking stick have become so adapted to digesting the waxy leaves that they exist solely in creosote bushes. Desert iguanas clamber up the stems to gorge on the small yellow flowers that burst forth in spring, and many kinds of bees gather the nectar and pollen of creosote, including almost two dozen species that gather it from no other plants.

Though the plant itself may garner little affection from humans, there is one aspect of it that all desert dwellers love—the smell. If the merest trace of rain graces the lowlands, the air is suddenly suffused with a heady aroma, a pungent perfume emanating from the moistened resins on the creosote's leaves. It is elixir to the soul of a native and soon becomes so to any but the most olfactorily disadvantaged immigrant.

FAUNA

Listen to the Mockingbird

Why do mockingbirds sing? More precisely, why do they spend so much time and energy learning and mimicking the songs of other birds—even other animals, even machinery?

Scientists like to find rational explanations for behavior. When an animal engages in a particular activity, the biologist looks for an evolutionary advantage to that activity; specifically, they ask how the activity helps the animal to survive and produce offspring. It is axiomatic that all behavior has some such root purpose, at least among the lower animals (who could explain bowling in terms of survival value?). Occasionally, though, we hit stumbling blocks. Like mockingbirds.

Generally, birds sing for two reasons: to attract mates and to mark their territory. The mockingbird's song certainly serves both these purposes, but it goes so over the top as to defy logic. Several theories have attempted to nail down dispassionate answers to the question. One proposes that the varied song serves as a measure of the age and experience-cum-success of the male. In effect this theory says that if he has so much time to devote to learning new songs, he must be strong and well-fed—and thus a good choice for a mate.

Could be. However, no less an authority than *The National Audubon Society Encyclopedia of Birds* says that the function of the mimicry is "difficult to perceive." And in 1956 W. H. Thorpe, the author of *Birdsong—The Biology of Vocal Communication and Expression in Birds*, came right out and said it: there appears to be an element of "play" in mimic-song.

Whatever the reason, there is no denying the exuberance of a male mockingbird in full showoff mode. One was heard to mimic the songs of 55 different species of birds in an hour; another went through 32 species in ten minutes. Thrown in with this bewildering mix is likely to be the barking of dogs or the repetitive squeak of farm machinery. One individual in heavily photographed Yosemite reportedly mastered the sound of a motor-driven 35mm camera.

In January male mockingbirds will be vigorously defending their turf and advertising for mates throughout the desertscrub and in towns. They will sing from atop trees and cactus and telephone poles, regularly making the rounds of their territory. When a male and female have paired, they will share in building a nest in a tree or cactus. Beginning in March, the female will usually lay four or five bluish-brown eggs, which will hatch a mere 12 days later; the young will be fledged and ready to leave the nest less than 2 weeks after that. This rapid development gives the adults time to rear two or three broods in one season.

Other members of *Mimidae*, the mimic thrush family, occurring in Pima County include curve-billed thrashers (see December's section on resident birds), sage thrashers, Bendire's thrashers, and crissal thrashers.

Ménage à Trois

We all love the sight of a hawk soaring high on a thermal on a cloudless day. But three hawks flying in formation is even better. That's how you'll often see Harris' hawks, one of only two species of hawk in the world that practice cooperative breeding (the other is the Galapagos hawk).

A breeding pair of *Parabuteo unicinctus* often have a "helper" bird (usually one, but sometimes two or three), which assists the alpha pair in hunting and defending the nest. This helper is most often a male offspring of the pair, less often a female offspring, and sometimes an unrelated bird.

adult pair gains a helping hand in procuring food for the hungry young hatchlings. Three birds are a more effective deterrent against nest robbers. And the young helper bird presumably gains extra instruction and experience in hunting before setting out on its own. This doesn't, of course, explain the older helpers; perhaps these birds are unsuccessful at breeding, yet still gain from the cooperative hunting of a group situation. If this arrangement is so advantageous, why don't more species copy it? The answer is, "Who knows?" Evolution takes many paths to success; this route seems to work well for Harris' hawks.

You might see Harris' hawks nests in saguaros and palo verde trees; the female lays two or three eggs beginning in late January and February, extending into August. Often two successive broods are raised; the earlier in the season the first eggs are laid, the better the chances that a second clutch will be produced. In fact, nests have been found with a second set of eggs while the first offspring were still in the nest, not quite fledged. Sometimes the second set of eggs is laid in another nest while the first young are still being raised.

If the helper is a male relative, he will not breed with the alpha female. If he is unrelated, he might try to seduce her but is very rarely successful. Male helpers have little direct contact with the nestlings; their role is strictly hunting and nest defense. Female helpers, however, often brood the young and help feed them.

The helper arrangement is common among Harris' hawks; one study found cooperative units at 40 percent of the nest sites surveyed. Although the helpers are usually young birds that eventually leave and find mates, some males up to eight years of age apparently turn into professional uncles and have been found helping alpha pairs.

When the yardstick of "evolutionary fitness" is placed against this helping behavior, several distinct advantages are apparent. The

Above, *Harris' hawk: cooperative breeder*

Harris' hawks are democratic in their prey selection. Rabbits and ground squirrels form a large part of the diet, which is augmented by other rodents; however, the hawks also take birds such as quail and cactus wrens and, in several recorded instances, roadrunners, kestrels, and Cooper's hawks.

More Humble than Hubble

Most people think they need an expensive telescope to enjoy the pastime of astronomy. But there is a capable alternative, something more humble than Hubble: the binoculars you use for birding. No, you won't see the rings of Saturn or the comet impacts on Jupiter, but you can spot the four moons of Jupiter that Galileo discovered with his simple instrument (a lead pipe with two lenses)—and more.

The key is not in magnification but in light gathering. The objective (front) lens on even a modest 7x35 pair of binoculars has about 200 times the area of your dilated pupil. Although the image is not 200 times brighter, it is significantly enhanced. The light-gathering capability combined with the magnification gives you a cheap passport to the universe.

To exploit your binoculars to the fullest, it must be very dark. Your eyes have to be fully dilated (allow 30 minutes). You also need to maintain a stable position; try lying on your back. Consult star and planet charts for positions and dates. Positions of well-known stars and constellations are listed at the end of each chapter. (Star positions change through the seasons but return year to year; planet positions change every year. Consult the current month's issue of Astronomy *or* Sky and Telescope *magazine for the positions of the planets). Tip: use a red-filtered light for reading while viewing, so your dilated pupils remain open.*

Binoculars can bring the universe closer

Places to Visit in January

National Optical Astronomy Observatories

On clear days you can see them from Tucson, some 50 miles to the west: huge, gleaming-white domed and diagonal structures perched atop Kitt Peak in the Quinlan Mountains like a latter-day Stonehenge to technology. This impressive collection of telescopes belongs to the National Optical Astronomy Observatories (NOAO) and is open on selected winter evenings for public viewing. Each year we try to attend one; after an evening of contemplating the vastness of our universe, our earthly problems seem somehow smaller and in perspective.

Among the 16 scopes on the mountain, there's the odd-looking diagonal McMath-Pierce Solar Telescope through which you can view the sun as it sets, and the impressive 4-meter Mayall Telescope for dark-sky viewing (to put it into perspective, the average amateur astonomer's scopes are about 4- to 6-inches). Call the Kitt Peak Visitor Center at (520) 318-8732 about winter programs and daytime visiting hours.

The Quinlan Mountains rise out of the 3,500-foot grassland plains of the Altar Valley to 6,875 feet. (NOAO leases Kitt Peak from the Tohono O'odham nation.) A winding, narrow road brings you to the top: a beautiful *encinal* community of silverleaf and Mexican blue oaks, manzanita, and border piñon. We have seen large troops of coatimundis (members of the raccoon family, with long snouts and long, ringed tails) ambling up a side canyon just off the road. On the drive up, look for mountain spiny lizards basking on rocks near the turnoff to the picnic area. The mountain spiny lizard (*Sceloporus jarrovii*), a very dark 4- to 7-inch lizard that looks as if its body is covered in a tiny fish-net stocking, has an antifreeze substance in its blood, which (along with its dark thermally absorbent scales) allows it to emerge from its burrow even on a freezing January day.

Above, *mountain spiny lizard: "antifreeze" in its blood*

Wet Wash Walks

A soporific sun warms our backs as we sink up to our calves in the slushy sand. Spears of light shoot off the clear, cold water speeding down the normally dry washbed near the edge of suburbia at the foothills of the Rincon Mountains. As we move slowly upstream, crossing and re-crossing the shallower tendrils of flow—Tanque Verde Creek is a few inches to several feet deep and a hundred yards wide in wintertime between storms—yellow-rumped warblers flash their namesakes at us and electric-red vermilion flycatchers dance in the trees like Christmas lights. Hundreds of birds, refugees from the nearby snowy mountains, forage in the willows, cottonwoods, and mesquites.

You can access the creek by taking Tanque Verde Road to Wentworth Road; the creek crosses Wentworth about a mile to the south. Park along Wentworth, taking care not to block any driveways, and head upstream. In Pima County, legal right-of-way is granted along the watercourse but do not stray onto private land. Unless you have extremely cold-hardy toes, rubber boots are a must to enjoy this walk. And if clouds cover the mountains, stay away from all creeks because of the danger of flash floods.

Wings Over Willcox

Pre-dawn murkiness. The air hangs brittle and still at 30°F. To the east, the Dos Cabezas Mountains begin to glow from behind. Black and flat in silhoutte, they look like paper cut-outs of mountains. Several dozen cold feet stamp and shuffle in the cold dawn, virtually the only sound in the hundreds of acres of cornfield stubble except for the occasional bark of a farm dog. Slight impatience. Then we hear it. The first call, a sound as old as time. It could be a few hundred yards away or a mile. A clear, piercing bugle: *CHURIUP! CHURIUP! CHURIUP!* The first of ten thousand sandhill cranes glide into the surrounding fields of corn stubble to feed for the morning before returning to the safety of their roosts on the vast and shallow rain-fed waters of the Willcox Playa.

Each winter in southeastern Arizona (in Cochise County, about three hours from Tucson), the fallow winter agricultural fields and the huge shallow lake south of the town of Willcox host tens of thousands of waterfowl, which fatten up for their long spring migrations north to their breeding grounds in the Rockies, Canada, and Alaska. The sandhill cranes may be the oldest migratory bird represented in the fossil record: about 10 million years old, by some accounts. Thousands of Canada geese also share the waters and fields, as do a few hundred snow geese. The best times to see the birds are during their flights to and from the cornfields, at dawn and then just past noon. The Wings Over Willcox festival in mid-January features organized tours for viewing the cranes and other birds, natural history workshops, and displays. For information, contact the Willcox Chamber of Commerce and Agriculture at (520) 384-2272.

JANUARY SKIES

"Moon of the Cottonwood Blooming"

TRADITIONAL O'ODHAM NAME FOR JANUARY

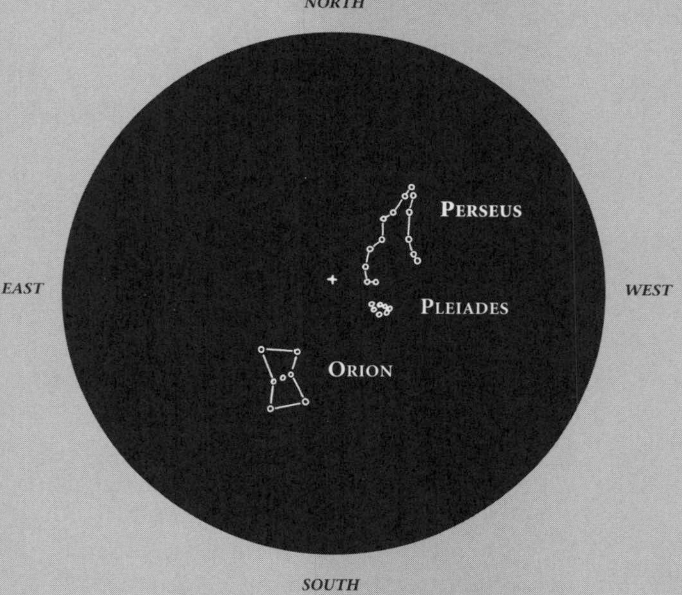

Star Chart for 32°N
Mid-month, 9 pm

FEATURE CONSTELLATION

Handsome Greek hero Perseus was the famous slayer of Medusa, the snake-haired she-monster whose single glance could turn one into solid stone. Perseus wore winged sandals and carried a polished shield and magic sack. With one blow, he beheaded Medusa and put her head in the sack; her blood spilled into the ocean and from the smoking foam sprang forth the winged horse, Pegasus, who then carried Perseus through more adventures: he rescued the beautiful Andromeda and saved the kingdom of King Cepheus and Queen Andromeda from doom. All these constellations appear in the winter sky, accompanying Perseus on his astronomical travels.

JANUARY AT A GLANCE

Desertscrub

❧ Desert succulents are busy sucking up as much moisture from winter rainfall as their roots and stems can hold.

❧ Woody plants are extending their roots and preparing to set new leaves.

❧ In lower desert riparian areas, Frémont cottonwoods (*Populus fremontii*) may be budding new leaves by mid-month, as well as blooming.

❧ Annual wildflowers and grasses are growing.

❧ Dry washes may have dramatic but short-lived floods if rains are heavy.

❧ Along flowing desert streams, look for mountain birds such as ruby-crowned kinglets, dark-eyed juncos, yellow-rumped warblers, and lark sparrows foraging in the rich habitat, waiting out the snow in their summer haunts.

❧ Packrats (white-throated woodrats) begin their breeding seasons.

❧ Curve-billed thrashers and northern mockingbirds sing their glorious territory songs and begin nesting late in the month.

❧ Harris' hawks begin laying eggs.

Desert Grasslands

❧ Wintering sparrows such as Brewer's and vesper are common.

Oak Woodlands

❧ Coues' white-tailed deer are mating.

Pine-Oak Woodlands

❧ Black bears give birth to tiny cubs, an average litter of two, which will nurse and grow in winter dens.

Coniferous Forests

Snow blankets the ground most of this month. Snowpack provides precious water for the coming spring both as groundwater seep and as runoff down rocky mountain canyons.

Special Events

❧ Flocks numbering in the tens of thousands of sandhill cranes, Canada geese and snow geese are wintering on the Willcox Playa in southeastern Arizona. The Willcox Chamber of Commerce and Agriculture's Wings Over Willcox festival is held in mid-month.

In the Sky

❧ The constellation Perseus blazes high overhead late in the evening, after twilight fades, along with the Pleiades star cluster (the Seven Sisters).

❧ Orion hunts high in the southern sky.

See the chapter Exploring the Nature of Pima County and Southern Arizona for definitions and descriptions of communities.

A February snowstorm creates perfect conditions for a ski jaunt to frozen Rose Canyon Lake in the Santa Catalina Mountains

february

WHITE IS THE *color of spring in the desert.*

It begins with a delicate flutter, a tumble of small white wings dancing down desert washes—spring is Sara orange-tip butterflies, named for the bright orange spots on the leading edge of their white fore-wings.

It cascades down rocky desert canyon walls, sweet and clear, the bright presence of orange blossoms—spring is the exquisite fragrance of desert mock-orange bushes, dripping from small, citrus-like white blossoms.

And it peeks from behind granite boulders, shoulders its way through the sugary western sand dunes, shines like miniature lanterns along trails and roads—spring is white petals of desert chicory, coursetia shrubs, desert onions, ajo lilies, prickly poppies, dune primroses, desert zinnias, and desert anemones.

So begins spring in the desert, heralded in early to mid-February on wings and petals of white. That is not to say there aren't other colors: pale pink fleabane and fairy duster, and fuchsia penstemon; yellow desert groundsel, bladderpods, and evening primroses; purple namas, phacelias, and verbenas; and creamy streptanthus, plantago, and dock. All these beauties among many others arrive mid- to late-February to blend their hues with the white harbingers. (See Appendix 1: Southern Arizona Desert Plants Blooming Calendar.)

Smelling new and promising, the days are bright with clean light, washed by the winter rains. We are drawn outside to just lounge in the sun like lizards. In fact, lizards are popping out all over the place after a few days of warmth. So are squirrels in the desertscrub and up to the oak woodlands. Antelope ground squirrels give birth this month and in March to between five and nine young in underground nest chambers lined with hair and grass. Although reptiles and mammals (including humans) may lounge, surrounded by wildflowers, in a balmy patch of sun, there's still a good chance of a dusting of snow.

Nevertheless, accompanied by some truly odd sounds, breeding and nesting are in full swing in the desertscrub. In town or in the suburbs, if you hear what sounds like someone using a jackhammer on metal, it's probably a Gila woodpecker using a metal pipe to amplify its rapidly drummed territorial messages. Gila woodpeckers will begin laying eggs in holes in trees and saguaros this month and next. When you're out hiking, you may hear what sounds like a bullet ricocheting past (zzzzziiiinNNGGG!!); that's the display call of a male Costa's hummingbird. Sit quietly for a while and search for a female entering and leaving a dense shrub thicket—a sure sign of nest-building. Costa's hummingbirds arrive this month to set up house and breed while flower production is high. Most will depart by July, following the flower blooms west and north along central and coastal California. The loud zing-pop! like a firecracker is a male Anna's hummingbird showing off his flight skills for a female. Anna's, our resident hummers, have been in full nesting mode perhaps since early December. And at night, the insistent thrice-asked question Who-who-WHO? is of course posed by a great horned owl, which will begin nesting this month.

In the grassy foothills and oak-filled canyons of southwestern Arizona, Mearn's (Montezuma) quail begin their breeding season. This upland bird forages with its strong claws, breaking up dirt and digging for tubers and acorns, which it cracks open with its powerful beak. Coues' white-tailed deer continue their mating; the Tohono

O'odham honor this important source of food by indicating February as Uhwalig Mashath, *"moon of the deer-mating odor." Later this month in oak woodlands around southern Arizona, spring will begin to show itself: melting snow moistens nearly every available creek bed, pale white-and-pink anenomes will be among the first annuals to sprout and brave the still-cold nights, manzanitas present their pink bell flowers, and birds like canyon towhees, rufous-sided towhees, and Bewick's wrens show up as they trail the leading edge of spring creeping up the mountainsides.*

In the pine-oak woodlands, many animals are dipping deep into their caches of food while they wait for spring to bring more bounty. One late February we watched two Arizona gray squirrels raiding an acorn woodpecker granary in a 40-foot ponderosa pine snag in the Catalina Mountains. Two woodpeckers arrived to drive them off but not before the squirrels stole a few acorns. Signs of spring are few and far between in these higher elevations; along riparian corridors trees such as thinleaf alder and Arizona walnut may begin to bloom before leafing out. But one February, we were astounded to find a female Anna's hummingbird building a nest in a silverleaf oak at an elevation of 6,000 feet. Temperatures at night surely dropped below freezing.

Little else is happening up above 7,000 feet in the mixed coniferous forests, where a hard crust of frozen snow still covers much of the forest floor. If you venture up into the snow for a quiet hike, one of the most abundant signs of life, especially if snow has not fallen in more than a week or two, is the litter left around ponderosa pine trees where Abert's squirrels have been feeding: tufts of pine needles shorn from larger twigs, peelings of bark, and the inner core of a twig, about 4 or 5 inches long, complete with teeth marks. These clippings are an important source of nitrogen for nutrient-poor forest floors. Also while you're out, look high in the pines for the now-conspicuous winter nests made by the squirrels in the fall; when the vegetation used to build the nests was fresh, they were invisible, but now that the pine boughs and other tree and shrub trimmings are dead, the nests stand out in sharp contrast.

FEBRUARY WEATHER

	Sunrise	Sunset	Avg. Relative Humidity/Tucson
February 1	*7:17 MST*	*5:57 MST*	*5 a.m. 59%*
February 28	*6:52 MST*	*6:20 MST*	*5 p.m. 27%*

Stations	Ajo	Tucson	Mt. Lemmon
Station Elevation	*(1,800 ft.)*	*(2,584 ft.)*	*(8,800 ft.)*
February Averages			
Max. temperature	*68.6°F*	*67.5°F*	*48.9°F*
Min. temperature	*35.3°F*	*40.2°F*	*21.0°F*
Precipitation	*.61 in.*	*.63 in.*	*1.92 in.*
Snow	*.04 in.*	*.19 in.*	*10.3 in.*
# days 100° & over	0	0	0
# days 32° & under	1	4	28
# days precip.>.01″	3	3	2
February Extremes			
Max. Temperature	92°F (1963)	92°F (1957)	65°F (1961)
Min. Temperature	22°F (1923)	20°F (1955)	-7°F (1963)
Max. Snow/month	0.50 in. (1923)	3.90 in. (1965)	18.0 in. (1963)
Max. Snow/1 day	0.50 in. (1923)	2.20 in. (1965)	20.0 in. (1982)
Max. Precip./month	3.20 in. (1931)	2.90 in. (1980)	4.81 in. (1963)
Max. Precip./1 day	1.66 in. (1920)	1.26 in. (1966)	4.81 in. (1963)

February Notes

February is a beautiful month in the deserts, with bright days that may warm up as high as the 70°s, tempting us with thoughts of spring. But beware: February will probably bring a day or two of freezing rain to the deserts and cold nights—not more than 40° on average. In the mountains, snow is a weekly reality, with a full month of below-freezing temperatures at night and day-time readings that climb meekly to the mid-40°s. The chances of temperatures reaching into the 80°s or even 90°s for a few days in the deserts are fairly good; and warming in the mountains can cause great floods in the washes. In 1980, Palisade Ranger Station in the Catalina Mountains reported over 10″ of rain for February. (Note: this station is not the one noted above for Mt. Lemmon.)

For information about data sources for these listings, see the Climate section of the chapter Exploring the Nature of Pima County and Southern Arizona.

In early February there is usually one good snowstorm that dumps enough snow for a ski jaunt to Rose Canyon Lake in the Catalina Mountains. It's a special trip worth the effort of getting up early to beat traffic. In late February we always plan to head out to Organ Pipe Cactus National Monument, in western Pima County, where spring gets a head start and some specialty wildflowers, like ajo lilies, sand blazing stars, and ghost flowers, hold court. And a hike on the Douglas Springs Trail in Saguaro National Park in late February to follow spring up the Rincon Mountains is a delight for the eyes and ears, as we are accompanied by the sound of cascading creeks and the sight of trailside flowers. ☙ ☙ ☙

FLORA

Early Bloomers

No matter how hard we try to anticipate it, the early spring bloom always takes us by surprise. One day there is nothing but promising green blotches of new growth carpeting the desert; the next, yellow and orange and purple flowers wink everywhere. We stop the car and get out, wondering how we could have missed all this just 24 hours earlier: three, four, a half-dozen species are blooming within a stone's throw—certainly they couldn't have coordinated a simultaneous outbreak.

The ones that first demand attention are probably desert marigolds, *Baileya multiradiata,* a common roadside showoff. The marigold blossom is bright yellow through and through, with numerous ray petals, and perched on foot-tall, woolly gray-green stalks. Like the blossoms of other members of the composite, or sunflower, family, the marigold blossom is actually composed of many tightly packed small flowers of two configurations. One type forms the fuzzy center of the bloom; another, each with a single large petal, forms the outer "rays."

Another yellow composite is *Encelia farinosa,* or brittlebush, a perennial that grows to small shrub size. Its flowers are similar in color to desert marigold, but the disk flowers are darker and the outer ray petals are only about a dozen in number; the bloom grows, as the name suggests, on brittle stalks that stick up about a foot above the

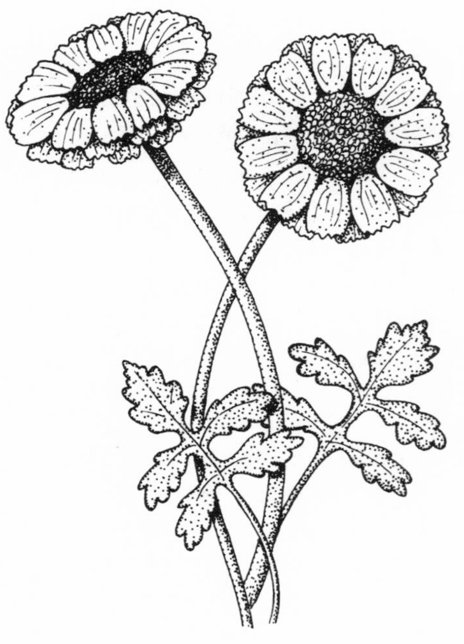

main plant. The brittlebush grows fat green leaves after a rain, but if a dry period ensues the big leaves drop off, leaving only small ones that lose less water to transpiration. In good years, brittlebush will turn entire hillsides into blazing yellow semaphores that can be seen from miles away. In a particularly lush wildflower year, a friend who is a helicopter pilot reported to us that there was yellow "everywhere" on the hillsides. Brittlebush, no doubt.

While hillsides glow with brittlebush, the flat plains of creosote in the lower valleys grow their own yellow carpets of small bladderpods (*Lesquerella gordonii*). The bladderpod's fruits ripen into hollow spheres that pop when squeezed. The flowers form a distinctive cross shape that gives the name Cruciferae to the family.

In lovely contrast to the yellow marigolds, brittlebush, and bladderpods, penstemon stalks begin to show varying shades of lilac, fuschia, and coral in late February. Although not often seen in huge monochromatic fields, *Penstemon parryi* delights in its own way as bright flashes of color catch your attention here and there, highlighting the shade under a mesquite tree or in brilliant contrapunto against a green saguaro trunk. The Tucson Mountain's King's Canyon in Saguaro National Park features a profusion of penstemon in most years.

In sandy areas of the lowlands the dune evening primrose (*Oenothera primiveris*) unfolds delicate white petals at sunset to attract its chief pollinators, several species of hawkmoth. Their jobs finished, the flowers wilt the next morning. Rarely will one see a poor photo of an evening primrose because photographers are obligated to catch the bloom during the best light of evening or early morning.

Growing among primrose can also be found sand verbena *(Abronia villosa)*, which forms low clumps of lilac, long-tubed flowers

Above, *desert marigold: a bright yellow showoff*

that are pollinated mostly by moths and butterflies.

Tucson residents who are used to the perfumed aroma of urban ornamental orange trees will sometimes be surprised to catch a whiff of the same fragrance while walking down a rocky desert wash far from town. This wonderful spice is produced by the desert mock-orange. *Crossosoma bigelovii* has an affinity for the steep sides of canyons; its white flowers resemble real citrus blooms and produce a similar heavenly odor. Mock-orange grows to small shrub size.

Visitors to the lower deserts near Ajo might be lucky enough to see ajo lilies, sprouting delicate, waxy blooms in the midst of the most hostile terrain (see sidebar).

Depending on rainfall and weather patterns, there may be other early bloomers: fleabane *(Erigeron divergens)*, desert groundsel *(Senecio douglasii)*, monkeyflower *(Mimulus bigelovii)*, nama *(Nama demissum)*, and desert star *(Monoptilon bellioides)*.

Saguaros and Freezing

One of the rarest—and loveliest—sights in the desert is a fresh snowfall topping cactuses and dusting mesquites with a whimsically incongruous frosting. But that cold white blanket carries a peril for the

Low Desert Beauties

Three of our most gorgeous wildflowers begin to present their wares this month in the low western deserts: ajo lilies, sand blazing stars, and ghost flowers. All three bloom February through late March.

Ajo lilies (Hesperocallis undulata) *are named for their garlic-like bulbs, which early settlers harvested (ajo is Spanish for garlic), but they are most famous for their large optic-white silk-like flowers with delicate yellow-pink stripes. Set on a straight stalk and surrounded by four or five undulating ribbony leaves, the flowers stand out brilliantly and eerily on sand-and-gravel flats at low elevations. At night, the white flowers call in the plant's most important pollinators, giant hawkmoths.*

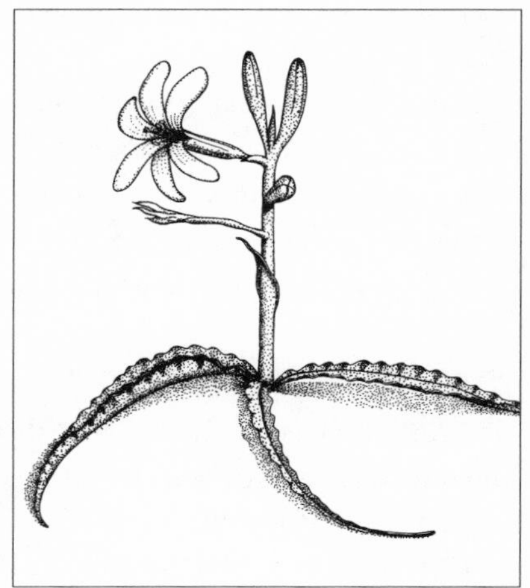

Ajo lily: delicate white flowers with yellow-pink stripes

*Sand blazing stars (*Mentzelia involucrata*) and ghost flowers (*Mohavea confertiflora*) look suspiciously alike. Both flowers have nearly identical cream-colored petals streaked inside with pale orange, and they often grow within a few feet of one another in sandy washes and rocky slopes; humans can tell them apart by their foliage (sand blazing stars have wavy, serrated leaves and ghost flowers have linear leaves), but bees can't tell the difference. A hungry bee dipping into a sand blazing star will find the promised sweet nectar; when it ventures into a ghost flower it will find nothing, but by the time the error is realized, the bee has already inadvertently pollinated the flower. By mimicking the nectar-rich sand blazing star, the ghost flower receives the benefits of nectar-feeding pollinators but does not have to invest energy into producing the expensive nectar.*

Look for these fascinating plants and the ajo lilies in Organ Pipe National Monument and Cabeza Prieta National Wildlife Refuge, both of which are in western Pima County.

larger cactuses, in particular saguaros. A saguaro can be 90 percent water by weight, and if that water freezes it will irreparably harm the cell structure of the plant. The critical factor is the length of time temperatures remain below freezing.

In February 1939 a record-breaking cold spell hit the Tucson basin, subjecting thousands of saguaros to many hours of temperatures in the 25°F range. What followed was disastrous—at least it seemed so to observers with a rather short-term perspective.

An unfamiliar type of bacterial rot (which was first thought to be

A snow-covered saguaro cactus

unrelated to the freeze) began decimating saguaros in the area, particularly in the heavily forested Saguaro National Park east of town. Officials resorted to bulldozing infected cactuses and burying them in an effort to stop the spread of the bacteria. It was all in vain; cactus after cactus died. The specter of extinction was even raised. The bacterial epidemic finally tapered off but photographs of the cactus forest taken before the event reveal the extent of the loss even today.

Subsequent research, particularly by Charles Lowe and Warren Steenbergh, indicated a connection between freeze damage and the bacterial infection. A healthy saguaro can defend itself against bacterial invasion by using the same callous tissue with which it seals woodpecker nest holes; a cactus that has been subjected to freezing temperatures or has suffered injury is vulnerable to invasion by the organism—often with fatal results.

However, the news is not all bad—if we can see the event from other than our anthropocentric view. Northern Pima County is also approximately the northern limit of the saguaro's range, and it is probably the cold that is the limiting parameter. Lowe and Steenbergh believe that what happened in 1939 is a perfectly normal, if infrequent, occurrence. Their research indicates that saguaro populations are subject to ups and downs, just like virtually every other species, and that catastrophic freezes—and subsequent outbreaks of bacterial necrosis—thin out the older and weaker members of the population from time to time. The

Granddaddy Saguaro

In the fall of 1992, the largest known saguaro cactus, dubbed Granddaddy, was diagnosed with fatal bacterial necrosis, brought on most likely by an intense freeze. In its prime it was the largest saguaro known (others were taller, none was as massive) and was believed to be nearly 300 years old, although the ages of saguaros are difficult to determine accurately. Protected in a remote section of Saguaro National Park's Rincon Mountain Unit, in its prime Granddaddy was estimated to have weighed more than 30,000 pounds. At chest height to a man its trunk was nearly 2-1/2 feet in diameter, and it raised 45 arms to the sky. This photo was taken in 1993 and nearly half its mass was gone by then.

disadvantage from our point of view is that it will be many decades before the cactus forest looks the way it did in 1939.

FAUNA

Cactuspeckers

Like most woodpeckers, their flight pattern is a vertiginous display—a combination half flapping, half free-falling swoop that creates a wild, multi-arced trajectory, like a child's drawing of a tempestuous ocean. A distinctive black and white ladder-backed pattern and the male's red cap identify the Gila woodpecker, a year-round resident of southern Arizona, as it hangs on the side of a saguaro or telephone pole.

Finding Gila woodpeckers is never a problem. *Ignoring* them—now that's a problem. Their piercing *EEK!EEK!EEK!* or *churr!churr!* is a constant reminder of their presence to hikers in the desertscrub. And many city dwellers spend several weeks in early spring waking at dawn to the machine-gun rattle of a woodpecker hammering away on a vent pipe on the roof, not, as some suppose, looking for nonexistent ferrous insects, but advertising his territory with the handiest amplifier he can find.

That cleverness extends to the Gila woodpecker's choice of hous-

SAGUARO ECOLOGY

Saguaro cactuses are the undisputed stars of the Sonoran Desert, and for good reason. A full-grown Carnegiea gigantea *can attain a height of 50 feet and weigh 8 tons—75 to 90 percent of which is stored water. It takes 30 years for a saguaro to grow to a height of 2 feet and 50 to 100 years for it to begin growing arms. Its fleshy trunks and arms provide shelter for many animals. Gila woodpeckers and gilded flickers excavate cavities for nesting, which are subsequently used by many other birds and even rodents; raptors use nests built in the cradling arms. On May evenings saguaros begin to open their 3-inch white flowers, which are visited by nectar-feeding bats; mornings find insects and birds gathering leftover pollen and nectar, and by afternoon the blooms close. In June and early July the flowers mature into ruby fruits containing 1,200 to 2,000 tiny seeds. The fruits split open, and pulp and seeds are eaten by insects, birds, and mammals. One saguaro will produce 40 million seeds in its lifetime, but fewer than one in 1,000 survives to become an established seedling.*

ing as well. This species was acquainted with the concepts of insulation and thermal mass eons before humans began constructing energy-efficient homes. The Gila woodpecker usually excavates its nest hole in the fleshy trunk of the saguaro cactus. The bird bores into the moist tissue and then down, creating a safe hollow. The cactus exudes a hard coating that seals the lining of the nest—and creates the "saguaro boots" that collectors love, which endure long after the rest of the cactus has died and disintegrated. The thick walls of the nest provide a thermal buffer which attenuates the temperature swings of the outside air. For example, at 3 P.M. on a 104° June day the temperature at the bottom of the hole might be 10° lower, while at 3 A.M. the next morning, when the outside temperature is 80°, the nest interior might be 88° or 89° (perfectly comfortable for a bird, which has a higher body temperature than humans). Extremes of winter cold are dampened as well.

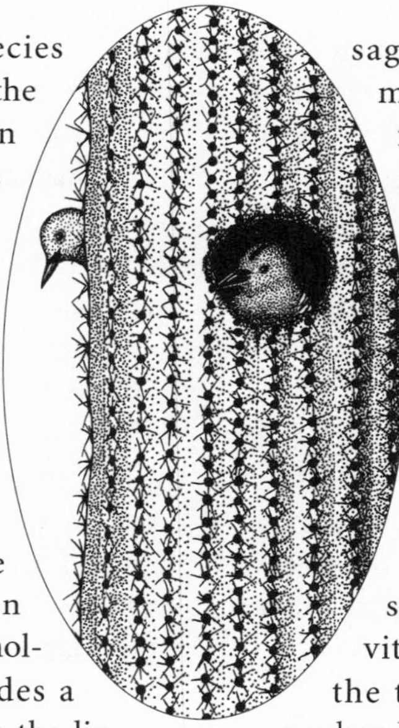

The woodpeckers do not drill nest holes *before* the nesting season but *afterward*. Why? Because the saguaro takes several months to coat the freshly excavated hole with its callous lining. So the nest the woodpecker builds this year is actually an investment in next year's housing.

Another kind of woodpecker—the northern flicker—also excavates nests in saguaros, but there is a vital difference between the two. The Gila woodpecker bores into the thick, lower part of the trunk and the resulting hole does not penetrate the woody skeleton of the cactus. The flicker, however, drills into the top part of the trunk, where the flesh is thinner, and often chisels right through the ribs into the heart of the plant. This incursion can severely weaken the structure—so much so, in fact, that the uppermost portion can topple. The resulting open wound leaves the saguaro vulnerable to bacterial necrosis, a fatal affliction. It is unclear how the flicker developed its potentially destructive habit or what the long-term effects might be on a saguaro population that is facing many other threats.

The woodpeckers' holes benefit many other species. Because

Above, *a male Gila woodpecker attracts a female to his nest*

woodpeckers construct new holes each year, the old ones are appropriated by a variety of freeloaders: elf and screech owls, kestrels, cactus wrens, doves and other birds, and sometimes mice and lizards.

The female Gila woodpecker lays two to four eggs in February or March. The eggs hatch in about two weeks, after which both parents take turns foraging for food, which includes insects, insect larvae, and cactus fruit pulp. The young are fed for a time even after they are fledged and able to fly.

Sky Island Bears

Very few animals engender such a polar range of human emotions as do bears. Our reactions range from atavistic terror to the warm fuzzies, a schizophrenia that is reflected in our literature. Scroll through the central reference list at the University of Arizona library; you'll find books for children bearing titles such as *Bear and Bunny Grow Tomatoes, A First Book of Bears,* and of course many tales of *The Berenstain Bears,* listed alongside adult works such as *Bear Attacks: Their Causes and Avoidance.*

Perhaps our schizophrenia reflects the mercurial nature of the bear itself, a nature that, just possibly, we recognize as paralleling our own. Bears can be by turn peaceful and dangerous, powerful and gentle, intelligent and stupid (or at least stubborn), dextrous and bumbling. A mother bear teaching her cubs to hunt is a study in patience and care; if you get between that bear and her offspring, you witness one of the deadliest animals on earth.

Of the two species of bear found in the lower forty-eight states—the grizzly (*Ursus arctos*) and the black bear (*Ursus americanus*)—the grizzly, unfortunately, no longer exists in Arizona, a victim of an early twentieth century drive to protect game and livestock by ridding the land of predators. The black bear, though, still lives here in relative abundance—about 2,200 to 2,500 inhabit the state.

In Pima County, black bears are creatures of the sky islands. Each of the three mountain ranges surrounding Tucson—the Catalinas, Rincons, and Santa Ritas—supports a small population of bears. Here, as in the colder parts of their range, the bears den through the winter. Contrary to popular belief, black bears don't actually hibernate; their metabolism doesn't slow enough to rate that term, and they can easily be awakened—a good point to remember.

The den is usually dug into the side of a hill in oak woodland or chaparral at 4,000 feet to 5,000 feet elevation in the shelter of a large boulder. The sleeping chamber is often augmented with soft grasses, and it is here, in February, that the females give birth to their cubs—tiny, helpless creatures weighing barely 8 ounces each. The usual number is two, and the female generally gives birth in alternate years, since the cubs may stay with her for up to a year.

Black bears are consummate omnivores. Their diet ranges from grubs, insects, berries, and small mammals up to the occasional deer. Infrequently beekeepers in remote agricultural areas will find a hive that appears to have been dynamited—bears really do love their honey.

Many animals have been accused of being stock killers over the decades—some with more validity than others. The black bear, however, is one of the most undeserving recipients of that title. Bona fide cases of black bears taking sheep or cattle are rare.

Although black bears can still find remote spaces in the wilderness areas of Pima County, there are concerns that these populations are becoming dangerously isolated. In the past it was common for bears to migrate between mountain ranges, assuring a steady variation in the gene pool. Now, if a bear ventures into the lowlands it is likely to be hit by a car or shot by frightened citizens. If the various populations become permanently separated from each other, inbreeding could cause problems in the smaller groups.

PLACES TO VISIT IN FEBRUARY

Organ Pipe Cactus National Monument

It starts early in February. A breeze wafts in from the west, brushing our faces. There it is: a touch of warm, a hint of green, a scent of flower? Then the craving sets in: Spring. It won't arrive in Tucson fully for many weeks, but we can go to it—by heading for the west deserts.

Head west on Ajo Way (Highway 86), through the nearly 3 million acres belonging to the Tohono O'odham nation; at the tiny town of Why, head south to Organ Pipe Cactus National Monument, almost at the Mexico border. On the drive, look for early spring bloomers such as desert chicory, penstemon, bladderpods, and verbena, and for crested caracaras. These bizarre-looking members of the falcon family are actually carrion eaters who sometimes venture into southern Arizona from their more southern ranges in Mexico. A pair reportedly has been nesting on the west side of the Baboquivari Mountains and you might see them patrolling the road for kills near Sells.

There is a large campground at Organ Pipe, but it fills up early in the day with wintering RVers (also known as Snowbirds). The best bet is to arrive early on a morning in mid-week to stake a site—or plan to head to the backcountry with a backpack. The campground sits in a bowl in the foothills of the Puerto Blanco Mountains, which are behind the visitor center. Radiating from the hills, flat plains of exotic desert sweep up to the skirts of mountains so jagged they look as if newly born from the depths of the earth. The plains are covered by a thorny forest of the namesake organ pipe cactuses, senitas, elephant trees and ocotillos, and in the early spring, beautiful wildflowers abound. Drive the 20 miles of Puerto Blanco Drive to look for exotic early bloomers like ajo lilies; ask at the visitor center for good sites (you might want to call before driving to the monument, if you want to time your visit with certain flowers). Attentive visitors might find signs of early Tohono O'odham camps. About half-way around the drive, very near milepost marker 10, look for *yerba de flecha* (*Sapium biocculare*), also called Mexican jumping bean. As in the true Mexican jumping bean (*Sebastiana pavoniana*), a small moth larvae moves around in the seeds and makes them "jump." The O'odham used the sap from the plant to poison arrow tips and lakes and streams to stun fish for easy hunting.

Don't miss Quitobaquito Springs, a true desert oasis on the Mexican border where water bubbles up and forms small lakes surrounded by improbable-looking cottonwood trees. The name of the springs comes from the O'odham for "reed-grown waterhole," *quitobac*. The reeds that surround the oasis are Olney bulrush (*Scirupus olneyi*). In the precious waters swim members of an endangered subspecies of desert pupfish (*Cyprinodon macularius*), a tiny and very ancient species of fish, perhaps one of the oldest still living. In the late 1960s someone introduced exotic golden shiners into the one-acre pond, perhaps for sport, but the result was the near-extinction of the pupfish. Park personnel removed the pupfish, killed off the shiners, then returned the pupfish to their small home.

Ski Rose Canyon Lake

A few times a winter, usually in February, the voice wafting from our radio alarm clock wakes us to the news that as we slumbered the night away, a storm passed through and dumped snow below 6,000 feet. That means skiable snow at

Microscopic Desert Dwellers

There is a whole world of microscopic life in the desert that we cannot see with a naked eye. We can, however, observe the telltale signs of their tiny everyday lives.

Desert varnish appears to us as dark reddish-brown and black streaks on rock walls, boulders, and even pebbles. Much of it looks like just water stains, but certain species of minuscule blue-green algae, lichens, fungi, and bacteria living in the outermost layer of the rock process minerals from water and the atmosphere. The by-products are depositions of oxidized minerals on the surface of the rock—black or dark brown from manganese and reddish from iron. Desert varnish is most prominent on canyon walls throughout the Southwest.

Desert pavements are naturally occurring fields of smooth pebbles set closely together into a layer of crusty, aerated soil, like cobblestones or a jigsaw puzzle. Often the pebbles are coated with desert varnish; scientists can age the desert pavement by the amount of varnish on the pebbles. It takes many thousands of years for desert pavements to form from the workings of wind, rain, and microscopic organisms. Once disturbed by a footprint or tiretrack, the pavement is quickly destroyed by erosion. Desert pavement can be found along El Camino del Diablo in Cabeza Prieta National Wildlife Refuge.

Cryptobiotic soil is often discussed in literature about the American deserts, and we're warned not to walk across it and destroy its delicate ecology. But how do we recognize it? Cryptobiotic soil, or "hidden living soil," comprises a pastry-like upper crust of dry, nearly sterile desert dirt and its principal component, blue-green algae. The algae is a nitrogen-fixer and therefore an extremely important element in providing nutrients for the animals living there: mites, fleas, and other nearly undetectable arthropods that carry on their complex lives just below the surface. Some are grazers, some are hunters. It may look like "dead" dirt, but it's actually a whole forest of life. Like desert pavement, it can be destroyed by disturbance. Avoid soils that are crusty and that collapse when you step on them. Cabeza Prieta National Wildlife Refuge has extensive areas of cryptobiotic soil.

Rose Canyon Lake in the Catalina Mountains! Oblivious to the cold, still-dark morning we leap out of bed, race to dress—long underwear, knickers, wool socks, sweaters—make hot chocolate, load the cross-country skis in the truck and dash off across the sleeping city to beat the crowds (most people won't make it up the mountain until noon; we always put chains on all four tires of our four-wheel-drive and proceed carefully).

Our reward is one of the finest ski jaunts in Arizona, and it's only 40 minutes from our desert home. We swoosh across untracked sugar-powder snow, along a mile of smoothly rolling road dropping to the 7-acre Rose Canyon Lake lying wrapped in its winter cloak of ice, a crystalline wonderland to a desert rat. We sit on a downed snag on our jackets and sip hot chocolate from a thermos and listen to the softly percussive *Wumps!* of heavily laden pine boughs dropping their burdens, hear the jitterings of titmice and chickadees high in the canopies, and watch the rising sun set the lake ice on fire. The trip back up the road to the truck is challenging and gets our cold blood moving again. We usually are just pointing our truck down the mountain as the first "early birds" begin to arrive.

Rose Canyon Lake turnoff is at milepost 17 on the Catalina Highway, the only access road to the Catalina Mountains; park along the road (bring a shovel in case the snowplow passes while you're at the lake).

Douglas Springs Trail, Saguaro National Park

Bright lavender buds of indigobush light our way and brightly cascading water provides musical accompaniment as we begin to climb out of the saguaro cactus forest on Tucson's far east side. Ahead on the slopes we can see desert grassland, and a few more miles up the trail, the dark telltale dots of oak trees invading the grass; then, beyond that, solid darkness: the montane forest 4,000 feet above.

Douglas Springs Trail in the Rincon Mountains provides one of the finest late-February hikes in southern Arizona, sampling the very best of nearly all of our plant communities. Protected by Saguaro National Park, the trail begins at the eastern end of Speedway Boulevard. The first few miles wind through thick saguaro cactus, mesquite and palo verde trees, and hackberry shrubs, climbing near and then across Aguila Creek, which cascades down polished rock slabs. Lupine, plantago, bladderpod, cryptantha, and dichylostema may be blooming. As the trail heads into the transition zone between the desertscrub and grassland, look for scars from a lightning-caused fire that burned hundreds of acres in the park in the early 1990s. Grasses introduced for cattle that grazed the range early this century have colonized the desert, providing dangerous fuel in an ecosystem that is not able to withstand conflagrations. Many cactuses and shrubs died.

The trail climbs 2,000 feet and 6 miles to Douglas Springs, a popular destination for backpackers. Beyond, it climbs 3,200 feet, via the Tanque Verde Ridge Trail, to Helen's Dome, where the views of the Tucson valley are breathtaking. Dozens of miles of trails cross the top of the mountain, offering myriad summer getaways and, for those prepared to snow camp, winter as well. Nearly 24 miles, the full round-trip hike to Helen's Dome is for the well prepared and hardy only. However, even if you go only a few miles you'll see several different plant communities. This wonderful trail should not be missed.

FEBRUARY SKIES

"Moon of the Deer-Mating Odor"

TRADITIONAL O'ODHAM NAME FOR FEBRUARY

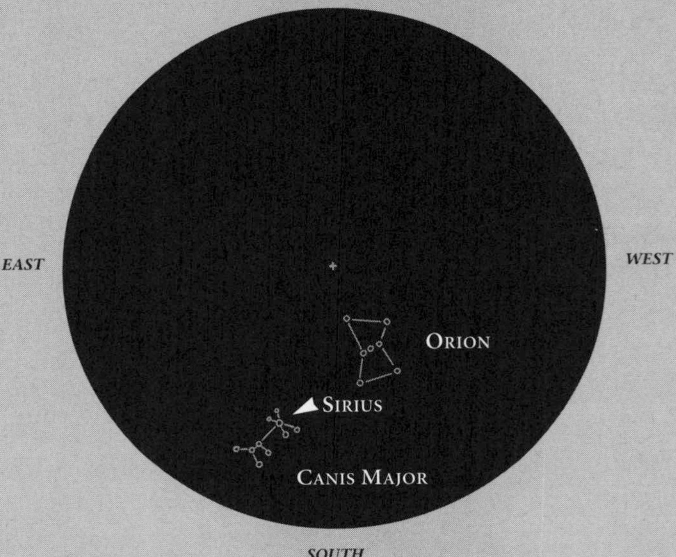

Star Chart for 32°N
Mid-month, 9 pm

FEATURE CONSTELLATION

In Greek myth, Orion the Hunter was the son of the sea god Poseidon and a mortal woman. As his name implies, he was a great hunter as well as a renowned warrior. Not content to pursue game and enemies, Orion had a reputation as a great pursuer of women. His most infamous exploit was a torrid affair with the goddess Diana, fittingly the patron of the hunt and keeper of the Moon. During her involvement with Orion, Diana forgot to carry the Moon across the sky in her chariot; for this dereliction of duty her brother, the sun god Apollo, became angry and tricked her into slaying her new lover with an arrow. Devastated, Diana beseeched Zeus to bring Orion back to life. Unable to do so, Zeus compromised and gave Orion a place of honor among the stars.

FEBRUARY AT A GLANCE

Desertscrub

❧ Some wildflowers begin blooming this month if the preceding months have been wet and mild. (See Appendix 1—Southern Arizona Desert Plants Blooming Calendar.)

❧ Sara orange-tip (*Anthocharis sara*) and Pima orange-tip (*A. pima*) butterflies herald the arrival of spring in the desert.

❧ On warm days you might see lizards basking in the sun.

❧ Antelope ground squirrels bear five to nine young in underground nest chambers lined with hair and grass.

❧ Some of the desert birds that begin mating and nesting this month are Gila woodpeckers, Costa's and Anna's hummingbirds, and great horned owls.

Desert Grasslands

❧ Mearn's (Montezuma) quail begin their breeding season.

Oak Woodlands

❧ Hardy wildflowers such as anemones (*Anemone* spp.) will be among the first annuals to sprout and brave the still-cold nights.

❧ Birds like canyon towhees, rufous-sided towhees, and Bewick's wrens begin showing up as they follow the leading edge of spring creeping up the mountainsides.

Pine-Oak Woodlands

❧ Temperatures are still cold and spring is a bit farther down the road.

❧ Along riparian corridors trees such as thinleaf alder (*Aldus tenuifolia*) and Arizona walnut (*Juglans major*) may begin to bloom before leafing out.

❧ Animals such as gray squirrels and acorn woodpeckers are dipping deep into their caches of food while they wait for spring to bring more bounty.

Coniferous Forests

❧ The temperature is still below freezing at night; a crust of snow covers much of the high country.

❧ Now is a good time to look for signs of Abert's squirrels: tufts of pine needles shorn from larger twigs, peelings of bark, and the inner core of a twig, about 4 or 5 inches long, complete with teeth marks, strewn under ponderosa pine trees. And look high in the pines for the now-conspicuous winter nests made by the squirrels in the fall; when the vegetation used to build the nest was fresh, they were invisible, but now the pine boughs and other tree and shrub trimmings are dead and stand out in sharp contrast.

In the Sky

❧ Sirius, the Dog Star of Canis Major, shines brightly in the south while Orion shows in the west.

See the chapter Exploring the Nature of Pima County and Southern Arizona for definitions and descriptions of communities.

march

F ULL-BODIED SPRING *bursts upon us in March—loudly, flagrantly, and fragrantly.*

We never seem to be quite prepared for this bonanza of sounds, sights, and smells. One day we are barely aware of the soft end of winter, the gentle sun, the quiet promise of spring days. Overnight the land presents an altogether differerent tune: an orchestra of arthropods begins with a chorus of buzzes and hums and zings and trills accompanied by the bright crystal cascade of snowmelt and culminates in the performances of innumerable avian Don Juans belting out arias from what seems like every tree, rock, and cactus. The desert joins the show by decking itself from sand dunes to mountain foothills with rainbows of wildflowers and budding green leaves; to the O'odham, this is the time of Chehthagi Mashath, *"green moon."*

It's hard to miss spring in March. Even if you don't venture out to find it, it will likely bumble right into you. Some of the most conspicuous March players are the bumblebees—big, fuzzy, and yellow and black—and the carpenter bees, of which there are two species common to Pima County. Big, metallic black or yellow, the carpenter bees buzz around loudly and haphazardly, often running into posts or people as they patrol cities and deserts for mates and suitable woody real estate to excavate their nest holes. Dead yucca and agave

Bees add to the explosion of color in March

bloom stalks are a favorite for one species. We can't help but like these harmless buffoons bouncing off our hats as we hike a foothills trail, making us part of the springtime symphony: Zzzzzzzzz-THWACK-zzzzzzzzz. Around us many more insects make their presence known, reminding us loudly of a very definite change of seasons. And if we fail to notice the noise, the sights and smells will surely arouse our senses.

Because, of course, the event for which March is most famous is the beautiful and improbable explosion of flower blossoms in the infamously harsh desert landscape, an affirmation of life and beauty in the looming shadow of the sixty-some-odd rainless, broiling days ahead. There really is nothing so arresting as a rocky desert hillside awash in the saffron blossoms of waist-high brittlebush, smelling as sharp and sunny as just-line-dried cotton sheets.

The sheer numbers and diversity of flowers this month and next are breathtaking—from fields of Lilliputian "bellyflowers" (ones you have to lie on your stomach to see) to the solitary and exquisite mariposa lilies. (For a listing of the more common flowers and their blooming schedules, see Appendix 1, Southern Arizona Desert Plants Blooming Calendar.) Each year we head out on a wildflower safari, trying to "bag" as many species as possible. Around 40 is average for a casual day's hunt, but a friend once listed nearly 80 on a trek through the Tucson Mountains in a good year. Some favorite beauties to shoot for this month and next include Coulter's and desert hibiscus, at least three species of lupine (bajada, Coulter's, and miniature), gilia, delphinium, owl's clover, tackstem, desert onion, desert chicory, goldfields, brittlebush, fairy duster, desert dandelion, Parry's penstemon, prickly poppy, indigo bush, and, of course, Mexican poppies. These latter tangerine-orange cups sometimes swaddle the foothills of Picacho Peak north of Tucson, offering the illusion of an orange blanket wrapping the feet of the peak. Wildflower enthusiasts travel for hundreds, even thousands, of miles to experience a "banner year." Of course, we think every spring has its special beauty no matter how many flowers bloom.

Taking advantage of the blooms of both flowers and insects are the early nesting birds, whose young may begin fledging this month: Anna's and Costa's hummingbirds, ruby-crowned kinglets, black-throated sparrows, verdins, Gila woodpeckers, curve-billed thrashers, and northern mockingbirds are among the busy parents. Pyrrhuloxias and cardinals will join in the family scene later this month and next, as will great horned owls, desert bighorn sheep, rock squirrels, and some of the lizards, such as side-blotched. This is also the month of the desert canines, when coyotes, kit foxes, and gray foxes all begin to whelp. Animals that begin their lives this month will experience cool and even cold nights, but the days may approach hot—although highs in the 70s are most common, often with tickling breezes.

Spring bird migrations are in full swing, a flurry of comings and goings. The great flocks of sandhill cranes, snow geese, and Canada geese in southeastern Arizona leave for the Rocky Mountains and Alaska. Wintering raptors like northern harriers and rough-legged and ferruginous hawks also head north. Just passing through will be thousands of migratory songbirds, traveling ancient, unseen trails from southern wintering grounds to northern summer-breeding ranges. Some will stop in Pima County. One we anticipate each year as our signature desert spring harbinger is the Lucy's warbler, a tiny gray bird that breeds along the mesquite-lined creeks and washes of the Sonoran Desert; in March its brilliantly trilled and whistled song may be heard throughout the day among the newly leafing mesquites. The Lucy's warbler nests in holes in trees rather than in twig nests on top of branches. Only one other North American warbler is a cavity nester.

Many owls and hawks also follow the ancient rhythms. The aptly named 5-inch elf owl arrives this month from Mexico to serenade prospective mates each night from saguaro-cavity nests. Turkey vultures are again common throughout the desertscrub and grasslands; Swainson's, black, and zone-tailed hawks return to grasslands and riparian areas; and the rare gray hawks begin building their nests along perennial streams in extreme southern Pima County and ad-

jacent Santa Cruz and Cochise counties, in the cottonwoods and velvet ash trees that are now bright green with new leaves. (For a list of popular species that arrive, leave, or visit our area in March and April, see the Flight Schedules chart, below; for a list of common southern Arizona birds and their habitats, see Appendix 2, Common Birds of Southern Arizona; also see April's Fauna section for a discussion on bird migration.)

March/April Flight Schedules for Popular Southern Arizona Birds

Winter Visitors Heading North	Arriving for the Spring/Summer	Just Passing Through (Migrants)
Snow goose	*Snowy egret*	*American white pelican*
Canada goose	*Blk.-bellied whistling duck*	*Osprey*
Mallard	*Turkey vulture*	*Least bittern*
Northern pintail	*Common black hawk*	*Marbled godwit*
Cinnamon teal	*Gray hawk*	*Long-billed curlew*
Northern shoveler	*Swainson's hawk*	*Baird's sandpiper*
Gadwall	*Zone-tailed hawk*	*Bonaparte's gull*
American wigeon	*American avocet*	*Ring-billed gull*
Common merganser	*White-winged dove*	*Rufous hummingbird*
Northern harrier	*Flammulated owl*	*Calliope hummingbird*
Sharp-shinned hawk	*Elf owl*	*Nashville warbler*
Ferruginous hawk	*Lesser nighthawk*	*Northern parula*
Merlin	*Common nighthawk*	*MacGillivray's warbler*
Sandhill crane	*Common poorwill*	
Common snipe	*Whip-poor-will*	
Belted kingfisher	*White-throated swift*	
Red-naped sapsucker	*Broad-billed hummingbird*	
Sage thrasher	*White-eared hummingbird*	
Vesper sparrow	*Blue-throated hummingbird*	
Sage sparrow	*Magnificent hummingbird*	
Savannah sparrow	*Lucifer hummingbird*	

Winter Visitors Heading North	Arriving for the Spring/Summer	Just Passing Through (Migrants)
Baird's sparrow	*Black-chinned hummingbird*	
Lincoln's sparrow	*Broad-tailed hummingbird*	
White-crowned sparrow	*Northern beardless-tyrannulet*	
Chestnut-collared longspur	*Greater pewee*	
	Western wood-pewee	
	Dusky-capped flycatcher	
	Ash-throated flycatcher	
	Western kingbird	
	Cassin's kingbird	
	Purple martin	
	Cliff swallow	
	Bell's vireo	
	Solitary vireo	
	Warbling vireo	
	Lucy's warbler	
	Grace's warbler	
	Painted redstart	
	Hepatic tanager	
	Summer tanager	
	Western tanager	
	Hooded oriole	
	Northern oriole	
	Scott's oriole	

Data taken from Harold R. Holt, *A Birder's Guide to Southeastern Arizona* (ABA Sales, book division of the American Birding Association, Colorado Springs, 1989); W.A. Davis and S.M. Russell, *Checklist of Birds of Southeastern Arizona* (Tucson Audubon Society, Tucson, 1994); and *Davis and Russell's Finding Birds in Southeast Arizona* (Tucson Audubon Society, 1995). For information about southern Arizona birds' habitats and statuses, see Appendix 2; see April's Fauna section for a discussion on bird migration.

In the grassland foothills and oak woodlands Mearn's quail begin hatching this month. Many shrubs are blooming in the higher desertscrub up into the oak woodlands, including desert lavender, an unlikely whiff of the English countryside in the desert; Mormon tea, on male and female plants; hop bush; and samota. Some of the oak trees may set blooms this month in lower and warmer elevations, and offering their fruit to birds and mammals are wolfberry shrubs, also called tomatillos, *or "little tomato plants," and manzanitas, "little apple plants." Early wildflowers in the higher elevations, up to the oak woodlands, may include Lewis flax, Arizona penstemon, dichylostema, various daleas, Greene's vetch, and common monkey flowers. Along watercourses, look in cottonwood and ash trees for the gauzy homes of tent caterpillars as the temperature warms up. Fifty or more dark forms squirm inside elliptical silky enclosures; at night they stream out of the nest onto the host trees and feed on the new leaves; at the bases of the trees you can find a litter of munched-on leaves.*

The gentle hand of spring is just touching the pine-oak woodlands above 6,000 feet in most areas. Hardy columbines are sprouting, insects swarm over creek pools, and bird song, a rarity in winter, is now common. Ruby-crowned kinglets, bridled titmice, juncos, and nuthatches may begin courting and mating this month. Deciduous trees such as alders, walnuts, and maples are just beginning to bud. Higher up, in the mixed conifer forests, patches of crusty snow still cling stolidly to the damp mat of old pine needles on the forest floor. There is a hint of spring: brown creepers are more active now, spiraling up the trunks of ponderosa pines looking for early insects, as are red-shafted flickers and, later in the month, the classic spring birds, American robins, which waited out the winter in the lower canyons of the mountains.

There is so much happening in the wilds in March that we are hard-pressed to decide where to explore. Besides a mandatory wildflower safari out Ajo Way (Highway 86), we also plan a climb of the famous Picacho Peak to enjoy the poppies. If we had to pick just one

MARCH WEATHER

	Sunrise	Sunset	Avg. Relative Humidity/Tucson
March 1	6:51 MST	6:21 MST	5 a.m. 53%
March 30	6:14 MST	6:42 MST	5 p.m. 23%

Stations	Ajo	Tucson	Mt. Lemmon
Station Elevation	(1,800 ft.)	(2,584 ft.)	(8,800 ft.)
March Averages			
Max. temperature	73.6°F	71.9°F	53.9°F
Min. temperature	48.8°F	43.8°F	25.3°F
Precipitation	.79 in.	.71 in.	1.55 in.
Snow	0 in.	.4 in.	7.9 in.
# days 100° & over	0	0	0
# days 32° & under	0	1	29
# days precip. >.01"	3	4	3
March Extremes			
Max. Temperature	96°F (1916)	92°F (1950)	68°F (1960)
Min. Temperature	27°F (1971)	20°F (1965)	-1°F (1962)
Max. Snow/month	0 in.	5.7 in. (1964)	23.5 in. (1962)
Max. Snow/1 day	0 in.	4.0 in. (1964)	8.0 in. (1962)
Max. Precip./month	3.17 in. (1952)	2.26 in. (1952)	3.65 in. (1982)
Max. Precip./1 day	1.82 in. (1944)	1.19 in. (1952)	2.00 in. (1982)

March Notes

In March we finally begin to feel the lengthening of the days and the warmer touch of the sun, although the wind can make it seem cooler. With desert highs averaging in the 70°s, lows in the mid-40°s—even higher by the end of the month—there is now no doubt spring is here. Shorts and t-shirts are de rigueur. During low desert hikes it can seem surprisingly hot if the mercury climbs above 80°. Averages indicate that there will be more bouts of rain—three or four days—and usually one last freezing night in the deserts, although winter still has its hold on the mountains where half a foot of snow may still fall and it may freeze every night. March can be a windy month; in 1934 just north of Pima County a state wind speed record of 84 mph was recorded.

For information about data sources for these listings, see the Climate section of the chapter Exploring the Nature of Pima County and Southern Arizona.

trail to hike for maximum wildflower blooms and bird activity, we might succumb and recommend Romero Canyon Trail in Catalina State Park, but in March spring beauty is everywhere.

FLORA

Wonderful World of Wildflowers

Wildflower watching can be as leisurely as strolling along desert trails and taking in the colors and scents or as challenging as hunting down species that are new to you and keying out their characteristics in plant guides. Whatever your style, the immense pleasure of finding flowers in the desert landscape is one of nature's best gifts.

A Rose by any Other Name. . .

We were enjoying a springtime hike with friends, one of whom is a field biologist, a specialist in plants. We passed a desert honeysuckle shrub in full bloom, its red-orange trumpets piping an invitation to all hummingbirds in the vicinity. Someone inquired about the plant's name and our friend rattled off, "Anisacanthus thurberi" *and hiked on. A puzzled look clouded the inquirer's face—to nonscientists, scientific names are all Greek or, more precisely, pseudo-Latin. And scientists' insistence that only scientific names be used to identify plants frustrates beginning wildflower enthusiasts, who may be convinced it's all a conspiracy to keep Common Man from tainting True Science.*

Believe it or not, there are actually some very good arguments for using the binomial system—genus given first, then species—rather than common names to describe plants. The binomial system provides useful categories of plants that indicate how they are related; there can be many plants in a genus *grouping because they are closely related, but there is always only one plant per* species *name. A plant's scientific name tells us what else it is related to as well as* specifically *what it is, anywhere in the world, no matter what language humans speak.*

However, plant common names are by no means standardized throughout the world, or throughout North America, or even throughout the Southwest. So, there may be several to a half-dozen common names used to describe one plant and of those names one or two might even also be used to describe a completely different plant. For example, Natt Dodge in his excellent guide Flowers of the Southwest Deserts *explains that the name "greasewood" is applied to any shrub that has resinous leaves and that "sage" is used to describe more than a half-dozen desert shrubs even though true sagebrush grows above 6,000 feet in the cold Great Basin desert. Our desert honeysuckle in the story above is also commonly called chuparosa, but so is the plant* Justicia californica, *which has similar flowers but does not grow commonly in southern Arizona.*

So use the most current scientific names to communicate most accurately what you see, but don't abandon common names because many times they can provide interesting clues to a plant's human history. Rhus aromatica *is called both squawbush and lemonadeberry, both names telling something interesting about the shrub, which grows in the mountains of the Southwest. Indian women used its stems extensively in basketmaking, and in the summer the berries were mixed with sugar to make a tasty lemonade-like drink.*

Remember: a rose by any other name is but a rose.

According to Carnegie Desert Laboratory ecologist William G. McGinnies, who monitored flowering plants for 20 years and wrote *Discovering the Desert and Flowering Periods for Common Desert Plants,* the last half of March is the peak season for flowers of non-woody perennials and spring annuals in the desert. Keep in mind that the absolute peak may vary a week or 10 days from March 20 according to temperature and precipitation during the preceding 5-month period—later if it has been dry or very cold, earlier if it has been moist and temperate. And the relative abundance of flowers will depend on a good amount of rain in fall and winter.

Many of the plants that bloom in March—ephemeral or "annual" wildflowers—belong to the "drought-escaping" group of plants characterized by Forrest Shreve early in this century. Shreve put desert plants into one of three groups based on how they evolved to survive in a drought-dominated environment; the other two groups are "drought-evaders" (such as brittlebush), which drop leaves or go into semidormant states during dry periods, and "drought-resisters" (such as cactuses), which can store water and remain relatively unaffected by the desert's extremes. The seeds of ephemeral wildflowers, the "escapers," germinate, grow, bloom, and fruit only after sufficient rainfall, either in late winter or late summer. These species survive by packing themselves away into safe little seed packages for the difficult times of the year. In general, the ephemerals that are blooming now, reliant on cool and wet fall weather to germinate, are plants related to northern and Californian species; those that thrive in the moist heat of the late summer monsoon season are related to Mexican or Central American tropical species. (See Appendix 1, Southern Arizona Desert Plants Blooming Calendar, for listings of blooming periods for common desert annuals and shrubs.)

So what is a flower? We see flowers' colors and beautiful forms, but what exactly are we seeing when we gaze on what we call a flower?

Most of the time what we see is a structure enclosing the sexual apparatus of the plant, usually both the female and male parts, although some plants have separate male and female flowers. The structure comprises outer petals and sepals, and inner pistil, stamens, and anthers (see illustration). There are as many kinds of structures as there are flowers in the world. These structures evolved to be pollinated in the most effective way possible by adapting to the most available pollinating agent, be it wind, moths, bees, flies, bats, or hummingbirds. For example, some species of penstemon flowers are just long enough for a hummingbird's tongue to reach the nectar but short enough so that the bird's forehead pushes against the pollen, transferring it from plant to plant. Flowers that are specially adapted to bird pollination are called *ornithophilous*. And many white flowers, which open only at night and are pollinated by a specific night-flying species (a moth or bat), have evolved to accommodate the physical characteristics of those species.

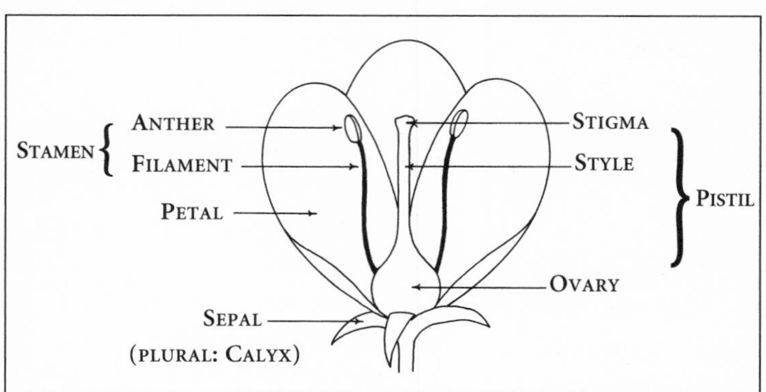

Parts of a flower

Sometimes what you see is not what you get—that is, what you're seeing is not actually a flower but many tiny flowers that make up a shape that looks like a flower, like desert marigolds (*Baileya multiradiata*) in the Compositae family, or the actual flower is tiny and inconspicuous and the colorful "petals" are over-evolved sepals or bracts, such as those in Indian paintbrushes (*Castilleja* spp.).

As amazing as structure, perhaps more so are the "strategies" of some flowers. Some close after successful pollination, such as desert willow (*Chiliopsis linearis*), or they change color, such as with some lupines (*Lupinus* spp.), to signal to their pollinators that the store is empty. And two of our most beautiful and sought-after flowers, owl's clover (*Orthocarpus purpurascens*) and Indian paintbrush (*Castilleja* spp.), are *hemiparasitic,* or partial parasites. They ensure success by attaching themselves to the roots of grasses or oaks and draw minerals and water from them, although they carry out their own photosynthesis.

Nearly every flower has an interesting story to tell. On your next hike, take along an inexpensive magnifying glass, and even if you can't tell a sepal from a stamen, you will be utterly amazed at the complexity of flower structures. See the bibliography for listings of flower books, most of which describe fascinating details of flowers and their life histories.

Desert Pines

Mormon tea shrubs (Ephedra *spp.*) *are fairly common in the Southwest on flat low-elevation plains, on sand dunes, and on rocky slopes as high as the oak woodlands. They are blooming this month and next; male and female flowers are borne on separate plants. The common name comes from a medicinal brew Mormon settlers in the last century made from the stems; presumably they learned the technique from the Navajos, who roasted the stems first because they believed it enhanced the flavor.* Ephedras, *of which there are four species in the Southwest, are ancient cone-bearing relatives of conifers; their tiny scale-like leaves conserve moisture and their straight, green-jointed stems carry on photosynthesis. The cones are small and soft, and the medium-sized shrubs in no way resemble their lofty cousins the pines. Around Pima County, you are most likely to encounter Mexican Mormon tea,* Ephedra trifurca.

FAUNA

Desert Dogs

The Bantu tribes of southern Africa have a word they use to describe someone who is exceedingly clever, fond of practical jokes, and perhaps a bit of a rogue. Such a person is known as a skelm.

It would be hard to imagine a more total war than the one waged against the coyote over the past century, nowhere more intensively than Arizona. Coyotes have been shot, poisoned, trapped, and purposely run over by trucks; their young have been burned in their dens or pulled out with fishhooks and clubbed or stomped to death. (Other campaigns in the same war wiped out the wolf, grizzly bear,

COYOTE

The coyote is known as Ban *in the Tohono O'odham language, and he is both coyote and Coyote. The latter is a legendary trickster, buffoon, skelm—responsible for a lot of mischief in the desert lands. Many common names of desert plants include Coyote's mark: coyote cotton* (Gossypium thurberi), *coyote melon* (Cucurbita digitata, *or* palmata, *and* Apodanthera undulata), *coyote tepary beans* (Phaseolus acutifolius *var.* latifolius) *and coyote devil's claw* (Proboscidea parviflora). *To the Tohono O'odham, these were all good cultivated crops until Coyote got hold of them and they spoiled: wild cotton's fiber is too short to spin, the melon is bitter, and the beans and devil's claw too puny. According to ethnobotanist Gary Paul Nabhan, by contrasting the cultivated and wild plants, the O'odham are emphasizing that they should care for their heirloom seedcrops lest they deteriorate in quality. But the bag of Coyote tricks found in wild relatives of cultivated crops is useful today: genes from wild cotton, grape, melon, and beans have been used to improve the health of cultivated crops.*

and jaguar in our state and severely reduced the numbers of mountain lions and black bears. Poisoned carcasses set out as bait have killed everything from golden eagles to foxes.)

In response, what have coyotes done? Well, they've done what any self-respecting *skelm* would do—increased their population and expanded their range.

When the western line of Anglo settlement in the United States was still drawn at the Appalachians, the coyote (*Canis latrans*) was unknown east of the Mississippi River. But during the 1800s and 1900s, as the wolf and grizzly were steadily extirpated, the coyote deftly filled their niches, colonizing many northeastern states and pushing farther north into Canada and Alaska. As urban centers grew into the surrounding countrysides, the coyote learned how to survive on the very fringes of even our most congested cities.

Desert coyotes, like the desert varieties of many other animals, are smaller than their eastern and northern cousins, with shorter and lighter-colored fur. Like coyotes everywhere, however, they are consummate omnivores. The carnivorous part of their diet ranges from deer to insects, with a predominance of rodents and rabbits—which they chase at speeds up to 40 miles per hour. In addition, they will eat an amazing variety of plant material. In late summer and fall, when prickly pear cactus fruit has set, you will see piles of bright red coyote poop in the middle of many rural roads (this well-known penchant for defecating on the center line of human rights-of-way has an overtly defiant air to it). Coyotes will also eat mesquite beans and other fruits, nuts, and seeds. And occasionally they will take down a domestic calf or sheep, further undermining their poor reputations with ranchers.

Coyotes are thought to be monogamous and to mate for life. The den is dug into the side of a wash or hill; 5 to 10 pups are born in late March, April, or May. The pups may stay with their parents for up to a year, learning a vast portfolio of skills.

The average desert coyote weighs about 25 pounds, which seems astonishingly small (we knew a house cat that weighed 23). Yet other desert canids are even smaller: adult gray foxes weigh about 9 pounds—the same as an antelope jackrabbit, and kit foxes average half that—little more than a fat cottontail. This hierarchy of size corresponds roughly to the frequency with which each species is seen in southern Arizona. Travel in the desertscrub and grasslands with any regularity and you will certainly hear coyotes and probably see them trotting away unhurriedly in the distance; they are found from low deserts into coniferous forests. Gray foxes are more secretive and rare, occurring most commonly in oak woodlands, although they have been seen in deserts up through forests. Many people live in southern Arizona their entire lives and never spot one. The diminutive kit fox, the shiest of all, inhabits low deserts and desert grasslands.

Ironically, the kit fox (*Vulpes macrotis*) is the only genuine carnivore of the trio. Its range roughly parallels that of the various species of kangaroo rats that comprise most of its diet. Pocket mice are also fair game as is the occasional rabbit—which must provide quite a battle. Kit foxes also prey on arthropods, including scorpions and centipedes, which they are adept at dispatching while avoiding the pointy ends (they usually crush those first, then munch leisurely on the rest). The kit fox locates this prey with help from its huge ears, which look as though they could home in on a mouse cracking seeds from 100 yards. These enormous appendages give the kit fox's face a decidedly outlandish but unbelievably cute appearance. Kit foxes are largely nocturnal; they spend the daylight hours in a burrow. In March or April the female gives birth to 4 or 5 young.

Although kit foxes are confined to the Southwest (barely reaching Oregon), the gray fox (*Urocyon cinereoargenteus*) is much more widely distributed. Its range includes all of the 48 states except for the upper midwest and northwest. Adaptable to a variety of habitats like its bigger cousin the coyote, it is also an accomplished omnivore.

The gray fox has a talent rare among canids—it is an excellent tree climber and will use this ability to escape danger or to search for birds' nests to rob of eggs or fledglings. It will also den in a hollow tree; failing that, a rock crevice or depression under a large boulder will suffice. The litter of 4 or 5 is born in March or April.

Desert Owls

One lovely spring morning we were on our way home from a visit to the Arizona–Sonora Desert Museum, headed back up the Gate's Pass Road. As we came around a curve, a movement on the shoulder caught our eyes. Thinking that it couldn't have been what we thought, we stopped the truck and walked back. Sure enough, there it was—a little western screech-owl, a scarce 8 inches tall, apparently hit in flight by a car and stunned, barely able to stand. We easily caught it and examined its fragile little body for signs of damage. One was immediately apparent: the left eye had a bloody contusion under the iris.

We didn't hold much hope—birds with impact trauma like this seem to die of shock very easily—but we took it back to the museum, since at that time they sometimes accepted injured animals for rehabilitation. (They no longer can accommodate wild injured animals; there are several licensed wildlife rehabilitation centers in southern Arizona today.) They agreed with our prognosis, but said they'd do what they could. The museum has a policy of not furnishing information about animals brought in for rehabilitation, so we learned nothing of the fate of "our" owl.

A few years later we were visiting the museum, and walked by an interpretive stand near the raptor enclosures. A docent was giving a lecture about the screech-owl perched on her finger—a screech owl with a funny dark spot on its left eye. Our accident victim looked fat and happy; the occlusion in its eye, which might have fatally hampered its hunting ability in the wild, was obviously no handicap here.

The western screech-owl (*Otus kennicottii*) of the Sonoran Desert is physically identical to other members of its species that range throughout the West and into British Columbia. But the local birds have thoroughly adapted to life in a hot climate. They appropriate abandoned woodpecker holes in saguaros for their own nests, waiting out the heat of day in well-insulated darkness, then venturing out to hunt after the sun is down. They get all the moisture they require from their prey, which includes insects, small mammals, and reptiles.

Screech-owls are year-round residents of Pima County. The same saguaro holes that shelter them from summer heat provide a buffer against winter chill. After mating in March, the female lays 2 to 5 eggs in the unlined cavity, and the male feeds her and often roosts with her while the eggs are incubated. Usually 4 or 5 chicks are hatched and are ready to leave the nest in about a month. (Incidentally, western screech-owls don't screech—their call is a very soft series of whistled hoots, often described as a "bouncing ball" call.)

Another owl, which competes with the screech-owl for empty nest holes, is the most abundant owl in Pima County during the summer—but you're more likely to hear than see them. We think of house finches as pretty small birds, but if you stood one next to an elf owl (*Micrathene whitneyi*), the finch would actually look down on the tiny raptor. Barely 5-1/2" tall, the elf owl is the smallest owl in the world, and only occurs in the extreme southwest of the United States, mainly in Arizona.

Elf owls winter far south in Mexico. In spring, beginning this month, the males return to Arizona before the females and search out suitable nest holes in saguaros or sometimes in deciduous trees, such as sycamores. They then perch in the holes and call to attract a prospective mate, belting forth a remarkably loud chirping song beginning at dusk. Once a female has accepted the invitation, she spends most of her time in the hole, receiving food from the male. The eggs, usually 2 to 3, are laid in May or early June; the young hatch about 3-1/2 weeks later and are ready to fly in another 3-1/2 weeks.

A 1-1/4-ounce raptor is necessarily limited in its choice of prey. Elf owls feed mostly on insects, snatching moths in mid-flight and pouncing on grasshoppers on the ground. They tackle scorpions as well, crushing the stinger before dining on the rest. Now and then a small snake or lizard is added to the menu.

Not much bigger than the elf owl, but far rarer, are ferruginous pygmy owls (*Glaucidium brasilianum*), whose range barely extends into Arizona from Mexico. Ferruginous pygmy owls inhabit desert lowlands; in fact this elevational preference is the easiest way to distinguish them from the very similar northern pygmy owl, a more common resident of higher woodlands and mountains throughout the West.

The most often seen, and largest, owls in southern Arizona are great horned owls (*Bubo virginianus*), hawk-sized birds found throughout the United States and far north into Canada. Their size and habit of roosting in the open, even after dawn and before dusk, make them easy to spot. When flushed they flap away on eerily silent wings.

Continuing the owl propensity for using housing constructed by others, great horned owls use the abandoned stick nests of hawks in the arms of saguaros or trees, although sometimes the eggs are simply laid on a bare rock ledge. These owls are also comfortable in urban environments and are often seen in downtown Tucson; several have nested on the University of Arizona campus, where their distinctive *who!who-who!* spooks students headed for night classes.

As their range indicates, great horned owls exploit a wide range of prey species. In northern Canada they hunt snowshoe hares; in the desert likely targets include woodrats, kangaroo rats, rabbits, and snakes.

We've discussed the smallest, largest, and rarest, but the most beautiful owl is certainly the barn owl (*Tyto alba*), with its softly patterned feathers and unearthly dished face. That odd face has a purpose, though—the shape helps funnel faint sound waves to the owl's sensitive ears, aiding it in tracking prey with deadly accuracy in utter darkness.

Barn owls, another widely distributed species, are fond of nesting in deserted manmade structures. In southern Arizona they frequent the many abandoned mine shafts scattered throughout the countryside, laying their eggs after mating this month on ledges 10 or 15 feet below ground level. Barn owl chicks, in contrast to their parents, are possibly the ugliest baby birds on earth.

One last category can only be described as the strangest: owls that live underground. Burrowing owls (*Speotyto cunicularia*) use holes dug by other animals such as ground squirrels, prairie dogs, and even desert tortoises and badgers. The owls often stand guard at the entrance to the burrows, looking rather comical on their long, unfeathered legs.

Females lay 7 to 9 eggs in their subterranean nest chamber, from March through early summer. The alarm call of the young birds mimics the sound of a rattlesnake—certainly an effective deterrent for most intruders.

Desert Tortoises

*Look into the eye of a desert tortoise and you might see a dinosaur looking back at you. Relatives of modern tortoises and turtles first appeared in the fossil record of the Triassic period, the beginning of the age of dinosaurs over 200 million years ago. In the geographically isolated and arid Southwest, there are only five native turtles. Of these, two are terrestrial: the desert box turtle, a grassland species, and desert tortoise (*Xerobates agassizii, *formerly* Gopherus*). The desert tortoise is the largest native North American land turtle—up to 9 pounds—and can live to a hundred years in a range a few miles square amid moist rocky slopes in the Sonoran and Mohave deserts, eating grasses, herbaceous and succulent plants, and fruit. Emerging this month after hibernation in deep burrows, which they dig with huge foreclaws, the desert tortoises will seek out mates for breeding. Young tortoises hatch August to October and weigh just 1 ounce; because of their soft shells, they are at extreme risk of predation. In Arizona, desert tortoises are being closely monitored by Arizona Game and Fish—they may be in jeopardy because of habitat loss and hunting by collectors. It is illegal to capture a desert tortoise to keep as a pet; the Arizona–Sonora Desert Museum sponsors an adoption program for "rescued" tortoises that cannot be returned to the wild.*

PLACES TO VISIT IN MARCH

Romero Canyon Trail

It is just before dawn as we begin to climb out of the mesquite bosque after splashing across the ankle-deep ice water of Sutherland Wash. The sun is trying to crest the heavy wall of Pusch and Romero ridges ahead of us. Railroad-tie stairs make the steep climb safer and forestall erosion; at the top, we can see desertscrub chase rolling grassland up the trail. We know that after about 2 miles the trail, out of sight over the first ridge, breaks into oak woodland near our destination, Romero Pools.

Even in the chilly air—it's about 50°F—we can hear the *ZZiinngg!* call of Costa's hummingbirds courting prospective mates. Later we will see a handsome male flashing his brilliant purple head atop a mesquite snag. We see several just-fledged birds, including black-throated sparrows and cactus wrens. Amazingly, we realize that there are hundreds, no, thousands, of insects darting around, their wings backlit by the sun, which has broken free of the rock crags above. In winter, the air here is so still and quiet. Now it is alive with the zing and flash of insects and birds celebrating spring.

This trail is one of the best in the Santa Catalina Mountains for enjoying the wildflower season. Head to Catalina State Park, to the end of the road; the trail heads east from there. The peak blooming period is usually around March 20, give or take a week (later if it's been cold, earlier if it's been wet and warm). In just under 3 miles the trail winds from a riparian mesquite bosque at 2,800 feet to an oak woodland at 3,600 feet, so you can catch a wide range of bloomers. Along this trail, one can find—in addition to the more common species (see Appendix 1, Southern Arizona Desert Plants Blooming Calendar)—mariposa lilies and Coulter's hibiscus, two elegant beauties, which sometimes bloom this month but more commonly in April. Mariposa lilies (*Calochortus kennedyi*) boast large ripe-tomato-red cups borne on single 6-inch-tall stems, with leaves that look like those of onions. They stand alone, arrogantly, in their beauty. Coulter's hibiscus (*Hibiscus coulteri*) is a woody shrub; the blossoms are large and elegant, the color of freshly whipped butter. If you hike the trail too early in the day, the blooms of these plants may not be open; after 9 A.M. seems a good time but be prepared for a hotter hike out, as temperatures can get up into the high 80°s in March.

The pools make a fine spot for a picnic; there are dozens of cascading waterfalls pouring into deep inviting pools. Plan to spend at least an hour lounging in the exquisite spring sun.

Wildflower Safari

It started out innocently enough. An annual drive in mid-March out Ajo Way (Highway 86), west across the Tohono O'odham Indian Reservation, lunch at our favorite O'odham restaurant in Covered Wells, up Indian Route 15 to Casa Grande, and back to Tucson via Interstate 10. This is some of the best spring wildflower country in the state. In most years the oranges of Mexican poppies and globemallows, the pinks of verbenas and owl's clover and Parry's penstemons, the yellows of brittlebush and goldfields, and the brilliant white of desert chicory and prickly poppies splash the roadsides like a Mary Cassat painting. We don't remember just when our leisurely drive changed to a challenging annual safari to see if we could beat last year's "bag." We do know, however, that the safari is addictive and fun.

We leave Tucson around 7 A.M. and begin "bagging" just after Kitt Peak road (Highway 386). We stop every 5 or so miles, in varying habitat such as rocky hills or sandy washes, and spend 20 or 30 minutes combing each area for flowers. If we find ones unknown to us, we try to identify them with four or five flower guides; but if we can't, we'll take good notes about color, numbers of petals and stamens, flower shape and leaf and stem shapes and make drawings so we can look them up at a rest stop or back home (we only count species

Past Kitt Peak Rd.
2-3 miles West

yellow center delicate violet

12 Erigeron divergens - fleabane
13 Sphaeralcea ambigua - mallow
Bright red here!
14 Ipomopsis longiflora - Blue trumpets
15 Gilia sinuata - Gilia (desert)
Purple

pale blue violet

straight long corolla tube

on long stems

16 Calliandra eriophylla - fairy duster
17 Baileya multiradiata - desert marigold
18 Lesquerella gordonii - bladderpod
19 Encelia farinosa - brittlebush
20 Eschscholtzia mexicana - Mexican poppy
21 Rumex hymenosepalus - Dock
22 Plantago insularis - plantago

Large Wash, near Covered Wells

23 Salvia columbariae - Chia (smells like mint - in family)
24 Glandularia gooddingii - desert verbena
25 Penstemon parryi -
26 Lepidium - Peppergrass

At Gu-Achi Trading Post

27 Dichelostemma pulchellum - Desert hyacinth
Bulb, onion-like ; lavender
28 Lotus humistratus - Hairy deer vetch
flower = tiny gold, hairy leaves
29 Eriophyllum lanosum = pygmy white daisy 1½" tall

Notes from a "wildflower safari"

that we can positively identify). In an average year we end up with around 35 separate species, including 3 or more of the same genus of lupines (*Lupinus* spp.), penstemons (*Penstemon* spp.), and globemallows (*Sphaeralcea* spp.). (See Appendix 1, Southern Arizona Desert Plants Blooming Calendar, for a list of species you might see; roadsides can be excellent wildflower "beds" because the tarmac surface concentrates rain runoff.) Depending on our whim, we either drive straight out Ajo Way past Sells and stop for Indian tacos in Covered Wells (marked incorrectly as Quijotoa by the highway department), then return by the same route and take a side trip up Kitt Peak road to look for early-blooming scarlet sage (*Stachys coccinea*) and Greene's deer vetch (*Lotus greenei*). Another option is to take Indian Route 15 north at Covered Wells to Casa Grande, and head home on I-10 with a stop to see the poppies at Picacho Peak (see below).

Visitors once asked us for a recommended "wildflower drive," so we enthusiastically described our favorite route. We happened to see them again and they reported that they had seen "a few flowers," but they were clearly disappointed. Going 55 miles an hour and looking through their windshield, they expected to see as many flowers as we did at a walking pace. Beauty really is in the eye of the beholder.

Poppies at Picacho Peak

Besides the stately saguaro cactus, springtime poppies are perhaps southern Arizona's most famous botanical attraction. Splashed across the desertscrub from March through April, artfully arranged around bright green cactus and palo verde trees and dramatic granite and sandstone rock, masses of glowing orange California and Mexican poppies draw people from around the world. If you subscribe to *Arizona Highways* magazine, the most likely image in your mind of poppies in the desert is of a brilliant orange carpet sweeping up to the base of the dramatic spire of Picacho Peak, 40 miles northwest of Tucson. But bear in mind, vast carpets of the flowers are rare; they occur perhaps every five or six years. You are more likely to see small but beautiful patches—more like area rugs than carpets.

If you visit, plan to climb the short but very steep trail to the top. The views are worth the extra effort. The peak is within a state park, which also has a campground. There is also a commercial campground and a few mini-mart stores.

MARCH SKIES

"Green Moon"

TRADITIONAL O'ODHAM NAME FOR MARCH

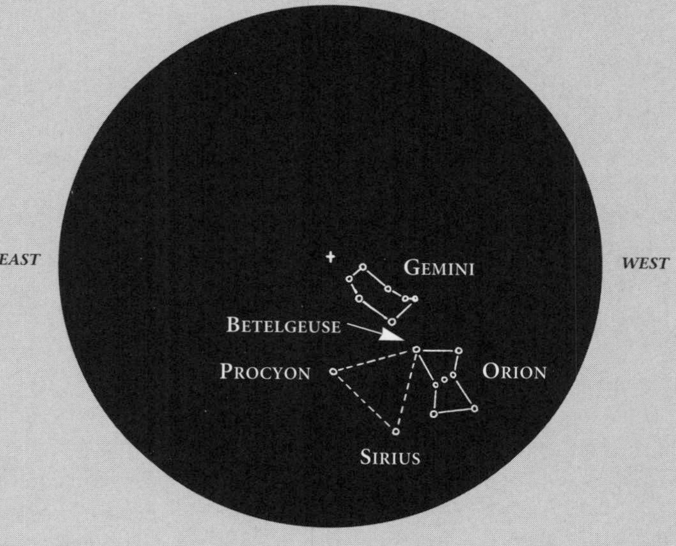

Star Chart for 32°N
Mid-month, 9 pm

FEATURE CONSTELLATION

Castor and Pollux are the famous twins of the Gemini constellation, the sons of the Greek god Zeus and Queen Leda of Sparta; their sister was Helen of Troy. Castor, who was mortal, and Pollux, who was immortal, were inseparable and shared many adventures, including a quest for the Golden Fleece. But their happiness ended in tragedy when Castor was killed in battle. Pollux implored his father to let him join his brother in Hades, the underworld; Zeus was so moved by their brotherly fidelity that he allowed Castor to join his brother in the heavens for half the year and for the remainder of the year return to Hades, where Pollux joined him.

MARCH AT A GLANCE

Desertscrub

❧ If it has been wet and mild, expect a wildflower bonanza. See Appendix 1 for Southern Arizona Desert Plants Blooming Calendar.

❧ Several species of carpenter bees are very active. *Xylocopa californica* is more common in the desert, where nest sites of yucca and agave bloom stalks occur; both sexes are black. Look for them around blooming desert lavender shrubs (*Hyptis emoryi*), one of their favorite plants. *X. varipuncta* is larger than *X. californica,* and the females are black while the males are golden-orange with green eyes. *X. varipuncta* prefers chinaberry and mulberry trees.

❧ When the brittlebush (*Encelia farinosa*) is blooming, look for iron-cross blister beetles (*Tegrodera erosa*), which feed on the blooming plant. The beetles are black, yellow, and red and have a black cross-like pattern on their backs; a chemical in their bodies called cantharidin can cause skin blisters.

❧ Desert owls—elf, western screech, barn—begin their mating this month.

❧ Birds tending to newly fledged young include Anna's and Costa's hummingbirds, ruby-crowned kinglets, black-throated sparrows, verdins, Gila woodpeckers, curve-billed thrashers, and northern mockingbirds. Pyrrhuloxias and cardinals will join in the family scene later this month and next, as will great horned owls.

❧ Spring bird migrations are well under way. See the Flight Schedules chart in this month's opening essay for a list of popular species that leave, arrive, or just pass through this month.

❧ Desert bighorn sheep, coyotes, kit foxes, gray foxes, rock squirrels, and some of the lizards, such as side-blotched, are having young.

❧ Desert tortoises are emerging from hibernation.

❧ Red-spotted toads begin mating, calling loudly near waterholes and creeks.

Desert Grasslands

❧ Mearn's quail begin hatching.

❧ Burrowing owls begin mating this month.

❧ Desert box turtles emerge from hibernation and begin to seek out mates for breeding later in the spring.

❧ Mule deer males return to solitary life and are shedding their antlers; they will immediately begin to grow new ones for next year's rut. Mule deer may move up into the oak woodlands for the summer.

Oak Woodlands

❧ Many shrubs are blooming in warmer canyon woodlands, including desert lavender (*Hyptis emoryi*), an unlikely whiff of the English countryside in the desert; Mormon tea (*Ephedra trifurca*), on male and female plants; and hop bush (*Dodonaea angustifolia*).

❧ Some of the oak trees may set blooms this month in lower and warmer elevations.

❧ Wolfberry shrubs (*Lycium* spp.), also called tomatillos, or "little tomato plants," for their bright red pea-sized fruits, and manzanitas (*Arctostaphylos* spp.), "little apple plants," are offering their fruits.

❧ Early wildflowers may include Lewis flax (*Linum lewisii*), Arizona penstemon (*Penstemon pseudospectabilis*), dichelostemma, various daleas, locoweeds (*Astragalus* spp.), Greene's deer vetch (*Lotus greenei*), and common monkey flowers (*Mimulus guttatus*).

❧ In mild years, look for the gauzy homes of tent caterpillars (*Gloveria arizonensis*) in cottonwood and ash trees along watercourses. Fifty or more dark forms squirm inside elliptical silky enclosures; at night they stream out of the nest onto the host trees and feed on the new leaves—around the base of the tree you can find a litter of munched-on leaves.

❧ Like their mule deer cousins, male white-tailed deer are returning to solitary life and will shed their antlers to grow new ones for next year's rut.

Pine-Oak Woodlands

❧ Columbines (*Aquilegia* spp.) are among the first summer plants to sprout.

❧ Deciduous trees such as alders (*Alnus* sp.), walnuts (*Juglans* sp.), and maples (*Acer* sp.) are just beginning to bud.

❧ Ruby-crowned kinglets, bridled titmice, yellow-eyed juncos, and nuthatches may begin courting and mating this month.

Coniferous Forests

- Patches of crusty snow still cling stolidly to the damp mat of old pine needles on the forest floor.
- Brown creepers are more active now, spiraling up the trunks of ponderosa pines looking for early insects, as are red-shafted flickers and later in the month, the classic spring birds, American robins.

Special Events

- Spring Begins: The vernal equinox occurs March 21. See below.

In the Sky

- The constellation Gemini is high overhead, showing off its two stars, Castor and Pollux.
- Vernal equinox is March 21, one of two equinoxes during the solar year (the autumnal equinox is in September). During an equinox the sun passes the equator on its way north (vernal equinox) or south (autumnal equinox); daylight and darkness are of equal length on that day. (The sun does not actually travel north and south of the equator but appears to as the earth on its tilted axis orbits around the sun.)

See the chapter Exploring the Nature of Pima County and Southern Arizona for definitions and descriptions of communities.

april

LIKE A WARM *tide, spring rises steadily up the mountainsides. In the deserts, summer has been waiting on the horizon but now begins to move in day by day, inching its way along the backside of spring. As spring ascends, the dawn of summer is upon us.*

As though to prove it, the hillsides begin to glow warmly as blue palo verde trees set flower buds, waiting until around mid-month before bursting their full lemon-yellow upon us, and mesquite trees present their straw-colored catkins. The Tohono O'odham call this time "yellow moon," Oam Mashath.

Our summer doves, the white-winged, arrive singing the song of summer that later, mixed with the whine of cicadas and the drowsing heavy heat of May and June, means that summer is fully upon us. For now, their cooing call Who-cooks-for-YOU? *echoes through the desert hillsides and is oddly comforting.*

Gambel's quail feast on mesquite buds, and their flocks, or coveys (which include as many as 40 members in fall and winter) disband as they pair up to mate. The beautiful males, with their chestnut caps, black faces, and elegant teardrop-shaped head plumes, perch on high mesquite snags or shrubs and call almost sadly, plaintively. Southwestern folklore says that when the mesquites are fully leafed out, by early to mid-April, the frostless season begins. How-

The bright yellow flowers of the desert prickly pear cactus herald April's blossom show

ever, science tells us that the probability of freezing temperatures is 10 percent for April 10.

With summer comes snake season. Keep an eye out this month for our serpent friends, including western diamondback and mojave rattlesnakes, gopher and long-nosed snakes, and Sonoran whip-snakes, among many other species, in the desertscrub up into the oak woodlands. (See May's Fauna section for the ecology and identification of our venomous snakes.)

*The desert's most unusual plants bloom this month. In the west deserts you might be lucky to find sandfood (*Pholisma sonorae; *to the west of Pima County) and broomrape (*P. arenarium*) blooming in the rolling sand dunes below the desert shrubs on which they grow, for each of these bizarre-looking plants is a root parasite. They are rare now, possibly because the hunter-gatherer people—the Hia C-ed O'odham, the Sand People—who for millennia harvested the flower stalks have nearly vanished as a race, having moved out of their traditional nomadic range of the Gran Desierto to live and intermarry with their relatives, the Tohono O'odham.*

The cactus blossom show begins this month as well. Desert prickly pear and beavertail cactus flame bright yellow and fuchsia, respectively; purple graces hedgehog cactus; and the blossoms of staghorn chollas, whose species name versicolor *might give you a clue, can be yellow, orange, or reddish-purple. Though the teddy bear cactus's yellowish-green flowers are inconspicuous and small, don't overlook this underappreciated plant as it quietly blooms this month. If the weather has been mild, look for creamy white buds atop the statuesque saguaro cactuses late in the month. Banana yuccas send up their short woody flower stalks this month, which are visited by yucca moths, their only pollinator.*

Beginning this month through the summer, riparian woodlands across Pima County resound with the songs and antics of more breeding birds than we can count. Bell's vireos invade the streamside thickets the way Arizonans flock to San Diego in the summer. You almost never see them, but their loud and unique song carries far (to us, Bell's vireos sound like they are counting rapidly up to six and back down, ascending and descending in pitch . . . one-two-Three-Four-FIVE-SIX! . . .SIX-FIVE-Four-Three-two-one*). Staccato tapping over and over may be a ladder-backed woodpecker marking its territory and attracting a mate. Hooded orioles, ash-throated flycatchers, solitary vireos, summer and hepatic tanagers, and Cassin's kingbirds arrive and begin breeding in the riparian corridors this month and next; look for them especially in groves of Arizona sycamores. The spectacular and rare elegant trogons, tropical birds of the quetzal family, return to a few of southern Arizona's moist riparian canyons this month to breed. (For more on migrating birds, see the Flight Schedule for Popular Southern Arizona Birds in the opening essay for March.)*

Most of the dozen hummingbird species for which southeastern Arizona is famous should arrive this month, primarily in the moist riparian woodlands of low- to mid-elevation canyons, although some will move up the mountains as summer rolls in, descending again in the fall before migrating south for the winter. In lower riparian woodlands the more common hummers will be broad-billed, black-chinned, and Costa's; magnificent, blue-throated, and broad-tailed will dominate in the higher mountain riparian woodlands. (See May's Fauna and Places to Visit sections for more on viewing hummingbirds.) Most Anna's hummingbirds depart this month for California, for a second breeding season through mid-summer; some of the Costa's will join them next month.

In the oak woodlands spring flowers are at their peak, including Lewis flax, monkey flower, Arizona penstemon, and indigo bush, while the creeks are beginning to succumb to the beginning of the first dry season even as spring starts its long climb up into the high country. Western wood pewees call their onomatopoeic song while Bewick's and house wrens flit about busily. Spring reaches well into the pine-oak woodlands this month, where Anna's and black-chinned hummingbirds are nesting, the warming earth continues to nurture the seedling promises of columbines, wild berries, and sum-

mer annuals, and the watercourses glow freshly green with the new leaves of velvet ash, Arizona black walnut, thinleaf alder, and cottonwood trees. Violet-green swallows and white-throated swifts play like acrobats along cliffs. Nights begin with the musical calls of whip-poor-wills, which migrate here in the summer, and later we hear the haunting calls of flammulated and whiskered screech owls.

In the mixed-conifer pine forests, hermit thrushes, house wrens, and yellow-rumped warblers are breeding and the "mountain hummers" begin to arrive. The aspens, maples, and Gambel's oaks might venture to put out leaves later this month, although we've seen many a late spring freeze knock them back to bare branches and force them to start all over again.

A hike up to Sycamore Basin in the front range of the Catalina Mountains is always on the agenda early this month. We like to relax in the cool shade with the songs of Bear Creek and the birds of spring in our ears. Another favorite nearby getaway is Ciénega Creek, east of Tucson; we walk among the stately sycamores and mesquites to enjoy the last of spring in the desert and welcome the breeding birds of summer. We might also venture out to Brown Canyon, in the shadow of Baboquivari Peak, which is a sacred mountain to the Tohono O'odham. Maybe we'll be lucky and see coatimundis, golden eagles, or the more rare zone-tailed hawks and sulphur-bellied flycatchers.

APRIL WEATHER

	Sunrise	Sunset	Avg. Relative Humidity/Tucson
April 1	6:12 MST	6:43 MST	5 a.m. 42%
April 30	5:39 MST	7:03 MST	5 p.m. 16%

Stations	Ajo	Tucson	Mt. Lemmon
Station Elevation	(1,800 ft.)	(2,584 ft.)	(8,800 ft.)
April Averages			
Max. temperature	82.0°F	80.5°F	62.1°F
Min. temperature	55.4°F	50.1°F	31.6°F
Precipitation	.29 in.	.31 in.	.36 in.
Snow	0 in.	.10 in.	.08 in.
# days 100° & over	0	0	0
# days 32° & under	0	0	15
# days precip.>.01"	1	2	1
April Extremes			
Max. Temperature	103°F (1962)	98°F (1965)	74°F (1959)
Min. Temperature	37°F (1938)	33°F (1976)	19°F (1961)
Max. Snow/month	0 in.	2.0 in. (1976)	.5 in. (1961)
Max. Snow/1 day	0 in.	2.0 in. (1976)	.5 in. (1961)
Max. Precip./month	3.19 in. (1941)	1.66 in. (1951)	2.10 in. (1963)
Max. Precip./1 day	1.44 in. (1941)	.74 in. (1952)	2.10 in. (1963)

April Notes

Temperatures in the deserts are creeping up the thermometer, but April is mostly a moderate month, with an average of about 80°F in the days and low 50°s at night. In the mountains, snow is still possible and for half the nights the temperature still drops below freezing. There may be a few days of sprinkles, but for the most part expect low humidity and clear, often windy days. Visitors are convinced the warm days mean summer is here to stay, but natives can usually recall at least one or two years in their lifetimes when it snowed in April in Tucson. In 1976 schools were closed and most of town shut down to enjoy more than an inch of snow that blanketed the desert; some cactuses suffered freeze damage that resulted in either death or disfiguration. Twisted and sagging saguaro arms are probably the result of one of these freezes.

For information about data sources for these listings, see the Climate section of the chapter Exploring the Nature of Pima County and Southern Arizona.

FLORA

Stately Sycamores

Anyone who has been to Sabino Canyon or other riparian areas in southern Arizona or southwestern New Mexico has experienced the cool shade of a sycamore tree and likely caressed its smooth white trunk or climbed high into the canopy and reclined on a gracefully curved limb. Shade is always precious in the desert, but the shade of the sycamore (*Platanus wrightii*) always has an extra-cool feeling to it.

This feeling might be partly psychological but part of it is very real—riparian areas, with their numerous broad-leaved trees such as sycamores and cottonwoods, transpire a great deal of water, cooling their surroundings by evaporation. Even when the watercourse in which they grow is dry on the surface, roots pull moisture from beneath the ground.

Several million years ago, one wouldn't have had to visit streams or canyons to find sycamores in Pima County—they formed extensive forests over what are today cactus-encrusted desert hillsides. During that period the climate was significantly cooler and wetter, and broad-leaved deciduous trees were the dominant species. As the climate slowly warmed and dried, these trees could no longer survive in open terrain, so their populations dwindled to the remnants we see today, huddled near reliable water sources.

The sycamore is the tallest tree of the desert lowlands, reaching 80 feet in height (its cousin, the eastern sycamore, is the most massive tree in the eastern United States). Its five-lobed leaves are large as well, up to 8 inches wide, and turn rich copper before dropping in the fall. The flowers, though, are inconspicuous and tiny, arranged in round heads about 1 inch in diameter, appearing now through June. When the seeds mature these heads form hard brown balls, hanging on stalks in clusters of three to five. Over time the hard balls break up into hundreds of individual seeds suspended on miniscule filamentous parachutes, which breezes can distribute.

Sycamores are of little value as browse for large mammals, but

Above, *sycamore leaves and catkins*

many species of birds nest in the canopy or in holes in the limbs and find excellent insect foraging on the leaves and twigs. Often sycamore trunks display neat rows of bore holes from woodpeckers searching methodically for hidden insects.

While they are ecologically crucial, the best thing about sycamore trees is their wonderful smell. Not quite sweet, not spicey, neither strong nor delicate, the scent of a sycamore is the smell of water and earth, *alive,* the way you imagine a tree ought to smell.

The Desert's Fountains of Life

Our Sonoran Desert is perhaps visually most identified by its postcard headliner, the giant saguaro cactus, a magnificent and bizarre plant that has a whole national park dedicated to its preservation. But standing stolidly by the saguaro's side, unnoticed and unappreciated, are the very plants that make life for saguaros—and over 165 other desert plants—possible. Desert legumes (members of the bean family), such trees as mesquites and ironwoods, provide the perfect microhabitats for the dispersal, germination, seedling establishment, and survival of other key desert plants. Rare desert species such as Sonoran pronghorn antelopes, desert bighorns, and masked bobwhite quail also depend on the desert legumes for shelter and food. In essence, they are the nurseries of the Sonoran Desert.

*Ironwood (*Olneya tesota*) is a very slow-growing, very hard-wooded tree. Live specimens of up to 800 years old have been identified, and dead trees may persist for almost 2,000 years. But these very qualities have endangered the future of ironwood. Vast tracts of desert are being cleared in the United States and Mexico to make way for urban expansion, and for food and charcoal production. The Seri Indians of Mexico's Sonoran coast use ironwood for their famous carvings of desert and sea animals. Non-Indian copycat carvers, who take huge quantities of ironwood from the desert and mass-produce carvings with power tools, have built up a sizeable industry as well, contributing to a significant depletion of ironwood in the state of Sonora. Without the plants that are the*

critical building blocks for the Sonoran Desert, we won't have sufficient regeneration of other plants, such as saguaros; a domino effect may be triggered as the species that depend on these plants, especially pollinators like moths and bats, diminish; the result—fragmented and endangered natural systems. (For more information on conservation projects involving desert legumes, contact the Ironwood Alliance Task Force; see Appendix 6, Southern Arizona Nature Resources.)

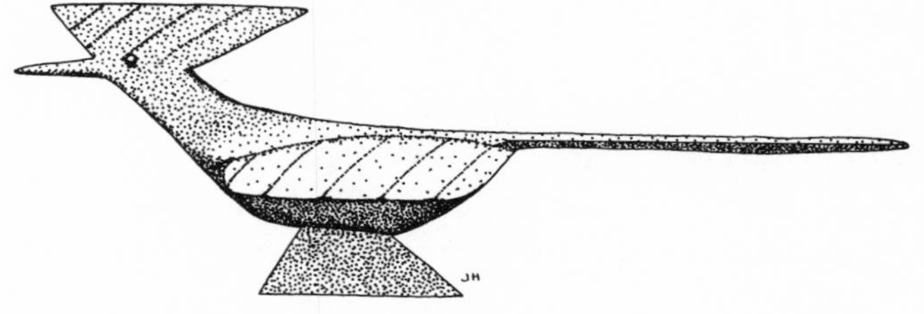

Seri Indian carving made from an ironwood branch

A Sticky Situation

To a casual observer, there would seem to be little mystery to sharp things on plants—they can hurt you, so you stay away from them. It follows that animals that might otherwise eat the plant will stay away as well, thus explaining why the plant grew such things in the first place. There is little doubt that spines originally evolved to protect the plant from being eaten. Support for this theory is found in Australia, where there are very few thorny plants—and no indigenous hoofed browsers such as those found in North America.

Yet anyone who has watched a group of javelinas shred a prickly pear cactus with apparent impunity, seen a range cow walking around with several cholla sections dangling from its lips, or watched a woodrat daintily nibbling new cholla buds while perched comfortably in the stickiest part of the cactus might question the efficacy of this defense. Scientists have observed for decades that spines and thorns seem to do little to deter many browsing animals, and researchers have subsequently searched for other evolutionary advantages to them.

Although many plants, such as mesquites, acacias, and palo verde trees grow thorns, the Cactaceae have invested in them to the near exclusion of all other foliage, and so it is cactus spines that have attracted the most scrutiny. And a clue lay therein for the researchers who were smart enough to look at the question from different angles: cactuses are predominantly plants of hot and dry climates. Might there be some cryptic advantage to growing spines instead of leaves in such an environment? As it turned out, there are several.

All green plants use chlorophyll to convert the sun's energy into carbohydrates. Usually chlorophyll is contained in leaves; however, leaves also give off large amounts of water—an expensive habit in the desert. So cactuses have shunned them, instead concentrating their chlorophyll in their trunks and limbs, the waxy skins of which lose less water to evaporation. Furthermore, it was discovered, those limbs receive a significant amount of shade from the spines—up to about 25 percent on average, and as much as 90 percent on the teddy bear cholla—helping to keep the internal tissues of the plant cooler and further reducing water loss. The spines also cut the flow of hot, dry, highly evaporative breezes over the surface of the cactus. This is accomplished with little metabolic cost, since mature spines are dead tissue, like hair or fingernails.

Another advantage to spines has been unwittingly discovered by everyone who has brushed too close to a cholla and experienced the pain of having a section of it imbed itself in the shin. When we stop to pry out the offending segment and fling it away in wrath, we have helped disperse the parent plant's genes—since that segment quickly roots and grows into a new cactus. When cholla segments cling to cattle or deer they can be dispersed for miles.

There is an additional benefit to spines—albeit not to the plant itself. For although in some situations spines don't seem to deter some browsers, they are a formidable hindrance to carnivores. Thus several species of birds brave the dangerous interior of the cholla to build their nests there, and woodrats often incorporate dozens of segments in their nest mounds, at least slowing down any excavating coyotes or badgers. Of course, if any of those segments managed to take root there would be a benefit returned to the cholla.

It's ironic to think that an adaptation presumably evolved for one purpose would prove to be more useful for another and that a device designed as a defense against animals can be utilized by other animals for their own defense.

FAUNA

The Long Commute

When one sees a few flocks of birds here and there overhead during migration in spring or fall, it's hard to imagine the extent of the phenomenon. Biologists estimate that in North America alone, about 5 billion birds shift their residences twice each year.

Why do they do it? The simplest answer is because they can. The ability to seasonally change habitats gives an animal a tremendous advantage over other animals that are tied to the same surroundings throughout the year.

For example, in summer the Arctic tundra explodes in productivity. Twenty-four-hour daylight provides energy for rapid plant growth and massive reproduction of insects—a paradise for nesting birds and other animals. But six months later the same region is suffering below-zero temperatures and has no daylight at all. The carrying capacity—the ability of the natural system to support a certain number of life forms—has been reduced to almost zero. Most large animals must hibernate to survive the cold months, and they barely survive the winter. Birds, however,

AVIAN DISEASE ALERT

Bird lovers who provide food and water for the many seed-eaters, especially around urban areas, should be aware of a deadly bird disease that is easily transmitted at feeders during the warm summer months. Trichomoniasis is caused by a pathenogenic species of Trichomonas, *a protozoa (there are many species of* Trichomonas, *many of which do not cause fatal symptoms). The deadly parasite often invades birds' upper digestive tract and can cause cankers in the beak, throat, and crop (different strains attack in different parts of the body). Eventually the birds cannot eat and they die of starvation; the disease is spread when infected birds try to pick up seed but spill it back onto the feeder where it is consumed by other birds. Trichomoniasis may also spread in bird baths, and some biologists are looking at the possibility that raptors that feed on other birds, Cooper's hawks and great horned owls among them, may also contract the disease. Birds of the* Columbiforme *family—doves and pigeons—are the most common carriers. If you feed birds and attract pigeons and doves, you may want to stop feeding during the warm months, April through September, or consider feeders that exclude Columbiformes. Water may be offered but change it daily and scrub the container well each time.*

simply leave, heading south in winter to sun themselves comfortably in milder locations—such as Pima County.

Other, more tropical species spend their summers in our area and winter in Mexico, South, or Central America to escape even our relatively mild Januaries. And still others only pass through Pima County in spring on their way from their southern wintering grounds to their northern breeding grounds, and in fall when they return south. Thus in winter we can find species here that summer farther north, in summer we can find species that winter farther south, and in spring and fall we can briefly find species that winter farther south and summer farther north. No wonder some birders are a little odd.

This enormous odyssey is not haphazard in its movement; the birds tend to follow several ancient "flyways." Pima County is on the western edge of the Central Flyway (the others are the Pacific, Mississippi, and Atlantic). Within these flyways, birds follow routes that cross favorable habitat for resting and feeding. Riparian corridors, with large trees and reliable water such as the San Pedro River still boasts, play an extremely important role in successful migration for most species. When these corridors are lost, through development, overpumping of groundwater, or other means, stress on migrating as well as resident species is greatly increased—especially in otherwise arid areas like the Sonoran Desert. Over 80 percent of all birds use riparian habitat, which naturally constitutes only 3 percent of all habitat nationwide. In Arizona, 95 percent of our riparian habitat has been reduced, altered, or destroyed by development and overuse.

Migrating species are especially endangered by habitat loss because destruction of their summer or winter territories can be disastrous as well. Many neotropical species—which summer in the United States or Canada and winter in Mexico, Central, or South America—are threatened by rainforest destruction in their wintering grounds, even though their breeding grounds in the north might be comparatively safe. Many birds we think of as "ours"—tanagers, orioles, warblers, and many, many others—are really just visitors from the south. If their home grounds are lost, we will see them no more.

Migration has other costs as well. It takes incredible amounts of energy to fly hundreds or thousands of miles twice each year, and some birds make the journey virtually nonstop. To accomplish this feat, some eat enough to double their body weight in the weeks preceding the journey—a process known scientifically as hyperphagia rather than simply overeating—adding on layers of fat to provide fuel for continuous flying. (This sounds like a foolproof plan for human dieters: eat all you want, but jog 3,000 miles twice a year.) The species that stop to feed and rest en route obviate the need for such reserves but increase their exposure to predation.

With all these disadvantages counterbalancing the benefits of migration, it's no wonder many species in temperate areas choose year-round residency as their strategy, toughing out the winters, enjoying the summers—and avoiding all that commuting.

Please Don't Call Them Cute

It's difficult—very difficult—to talk about raccoons, coatimundis, and ringtails without using the adjective "cute." But we'll try.

Procyonidae is a family within the order Carnivora. On a technical basis, procyonids differ from other carnivores in having teeth more adapted to an omnivorous diet and physiology adapted to climbing. Beyond that, though, the parameters seem to be pretty loose—lumped in with the above three members are animals as diverse as kinkajous and lesser pandas.

Most people are familiar with raccoons from books and movies. The common picture of the raccoon (*Procyon lotor*), crouched by a stream bank feeling around for crayfish, seems at odds with the southwestern landscape. Nevertheless, raccoons do very well here. They are generally restricted to permanent water sources—the Arizona range map for the species looks like an overlay of the hydrology chart—but otherwise have adapted well to a hotter climate. Their proclivity for nocturnal foraging helps them avoid the heat of day and unlike raccoons in the northern United States, which lie dormant in hollow trees through the winter, ours stay active all year.

Raccoons will eat whatever they can gather in the water, such as invertebrates, frogs, and fish as well as berries, nuts, and small mammals and birds—even carrion when options are low. Rock cavities and crevices are the preferred den sites for Arizona's raccoons, rather than the classic tree holes one usually associates them with. Three or four (sometimes one to six) young are born in April or May.

Another procyonid, but one with which most people are unfamiliar, is the coatimundi (*Nasua*

nasua). The reaction of most people at seeing one, whether in the wild or at the Arizona–Sonora Desert Museum, is utter astonishment. The coati looks more like a benign cartoon creature invented for a children's book than a real animal. Its long, faintly ringed tail sticks jauntily straight up in the air while the black nose on the tip of its extended snout seems to have a life of its own, probing the air this way and that. Coatis often travel in groups of a dozen or more animals and frequently mutter to each other with high-pitched little *eeps.*

Coatis in Arizona prefer oak woodland habitat, although they occasionally will range down into desertscrub. They are excellent tree climbers and will scale oaks and sycamores to escape predators, to nap, or to steal birds' eggs, though most of their foraging is done on the ground, where they root with those long noses for insects, larvae, lizards, snakes, and small mammals. Nuts and fruits of trees and cactuses are also on their menu. Most of the year coati troops comprise females; in April and May the males, which live solitary lives, will join them to mate. Up to six young are born after a gestation period of about 75 days.

Raccoons and coatis may be accomplished climbers, but the cliff-scaling feats of our region's third procyonid are extraordinary. We once saw a ringtail (*Bassariscus astutus*) disappear at a dead run over the lip of a 200-foot cliff at the Grand Canyon, apparently flinging itself to a certain death. Yet a cautious glance over the edge revealed a crevice 20 or 30 feet down the precipitous face, out of which a tiny head poked. This ringtail was thoroughly people-oriented, and it soon scampered back up the face to beg food—a performance we wouldn't have attempted without a rope and sticky climbing shoes. A good part of this skill is attributable to the ringtail's soft footpads and semiretractable claws; also, they can rotate their hind feet a full 180° to help keep a grip during descents.

Ringtails (also misnamed ring-tailed cats) are much smaller than their 20–25-pound raccoon and coati relatives—an adult might bend the scale at 2 pounds or so. They have pointed faces and distinctly ringed, bushy tails at least as long as their bodies. They show a great affinity for rocky hillsides and canyons, employing crevices and caves for dens. Miners used to tame

Ringtail: extraordinary cliff-scaler

them, feeding them scraps so they would hang around and kill scorpions and mice. Ringtails are efficient predators—their diet only includes a few fruits and berries in season.

Ringtails give birth in May or June to a litter of two to four blind, helpless young. Within about 5 weeks they appear to be miniature versions of the adults but continue growing for another 4 months or so.

All of the procyonids show great proclivities to adapt to a human presence. Some retired biologist friends who live in Portal, in the Chiricahua Mountains, told us of a wild coati that was in the habit of climbing to their porch roof and hanging off the edge, in view of anyone standing at the kitchen window. This performance was aimed at getting free food—the preferred form of which our friends discovered was peanut butter sandwiches. As professionals in the field of ecology, both were aware of the hazards involved in feeding wild animals but admitted to us that they couldn't help themselves in this case. As the woman sheepishly put it: "He was just so darn *cute!*"

PLACES TO VISIT IN APRIL

Ciénega Creek

Just moments earlier we were immersed in dense weekend traffic on I-10: frantic, noisy, and gray. Now we are immersed in quite the opposite: soothing, quiet, and green. A yellow-breasted chat calls *touk-touk-touk!* from the top of a mesquite snag. The accipitrine shadow of a Cooper's hawk shoots straight as an arrow down the wet sand of the creek bed—we look up but the only sign of its passing is a wake of eerie silence. In a moment, the busy chittering of vireos and warblers continues as though uninterrupted by the shadow of death. Likewise, we have completely forgotten our urban baggage and amble on down the creek, soaking up the quiet and the green.

Ciénega Creek, just half an hour from east Tucson, is part of Pima County Parks and Recreation's Ciénega Creek Nature Preserve. Permits are required to enter the day-use-only riparian area, one of the few cottonwood-hackberry-mesquite watercourses remaining near urban Tucson. Early spring is an excellent time to visit, a chance to enjoy the last of the wet coolness before summer settles in and perhaps to see some migrating birds. Be prepared—there may be a lot of water underfoot and a lot of bugs. Contact Pima County Parks for information about parking as well as for permits, which are free. (See Appendix 6 for a listing of agency phone numbers.)

Brown Canyon and Baboquivari Peak

As we walked down the road near the Brown Canyon visitor center on the Buenos Aires National Wildlife Refuge, heading toward the nearby creek, the zone-tailed hawks went off like a burglar alarm. Extremely defensive of their nest territory, these notorious complainers will strafe and bomb anything that they deem unwelcome, which is just about everything.

Screeeeee! SCREEEE! We could hear them just ahead, but oddly, they were not heading our way. They were cruising the creekbed on the other side of the sycamore grove, screaming more and more urgently. Realizing something else must be bugging them, we hurried quietly to the edge of the bluff overlooking the creekbed. Nothing. Then we turned just in time to see two mountain lions stroll onto the road just beyond where we were standing. We stood breathless: one of the lions sniffed around and did some territory marking while the other, smaller lion play-pounced it; then they ambled slowly into the brush out of sight.

Brown Canyon is just that kind of place—wild, full of wildlife, a place where unexpected things happen. Although sighting mountain lions at all is extremely rare, especially in daytime, in Brown Canyon it's been reported with regularity. And in the early 1990s, just before the U.S. Fish & Wildlife Service bought the canyon, there was a reliable sighting of a jaguar in the upper reaches, in a rugged cleft now called Jaguar Canyon.

The canyon, formerly home to several small-scale cattle ranches, is being developed for public visitation. It is currently not open to the public except by guided tours; naturalist volunteers or refuge staff lead tours weekly, or groups can arrange tours. The hike to the visitor center winds through some of the most complete hackberry-mesquite-sycamore thickets left intact in the Southwest. In the spring they are filled with summer tanagers, yellow-breasted chats, Bell's vireos, Lucy's warblers, Bewick's wrens, northern beardless-tyrannulets, hooded orioles, Cassin's kingbirds, broad-billed, black-chinned, Anna's and Costa's hummingbirds, and such migrants as cedar waxwings, yellow-billed cuckoos, and numerous warblers. In the evenings, buff-collared nightjars, poorwills, whip-poor-wills, elf owls, western screech-owls, and great horned owls have all been heard.

The main canyon extends for about 2 miles beyond the visitor center, forking into two major drainages. Arch Canyon heads southwest up to a natural bridge of diked rhyolite; it's possible to bushwack beyond it, up over the boundary ridge to the base of Baboquivari Peak (there are numerous climbing routes on the peak; see sidebar). Jaguar Canyon slices northwest into the heart of the Baboquivari Mountains. These two oak-, sycamore-, walnut-, and hackberry-filled canyons nurture species found nowhere else on the 116,000-acre refuge, including sulphur-bellied flycatchers, whip-poor-wills, whiskered screech-owls, and plants such as border piñons and pine-needle milkweed. Above it all towers the spectacular Babo-

The Lure and Lore of Baboquivari

*To the O'odham people, Baboquivari Peak (*Waw Kiwulik, *"narrow about the middle," in the O'odham language) is a sacred mountain, a home of one of their most important legendary figures, I'itoi, who brought the People into this world. According to one version of the legend, after creating fire, deer, humans, vultures and a lot of mischief, I'itoi retired to the center of the earth in a cave complex whose entrance is below the sacred peak. O'odham basket weavers depict this maze as a spiral with a man inside it; the picture is an allegory of man searching for the deeper meaning of life.*

Ever since coming to this region, European explorers have fallen under the undeniable spell of the impressive peak—a 7,830-foot monolith of solid granite thrust up through the earth's crust more than 100 million years ago, perhaps the long-eroded base of an even older Jurassic volcano. Plenty of myth and mysticism surrounds the mountain, as so many of its Anglo climbers have experienced violent weather, eerie clouds, and dangerous lightning, and been regaled with stories by the O'odham. Indeed, much of the time Baboquivari stands shrouded in clouds, as though I'itoi likes to wrap himself in a cloak of vapor.

One of the first Europeans to see the peak was Captain Juan Mateo Manje of Father Eusebio Kino's expedition, who named the peak Noah's Ark in the late 1700s; in 1898 Jesus Montoya and Dr. Robert Forbes, an Arizona legislator, professor, and agronomist, climbed the mountain along the route now named after Forbes (he climbed the mountain six times, the last on his eighty-second birthday); and in 1957 Don Morris was among the first people to use modern rock-climbing techniques to scale the formidable Southeast Arete, a climb that attracts people from all over the world.

Baboquivari Peak

The lore of Baboquivari is rich, preserved in the oral histories of the Tohono O'odham, and continued in a modern recreational vein by writers the world over. Perhaps one of the more well-known people to scale the peak was Supreme Court Justice William O. Douglas, who in 1951 wrote: "It was a mountain wholly detached from the earth—a magic pillar of granite riding high above dark and angry clouds. Lightning briefly played around its base; and then it vanished as quickly as it appeared—engulfed by black clouds that welled upward in some wind."

Although at press time access to the mountain's top (the east half is owned by the U.S. government, while the west is owned by the Tohono O'odham nation) was still granted through private property easements on the east side of the mountain and by permit from the Tohono O'odham nation on the west, access to the peak may one day be restricted to Indians. The O'odham are negotiating with the U.S. government to repossess all of the mountain, a vital cultural resource for their community. For information on climbing the peak, see Bob Kerry's Backcountry Rock Climbing in Southern Arizona *(Backcountry Books, Tucson, 1993).*

The best vantage from which to view the peak is Brown Canyon on the Buenos Aires National Wildlife Refuge, on the east side of the Baboquivari Mountains (see Places to Visit). The peak is always impressive but it is especially beautiful when summer storms wrap themselves around it and lightning dances on the ridges.

quivari Peak, Arizona's most massive rock pinnacle.

Call the Buenos Aires National Wildlife Refuge for more information. (See Appendix 6 for a listing of agency phone numbers.)

Sycamore Basin

Spring is not complete without a sycamore "fix," and where better to get one than Sycamore Basin, a peaceful valley nestled above Sabino Canyon in the Santa Catalina Mountains? We bask in the warm sun on silky water-washed rocks, the voice of Bear Creek in our ears, the spicy warm fragrance of sycamore leaves in our noses. Summer tanagers *kiti-chuck-kiti-chuck* in the canopies, a rock squirrel stands up behind us and scolds loudly, a young white-tailed deer comes to drink, never making a sound.

There are three ways to get to Sycamore Basin. From the Sabino Canyon visitor's center, take the Seven Falls Trail in lower Bear Canyon up past the falls to a spur trail to Sycamore Basin and Reservoir (there is a small manmade lake on Bear Creek in the basin), a mostly uphill hike of 8 miles. Or from the visitor's center, take the tram (there is a fee) to Upper Sabino Canyon; take the Sabino Canyon Trail to the Sycamore Canyon Trail into the basin, about 5 miles. And finally, you can drop down into the basin from Soldier's Camp off the Catalina Highway, a hike of about 1 mile. Getting an early start is always a good way to beat the crowds, although you can almost always find a spot alone by hiking up the creek. Be prepared for bugs, too.

APRIL SKIES

"Yellow Moon"

TRADITIONAL O'ODHAM NAME FOR APRIL

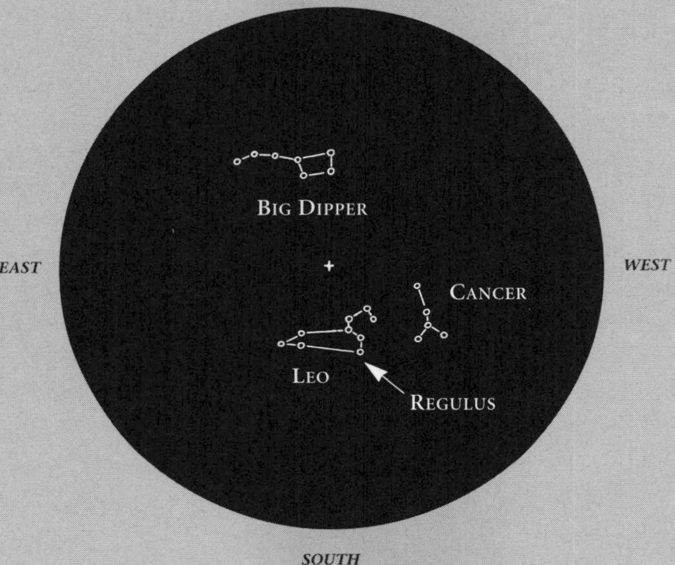

EAST *WEST*

SOUTH

Star Chart for 32°N
Mid-month, 9 pm

FEATURE CONSTELLATION

Cancer, the Crab, was one of the giants that the goddess Hera sent to test Hercules during his twelve labors. The Crab was to assist the many-headed Hydra in defeating Hercules, but he killed them both, accomplishing the second of his tasks on his way to immortality. The constellation we know as Cancer has also been called the Gates of Humanity because it was believed that when a person was born the soul first passed from heaven through its stars to enter the newborn babe. When a person died, their soul exited earth and into heaven via another gateway in the constellation of Capricorn, the opposite zodiac sign to Cancer.

APRIL AT A GLANCE

Desertscrub

❧ Blue palo verde trees (*Cercidium floridum*), catclaw acacias (*Acacia greggii*), and mesquite trees (*Prosopis* spp.) present bright yellow blooms.
❧ Ocotillos (*Fouquieria splendens*) will be blooming.
❧ Sandfood (*Pholisma sonorae*) and broomrape (*Pholisma* spp.) bloom in the sand of the far west deserts.
❧ The cactuses begin blooming this month. Look for prickly pear, cholla (*Opuntia* spp.), and hedgehog (*Echinocereus* spp.) blossoms. Saguaros will be topped by fat buds, and some will open toward the end of this month.
❧ Banana yuccas (*Yucca* spp.) send up their beautiful creamy flower stalks.
❧ White-winged doves return from their winter territories. Gambel's quail break up their coveys and begin mating.
❧ Arriving this month and next along riparian corridors to breed are hooded orioles, ash-throated flycatchers, solitary and Bell's vireos, summer and hepatic tanagers, Cassin's, tropical, and thick-billed kingbirds, and broad-billed, black-chinned, and Anna's hummingbirds, among many other migratory birds.
❧ Butterflies will be common again. Look for great blue hairstreaks, Leila hackberry butterflies, Eufala skippers, common and Isola blues, and queens, among many others, in all communities.
❧ Snakes are out in force. It's a good time to remember to watch where we put our feet and hands.
❧ Reptiles such as desert iguanas and lesser earless and western whiptail lizards begin breeding this month.
❧ Bobcats bear their litters this month, as do their important prey species: round-tailed and Harris' antelope ground squirrels.

Desert Grasslands

❧ Breeding begins for summer and resident sparrows, including Cassin's, grasshopper, Botteri's, lark, black-throated, rufous-crowned, and rufous-winged.
❧ Raptors to look for include Swainson's hawks, which arrive to breed here, and resident but rare white-tailed kites.
❧ Chihuahuan ravens may begin nesting this month.

❧ Pronghorn antelope will drop their fawns this month through May or June.
❧ White-tailed and mule deer will shed their antlers.

Oak Woodlands

❧ Flowers such as Lewis flax (*Linum lewisii*), Arizona penstemon (*Penstemon pseudospectabilis*), common monkey flowers (*Mimulus guttatus*), and indigo bush (*Dalea parryi*) are at their peak. Many flowers in the milkweed family bloom late this month; they are a favorite food and larval plant for numerous butterflies.
❧ Birds such as western pewees, Bewick's and house wrens, Scott's orioles, Cassin's kingbirds, and summer tanagers will be common in the woodlands, especially near creeks.
❧ Look for two-tailed swallowtail butterflies now through fall.
❧ Solitary male coatimundis briefly join tribes of females this month, which marks the beginning of their breeding season.

Pine-Oak Woodlands

❧ The warming earth continues to nurture the seedling promises of columbines, wild berries, and summer annuals.
❧ The watercourses glow freshly green with the new leaves of velvet ash (*Fraxinus velutina*), Arizona black walnut (*Juglans major*), thinleaf alder (*Alnus tenuifolia*), and cottonwood (*Populus* spp.) trees.
❧ Anna's and black-chinned hummingbirds may be nesting, along with red-faced and Virginia's warblers, painted redstarts, greater pewees, and hepatic tanagers. The spectacular elegant trogons return to a few of southern Arizona's moist riparian canyons this month to breed.
❧ Look also for violet-green swallows and white-throated swifts performing like acrobats along cliffs; nights begin with the musical calls of whip-poor-wills, which migrate here in the summer; later in the night, listen for the haunting calls of flammulated and whiskered screech-owls.
❧ Black bears emerge from hibernation, urinating and defecating for the first time in four months.

Coniferous Forests

❧ Hermit thrushes, house wrens, olive and yellow-rumped warblers, ruby-crowned and golden-crowned kinglets, hairy woodpeckers, and Steller's jays begin preparations for breeding; soon the "mountain hummers"—magnificent, blue-throated, and broad-tailed—begin to arrive. Keep your eye out for band-tailed pigeons, as well.

❧ The aspens (*Populus* spp.), maples (*Acer* spp.), and Gambel's oaks (*Quercus gambelii*) might venture to put out leaves later this month.

Special Events

❧ Earth Day is April 22. The Arizona–Sonora Desert Museum often plans events around this day.

In the Sky

❧ The constellation Leo strides high overhead led by its bright white "king star," Regulus.

❧ The Big Dipper in now high in the northeast; and Cancer rises between Leo in the east and Gemini in the west.

See the chapter Exploring the Nature of Pima County and Southern Arizona for definitions and descriptions of communities.

A young Harris' hawk sits atop the white waxy blossoms of a saguaro

may

AS THE TEMPERATURE *builds like an oven set on bake, and the sky dries and shrinks away into a sheer cerulean dome, the dried husks of spring's ephemeral flowers tumble across the desert on thirsty winds and many of the breeding birds follow the swiftly retreating creeks up into the mountains.*

May is hot. May is dry. May is also magnificent, for it is when the native desert awakes. Just when we think everything has died or shriveled up to hibernate through the drought of May and June, we wake to find a vast tide of yellow splashing down the foothills and across the desertscrub basins—the glowing blossoms of foothills palo verde trees. Soon the yellow is joined by the delicate, smoky lilac of ironwood blossoms; toward June, smoke trees also open and offer their soft lavender buds. In the shimmering midday heat, the colors melt into a living desert tapestry, and the perfume of mesquite, mimosa, and acacia catkins sends the senses spinning.

Look up and you see the crowning glory of summer held aloft on the tops of the giant saguaro cactuses. One by one, in the waning hours of the day, the saguaros will unfold their 3-inch waxy white blossoms to the sky, a dozen or more per arm, calling in nocturnal pollinators with promises of nectar-filled moons. Lesser long-nosed and Mexican long-tongued bats migrate north following the blooming and fruiting of the giant cactuses—the saguaros, cardóns, and organ pipes—as well as the agaves. Hawkmoths, another nighttime flier, also feed on the nectar of night-blooming plants, particularly those in the cereus family, many of which produce flowers this month. Each saguaro flower will stay open only until the next midday, democratically allowing diurnal creatures like white-winged doves and bees to partake of whatever nectar and pollen the bats and moths missed.

This month or next the elusive Arizona queen-of-the-night cactus, a night-blooming cereus—which grows tucked under desert shrubs such as mesquites, ironwoods, or creosote—will surprise us for just a few nights with beautiful white blossoms borne along stems that look like dead sticks. No one knows why, but all the plants in a population will bloom nearly at once and for a very short time.

But not all the action is at night, even when the heat comes on strong. Tough desert birds like white-winged doves, roadrunners, Gambel's quail, and black-throated sparrows are active all through the day; we've even found white-winged doves nesting in full sun atop mesquite snags. Oldtimers say the bigger the flocks of white-wings arriving by May, the better will be the crop of saguaro fruit. Later in the month you may see adult Gambel's quail pairs parading their newly hatched, thumb-sized chicks all in a row, and you may hear the soft cooing of nesting roadrunners in the early morning. Most desert lizards—roadrunners' preferred meal—are laying eggs this month, including desert horned lizards and the big desert spiny lizards; and Gila monster eggs, laid 10 months ago, begin to hatch. Some of the desert legumes, like the blue palo verdes and mesquites that began blooming last month, will begin to set their bean pods, making May U'us Wihogtalig Mashath, *"moon of the bean tree," to the Tohono O'odham.*

In the low light of dawn and of sunset the grasslands appear to have been planted with hundreds of 10-foot-tall candles, bright lights illuminating the rolling hills. These are the blooms of soaptree yuccas, huge flower stalks laden with hundreds of creamy white bell-flowers that attract yucca moths. Large groups of common nighthawks swoop gracefully among them, searching for insects. Pronghorn antelope con-

tinue to give birth to their fawns while scaled quail begin breeding—normally shy males will sing from tree snags and fenceposts. Along washes wild cotton has leafed out and is preparing to set its large white blooms.

In water holes, springs, and creeks the small Sonoran mud turtles will breed amid the drum-like staccato songs of canyon tree frogs, which are also breeding from the grasslands up into the pine-oak woodlands. Although they're called treefrogs, look for them on rocks near permanent water. The big white flowers with yellow centers lining roadsides and washes are prickly poppies, or "cowboy's fried eggs."

The mid-elevation lizards and toads, like Clark's spiny lizards and red-spotted toads, both common in the moist oak woodlands, are very active in May when the days are pleasantly warm and the nights still cool. The Clark's bear live young beginning late this month all through November. The red-spotted toads, normally nocturnal, may be seen throughout the day this month as they seek out mates mostly close to permanent water to which they retreat with hollow ploops! *when startled. In riparian areas the Arizona grape will be twining energetically over shrubs and trees, and high above, the incredibly noisy Cassin's kingbirds will build their nests in sycamore trees and defend them vigorously against hawks and ravens. Large, brilliant red tubular flowers borne atop what appear to be dead stems are coral bean flowers, one of the most spectacular of the Southwest's hummingbird-adapted plants.*

Up in the pine-oak woodlands the days are especially beautiful—warm but not hot, with cool breezes in the mornings and evenings. Mountain spiny lizards bear live young this month and next. Early summer flowers like Fendler's globemallow, with its deep pink flowers, and the lovely yellow columbine may grace trailsides and stream banks. Birds like black-headed grosbeaks, painted redstarts, and American robins fill the tree canopies with breeding songs, although none can outsing the Scott's orioles with their arresting flute-like airs.

Springtime is in full swing now in the coniferous forests, although a few nights will still drop into freezing and a surprise snowstorm is not impossible. Maples, red-osier dogwoods, and aspens sport their

MAY WEATHER

	Sunrise	Sunset	Avg. Relative Humidity/Tucson
May 1	5:38 MST	7:04 MST	5 a.m. 34%
May 30	5:19 MST	7:24 MST	5 p.m. 13%

Stations	Ajo	Tucson	Mt. Lemmon
Station Elevation	(1,800 ft.)	(2,584 ft.)	(8,800 ft.)
May Averages			
Max. temperature	90.3°F	88.8°F	69.2°F
Min. temperature	62.7°F	57.4°F	34.8°F
Precipitation	.09 in.	.15 in.	.24 in.
Snow	0 in.	0 in.	0 in.
# days 100° & over	3	1	0
# days 32° & under	0	0	6
# days precip.>.01"	1	1	1
May Extremes			
Max. temperature	111°F (1951)	107°F (1951)	82°F (1959)
Min. temperature	38°F (1915)	38°F (1950)	28°F (1959)
Max. snow/month	0 in.	0 in.	0 in.
Max. snow/1 day	0 in.	0 in.	0 in.
Max. precip./month	1.26 in. (1972)	.67 in. (1979)	.92 in. (1982)
Max. precip./1 day	1.26 in. (1972)	.50 in. (1967)	.52 in. (1960)

May Notes

Dry and hot characterizes May in the deserts—at least a day or two over 100° with a sprinkling of rain if any. The mountains celebrate spring with balmy days in the 60°s or 70°s and chilly nights. High pressure systems hold off moisture for southern Arizona during May, while temperatures build. In 1994 there were 99 contiguous days of 100° or over; the record of 100 days over 100° held by one day. Other than high temperatures and lack of rain, not much happens weatherwise in May. Toward the end of the month occasional dust storms will cause brief closures of I-10 north of town.

For information about data sources for these listings, see the Climate section of the chapter Exploring the Nature of Pima County and Southern Arizona.

new leaves, and snowberries are leafing out. Magnificent, blue-throated, and broad-tailed hummingbirds will arrive this month, moving up into the high country with the imminent blooming of flowers such as bouvardia, scarlet sage, skyrocket, and scarlet penstemon. They will breed in summer. Overturned rocks and shredded logs are signs of a hungry black bear, perhaps a female with her new cubs. Male Abert's squirrels, normally solitary, compete vigorously for mates this month with high-pitched "barking," lots of tail-flicking, and aggressive chasing. One of Arizona's largest rodents, the porcupines, will bear their young this month mostly in the high country, although they are also found in low-elevation riparian areas; young porcupines are born with soft spines but within a day their spines stiffen and they can follow their parents.

In May we split our time between the deserts and the mountains. A trip to the Santa Rita Mountains and Madera Canyon to "catch" the hummingbird and trogon arrivals is always a treat, and we spend at least a couple of nights watching the bats and moths flicker around the white flowers of saguaros and yuccas. We might also look for night-blooming queen-of-the-night cactuses, and after a season without some of our favorite desert animals, we plan a few excursions to look for snakes.

FLORA

Birds, Bees and . . . Bats?

The yucca flower waits in the darkness of a warm May night, its waxy, creamy-white petals unfolded, one of several hundred such blooms filling the stalk that rises 6 feet above the parent plant. Within the flower stands the ovary and its repository of ovules, the unfertilized seeds. Beside the ovary stand the stamens, delicate filaments capped with sticky heads of pollen, the sperm of the plant.

Suddenly a small white moth lands on one of the petals. Deliberately she clambers into the interior of the flower and, using a pair of highly specialized appendages, gathers pollen from the stamens, rolling it into a tight ball which she holds under her head. The moth then clambers out of the flower and flutters away.

Still the flower waits patiently. Soon another moth alights—but this one is already carrying a ball of pollen, gathered from flowers on other yuccas. This moth ignores the stamens; instead she crawls to the top of the ovary, called the stigma, tears off part of her ball of pollen and carefully stuffs it into the narrow slits that head the passage to the ovary. Readjusting her position, she uses the pointed ovipositor on the tip of her abdomen to pierce the base of the ovary and deposit one of her own fertilized eggs among the ovules. Mission complete, she climbs out and flies away, leaving her developing egg—and a pollinated flower.

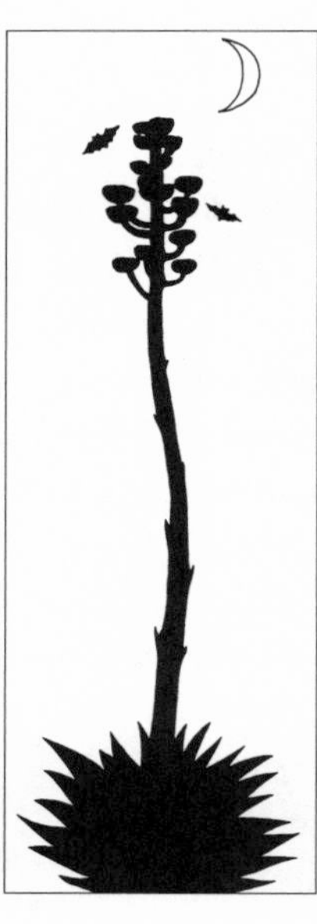

The yucca (*Yucca elata* and other species) and yucca moths of the genus *Tegeticula* illustrate a classic example of mutualism, a symbiotic relationship between two species from which both participants benefit. The pollen deposited by the moth fertilizes the seeds of the yucca, and they begin developing within the ovary—the fruit—of the plant. Meanwhile the moth's egg hatches and the larva begins boring its way through the fruit, eating the seeds. But not all of them. Enough are left to ensure descendents for the yucca.

Symbiosis is an ancient and vital strategy for many plants. The moth-yucca relationship is a type of symbiosis called mutualism—two species derive benefit from a specific association. A flowering plant that offers nectar as food for insects or birds is repaid when its pollen sticks to the heads or bills of the animal and is carried to pollinate another flower of its species or when other pollen is deposited in its own ovary. Among plants, this exchange is called cross-pollination; it ensures a healthy mix of genes. What is unusual about the yucca–yucca moth relationship is that it requires deliberate action on the part of the moth—in fact, the yucca cannot be accidentally pollinated by bees or birds because of the configuration of the flower.

White flowers, such as those borne by the yucca, are often a trait of plants whose pollination is carried out at night by moths or nectar-feeding bats; white is more visible at night than colors. The timing of these blooms offers another clue. For example, the flowers of cardón and organ pipe cactuses open after dusk and close soon af-

Above, *nocturnal pollinators visit an agave*

ter sunrise; their pollination is carried out almost exclusively by bats. Saguaro flowers are white as well and open at dusk—but they stay open through the next afternoon. Researchers have determined that saguaros are pollinated by both bats, at night, and by birds, mostly doves, during daylight hours.

Many species of agave are adapted to bat pollination. Certain bats, such as the lesser long-nosed (*Leptonicteris curasoae*), are physiologically adapted to feed on nectar, pollen, and ripe fruit rather than insects. These endangered bats migrate north from Mexico in the spring, following the blooming cycle of columnar cactuses into Arizona. In late summer and early fall they return south, feeding on agave blooms. One such agave, the Palmer's (*Agave palmeri*), is found throughout Pima County between 3,000 and 8,000 feet elevation. The magueys in our area have dark white flowers that open at night. However, north of the Catalina Mountains, beyond the migration range of the nectar-feeding bats, is another species, *Agave chrysantha,* which is indistinguishable from *A. palmeri*—except that its flowers are bright orange-yellow, bloom during the day, and are pollinated by hummingbirds.

Another, much harder to find night bloomer is the Sonoran queen-of-the-night (*Peniocereus striatus*), a night-blooming cereus of the west deserts. The multiple stems of the queen-of-the-night are less than a quarter-inch thick, and the cactus grows to only a couple of feet under desert plants such as ironwood and creosote. *Peniocereus* only blooms for a few nights each summer during the rainy season, and it is pollinated by moths such as the hawkmoth. The floral tubes of the blossom are exactly the right length for the long, nectar-sipping proboscides of the moths, and the anthers are positioned to thoroughly coat the foraging insect with pollen.

Bring on the Drought

Plants deal with the Sonoran Desert's fore-summer and fall droughts in three ways: they avoid it, like winter's and spring's ephemeral, or "annual," wildflowers; they tolerate it, like brittlebush, by going dormant during dry times, shedding their leaves and looking quite dead; or they ignore it, like the succulents, by storing water in their fleshy tissue all winter, like a savings account ready to use for a non-rainy day.

The succulents' mechanisms for ignoring the dry seasons and taking advantage of in-between rains are marvels of evolution. In order to snatch up as much water as quickly as possible after the desert's all-too-brief rains, most cactuses—even giant saguaros—have evolved extensive and shallow root systems, usually no more than 4 inches below the surface but sometimes radiating amazing distances from the plant. A small cholla may have a root system 30 feet in diameter. Instead of extensive roots, yuccas evolved spreading flat leaves that collect and channel rainwater onto the central root.

Many succulents photosynthesize through an extremely water-efficient method dubbed CAM, which stands for Crassulacean Acid Metabolism (after the plant family Crassula, in which the phenomenon was first discovered). CAM plants include most cactuses and yuccas found in dry climates with large differences in daily high and low temperatures. CAM plants utilize about one-tenth the amount of water to convert sunlight to energy than plants that photosynthesize the more common way, dubbed C3 (the trade-off is that CAM plants, such as cactuses, grow much more slowly). Most plants open their stomates during the day to photosynthesize—taking in carbon dioxide and releasing oxygen; CAM plants, however, keep their stomates closed during the day, photosynthesizing with stored carbon dioxide, opening them to respire at night when the temperatures are much lower and relative humidity higher. But when it gets really dry, as it does in May and June, CAM plants have the ability to "idle." They close up their stomates both night and day, becoming watertight and nearly sealed to gas exchange as well (the plant continues to metabolize very slowly, recycling the carbon dioxide and oxygen into its own system; it can do this for extended periods but will eventually use up its stored carbohydrates).

When rains do come, CAM plants react instantly because they have been "idling" rather than shut off. Within 5 hours of rain new rootlets have been found on agaves; within 24 hours full growth can be resumed. A drought-tolerating plant like brittlebush, which goes dormant for the drought, needs a few weeks to wake up after a rain.

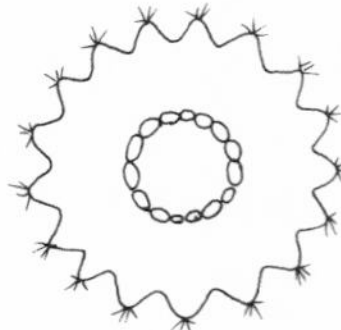

One of the pervading folklore stories about cactuses involves their legendary ability to store water: most "desert survival guides" suggest chopping up a cactus and chewing its pulp for water. But beware: not only will you likely expend far more energy getting the meager moisture than it's worth, but the pulp of some CAM plants contains toxic oxalic acid (such as the prickly pears and chollas), bitter alkaloids (such as plants in the cereus family), or substances that cause diarrhea.

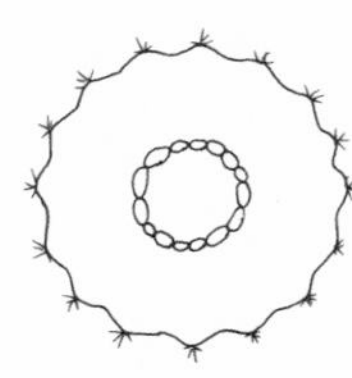

Cross section of a saguaro before and after the rains

When one sees a field of thousands of blooming flowers on a spring morning, it's easy to forget that all those flowers are fiercely competing to attract bees or other pollinators to ensure their own fertilization. By evolving to attract nocturnal flyers, plants like the cardón and agave are able to exploit a new niche—and, of course, since the moths and bats had to evolve at the same time, they were exploiting new niches as well, reducing competition and increasing the diversity of life.

Unfortunately, there is a growing threat to this ancient relationship. The use of insecticide sprays on agricultural fields and rabies control programs in Mexico, where many of the important pollinators for Sonoran Desert succulents spend a great deal of their life cycles, have seriously affected the reproductive rates of those succulents. In a national park along the U.S.-Mexican border, researchers found that insecticide spraying across from the park reduced hawkmoth numbers enough in one season that the subsequent cactus fruit set was alarmingly low. They have termed the process "chemically induced habitat fragmentation" and have found that several succulent species are suffering low rates of reproduction due to pollinator elimination. Other scientists working in the Sierra Madre feared that a rabies outbreak in 1994 might spell disaster for endangered nectar-feeding bats that winter in Mexico; often, whole bat colonies, regardless of their ability to carry the rabies virus, are exterminated.

FAUNA

Sympathy for the Devil

Pity the poor rattlesnake.

Forever damned by the biblical stigma of The Serpent, and by the even older loathing for creepy-crawly things passed on from each human generation to the next, the rattlesnake possesses an additional, unforgivable flaw: the means with which to defend itself.

About 8,000 people are bitten by venomous snakes each year in the United States. Usually seven or eight of these victims die, barely one-tenth of 1 percent—and many of those deaths result from improper or totally absent treatment. Nevertheless, the perception that rattlesnakes are not only creepy-crawly but dangerous results in their death by the thousands each year, at the hands of both legitimately concerned homeowners as well as those merely looking for an excuse to kill something.

Ironically, the rattlesnake's venom did not evolve as a defensive device. It was intended as a tool with which to procure food and thus is much more effective at killing kangaroo rats than humans. In fact, when biting defensively, a rattler often fails to inject venom at all—it's estimated that up to one-third of all bites on humans are dry.

When used against its intended prey, the venom can result in death within seconds for small animals; even a large rat will succumb within a few minutes. The snake then tracks down the animal by scent, using its nostrils and its forked tongue, which conveys particles to a receptor in the roof of the mouth known as the Jacobson's organ.

An important secondary function of the venom is its digestive properties. Because snakes cannot chew their food, they gain none of the enzymatic reactions that saliva produces. So it is a great advantage to the snake to have its meal breaking down from the inside at the same time it is being swallowed. When a snake swallows an animal larger than its head, the jaw is able to expand to an amazing circumference. Meanwhile the snake can breath through the glottis, a tube ringed with cartilaginous reinforcement that exits the front of the lower mouth like a snorkel.

As with all reptiles, a rattlesnake must periodically shed its skin because the epidermis is a ker-

Eight Venomous Snakes of Pima County

Coral snake (Micruroides euryxanthus) — *Rare; desertscrub to low oak woodlands; small, less than 20 inches; red bands touch yellow bands but not black bands; front of head entirely black.*

Western diamondback rattlesnake (Crotalus atrox) — *Common; desertscrub to coniferous forests; to over 6 feet; black and white rings around posterior 4-5 inches of tail; small scales between supraoculars.*

Mojave rattlesnake

Mojave rattlesnake (Crotalus scutulatus) — *Common; low desertscrub to low pine-oak woodland; to 4 1/2 feet; black and white rings around tail (black rings usually narrower); large scales between supraoculars.*

Black-tailed rattlesnake (Crotalus molossus) — *Common; oak woodlands to coniferous forests; to 5 feet; posterior 4-5 inches of tail black; often vivid pattern markings.*

Arizona black rattlesnake (Crotalus viridis cerberus) — *Common; oak woodlands to coniferous forests; to 3 1/2 feet; almost all dark gray or black.*

Tiger rattlesnake (Crotalus tigris) — *Uncommon; desertscrub up to grasslands, especially mountain foothills; to 3 feet; sometimes faint "tiger stripes" across back; small head.*

Sidewinder (Crotalus cerastes) — *Uncommon; southwest deserts; to 2 feet; hornlike projections above eyes; sidewinding gait at times.*

Speckled rattlesnake (Crotalus mitchellii) — *Rare; west deserts; to 4 feet; speckled, often faint cross bands on back; larger head than tiger.*

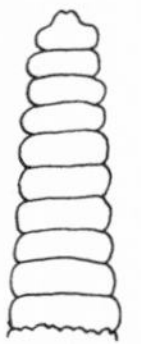

Rattle and cross section

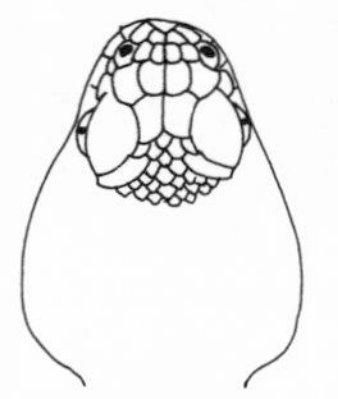
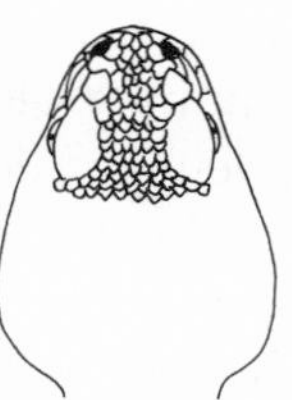

Mojave rattlesnake & diamondback rattlesnake

atinized material that cannot grow with the animal. (Actually most vertebrates, including humans, shed their skins regularly—it is simply a much more gradual event with us and usually goes unnoticed unless we buy a loofa sponge to assist the process.) The frequency with which a snake sheds has nothing to do with age; it is a function of how often the snake eats and how quickly it grows. The rattlesnake does gain a new rattle segment with each shedding, so on a snake with a perfect (unbroken) rattle you can tell how many times it has shed since birth.

Along with copperheads and cottonmouths of the eastern United States, rattlesnakes are members of the sub-family Crotalinae. These are the pit-vipers, so called because of the temperature-sensitive organs in front of each eye (they resemble extra nostrils), which help them locate food. So sensitive are these organs that a pit-viper can strike accurately at a warm object even if its eyes are taped.

Arizona is home to more species of rattlesnake—18—than any other state. (Surprisingly, rattlers occur in all the lower 48 states except Maine and Delaware, where they have been extirpated.) In Pima County we can find them in virtually any habitat, from the low western deserts—the sidewinders (*Crotalus cerastes*)—to the high mountains—the Arizona black rattlesnakes (*Crotalus viridis cerberus*). And although their prime period of activity is from spring through fall, rattlesnakes have been seen in every month of the year. But it is important to remember that rattlesnakes are shy and retiring and will in virtually any situation avoid confrontation with humans. Most bites are the result of carelessness or bravado on the part of the human—in fact, a statistically astonishing number of recorded bites involve young males with elevated blood-alcohol levels.

Many other cultures don't share the European abhorrence of snakes. Most native American tribes respect snakes, and may include them in ceremonies. Their folktales describe the rattlesnake as peaceful, only given to striking after the most egregious abuse—a far more accurate portrayal than frontier myths of vengeful mates and immortal severed heads.

On a practical basis, rattlesnakes serve as important low-level predators, vital controllers of rodents. Aesthetically, their movements and patterns are marvels of grace and symmetry. And philosophically, they are paradigms of evolution, creatures perfectly adapted to their environment.

Nature's Super Athletes

An adult broad-tailed hummingbird in reasonable cardiovascular shape has a resting pulse rate of around 600 beats per minute—10 heartbeats every second. During a courtship display or other strenuous activity that rate will more than double, powered by a heart proportionately larger than that of any other warm-blooded animal—a full 20 percent of the bird's body weight.

This furious pace is supported by a metabolism that if enlarged to human proportions would require around 200,000 calories a day to fuel—the equivalent of 30 chocolate cakes (our human-sized hummer's heart would be the size of a 1-gallon paint can). It's no wonder our feeders filled with pure sugar water evoke such fierce competition from neighborhood hummingbirds—they need a near-constant intake of calories just to stay alive.

Contrary to popular belief, though, hummingbirds do not subsist solely on flower nectar and the largesse of urban birdwatchers. They are, in fact, voracious insectivores as well, gleaning small insects around the flowers from which they gather nectar and perching in trees and darting out to snag gnats and mosquitos on the wing (a remarkable feat of dexterity considering the configuration of their beaks). These insects provide much-needed protein; a captive hummer fed only sugar water would quickly starve to death.

In view of their nutritionally tenuous grasp on life, it is surprising that many hummingbirds undertake daunting migration flights. Ruby-throated hummingbirds, the only hummer of the eastern United States, migrate from as far north as Canada to wintering grounds in Central America, often including a nonstop 600-mile leg across the Gulf of Mexico. They accomplish this feat by gorging on insects and nectar, doubling their 2-gram body weight with layers of fat in the weeks prior to the move.

The flight mechanism that facilitates not only marathon migration flights but also the hummer's unique ability to hover, fly backwards, and even sideway is the most highly developed of any bird. First, the flight muscles can account for one-third of the hummingbird's body weight, and they are unusually well-supplied with capillaries to ensure an adequate supply of oxygen. Unlike most birds, hummers have extremely strong elevator muscles, which power the wing on the backstroke. To hover, the hummingbird rotates the wing around a highly motile shoulder joint, turning the wing completely upside down on the backstroke so that it slices the air and cancels the tendency to push the bird forward. This elastic motion is repeated up to fifty times per second in the broad-billed hummingbird.

This ability to hover is even more remarkable when one considers that the shape of the wing itself is one more usually associated with falcons and swifts: a narrow, swept-back design like that of a high-speed aircraft. Indeed, certain species of hummers have been clocked at 50 miles per hour during courtship flights, indicating an impressive range of proficiency—like a stunt biplane with Mach-1 capability.

For nature to cram this much biomechanical sophistication into a package the size of a hummingbird borders on the fantastic. A female bee hummingbird from Cuba has a body the size of the end joint on your little finger and weighs roughly as much as a dime. She builds a nest the size of a thimble in which she incubates an egg no larger than a small pea.

Hummingbirds are in the family Trochilidae and are found only in the western hemisphere. Arizona boasts more species (at times as many as 16) than any other U.S. state, although this number represents but a fraction of the 320-odd known species, found mostly in the tropics. There are a couple of reasons why Arizona—and southern Arizona in particular—should be relatively blessed. We sit at the very northern tip of the summer range of many species such as the Lucifer, broad-billed, and magnificent, each of which only enters the United States in southern Arizona, New Mexico, or Texas. Our wide range of habitat is an advantage, as species such as the black-chinned gravitate to the desert canyons while the blue-throated and magnificent prefer higher elevations. One species, the Costa's, could rightfully be described as a Sonoran Desert native because its wintering grounds extend only to southern Sonora, Mexico, and its summer territory to central Arizona and southern California.

Another strong attraction is the 130-odd species of "hummingbird flowers" that bloom in the Southwest each spring. These plants, although evolved in many different families, share certain characteristics: their flowers are red and are usually set nearly horizontally, making access easy for a hovering bird. The flower petals often bend back at the tip, which further assists hovering by eliminating obstructions and, in addition, discourages landings by bees. The corolla tubes are long to accommodate a long beak, and the anthers are arranged to liberally douse the feeding bird with pollen—the whole reason the flower has gone to so much trouble to attract the bird in the first place. Hummingbird flowers of various species are favorite landscape plants for homeowners who wish for their own reasons to entice the little birds.

Ornithophiles

In western North America there are as many as 130 species of flowers especially adapted for attracting hummingbirds (plants that evolved to attract birds for feeding and consequently pollination are called ornithophilous*—"bird-loving"). Most of them look suspiciously alike: warm colors (red, orange, and sometimes yellow), long and tube-shaped, and suspended singly or in loose clusters. The flowers are red because hummingbirds can identify that color (most insects cannot) and learn to relate food with the color red. The nectar of typical hummingbird flowers is especially evolved for these energetic little birds: relatively large quantities and somewhat dilute (insect-adapted nectar is viscous and scant). Some flowers go to extremes to ensure the proper animals visit and thus carry out pollination; the skinny tubes of skyrocket flowers exactly fit the bills of hummingbirds, and their lobes are bent backward, allowing free access to hummingbirds but preventing bees from landing (though some bees and nectar-loving birds like orioles learned to "rob" the nectar by piercing the flower's base and* *extracting nectar from the bottom; conversely, hummingbirds will also "steal" nectar from bee-adapted flowers when available, such as those on the creosote and blue palo verde).*

In May, when hummers arrive en force *in southern Arizona, many of these ornithophilous flowers will be in full bloom. A few more common species you'll find in Pima County include:*

Bouvardia (Bouvardia glaberrima) — *Oak woodlands to coniferous forests.*

Coral bean (Erythrina flabelliformis) — *High desertscrub to oak woodlands.*

Desert honeysuckle (Anisacanthus thurberi) — *Desertscrub to oak woodlands.*

Hummingbird trumpet (Epilobium californica var. latifolia) — *Desertscrub to pine-oak woodlands.*

Scarlet penstemon (Penstemon barbatus) — *Oak woodlands to coniferous forests.*

Scarlet sage (Stachys coccinea) — *Desertscrub up to coniferous forests.*

Skyrocket (Ipomopsis aggregata) — *Coniferous forests.*

PLACES TO VISIT IN MAY

Tropical Delights

We'll never forget the first time we encountered an elegant trogon, one of the "specialty" birds people travel from all over the world to see in southern Arizona. We were ambling along the Old Baldy Trail next to Madera Creek in the Santa Rita Mountains, enjoying the cool shade of alligator junipers, sycamores, and walnuts. Hundreds of lemon- and lilac-colored butterflies clouded the trails. Suddenly a clear bugling call pierced the thick May air just across the stream: *OARK!-OARK!-OARK!-OARK!* Had a man dressed in a loin cloth swooshed across the canyon on a swinging vine, alighted in front of us, and proclaimed, "Me, Tarzan!" we would not have been surprised, so strong a jungle-image did the birdcall evoke.

We had heard a male elegant trogon, an exotic tropical bird related to the famous quetzals of Central America, a species that has been slowly edging its way into extreme southern Arizona's remnant riparian canyons each summer for the past century or so. Formerly called the coppery-tailed trogon for its flashy tail, this metallic green, white,

red, and gray bird is about a foot long and impressive in flight, as it feeds on fruit at twig-ends by hovering like a hummingbird. The bird we heard flashed into sight for a few seconds, then was gone. But the memory has stayed with us.

Just barely beyond the southeastern tip of Pima County and less than an hour from Tucson, Madera Canyon is a spectacular place for birding and hiking, although on looking at its heavily used picnic areas, crowded parking lots, and well-signed trails one would reconsider. Fear not. At peak times (weekends and holidays) simply arrive with the sun, or go in mid-week. Entrance to the canyon, on Coronado National Forest, is free, but the non-profit, non-government Friends of Madera Canyon sets up a drive-through information booth at which they ask for donations on weekends. Their free map is an excellent guide to the confusing web of trails.

The best place to see elegant trogons is along the creek, a mile or so up the Vault Mine Trail (also called Agua Caliente Trail). The aggressive hiker may take the Vault Mine–Agua Caliente Trail up to Josephine Saddle (almost 2,000 feet of climbing), then back via the Old Baldy Trail, a steep but beautiful 5-mile trip from the riparian stream up into pine-oak woodland and coniferous forest. Sulphur-bellied flycatchers, western wood-pewees, Hutton's vireos, zone-tailed hawks, and painted redstarts are all common in late spring and summer, and it's a good place to hear flammulated owls, spotted owls, western screech-owls, and whip-poor-wills after the sun goes down. Really aggressive hikers may want to power to the summit of Mount Wrightson (9,453 feet) via the Super Trail. The views from the rocky top sweep across southern Arizona and northern Mexico.

Don't miss the opportunity in Madera Canyon itself to see many of the dozen or so species of southern Arizona's summer humming-

Above, *Elegant trogon: an exotic metallic green, white, red, and gray bird*

birds. Find a comfortable rock in front of the nectar feeders at the Santa Rita Lodge or the Palisport Gift Shop and enjoy the show. Magnificent, blue-throated, and broad-billed will be the most common, along with black-chinned, Anna's, and Costa's; violet-crowned, white-eared, and Berylline are possible; rufous and Allen's might be seen July through September.

Another tropical genus that summers in our area are the tanagers. In Madera Canyon, four species are possible: summer, in the lower canyon; hepatic, in the middle canyon's oak-woodlands; western, in the higher coniferous forests; and the rare flame-colored, also up high.

A hike in Madera Canyon is like traveling to the tropics from Tucson in less than an hour.

Snake Drive

"There's one!" the person riding shotgun—navigator and principal lookout—cries when a slithering form appears on the road ahead. Before the Land Cruiser stops, the doors are open and we pile out, approaching the serpentine quarry on the road ahead with as much stealth as possible. A beautiful gopher snake, maybe 5 feet long, richly amber and brown in the early evening light, lies comfortably in the rapidly cooling sand. We admire him for five minutes, then one of us moves him gently off the road so that another, less-herpetophilic traveler won't squash him flat.

Back in the truck we continue on, hoping to see an elusive Mojave rattlesnake before the light is completely gone. A few tree roots growing sinuously across the road fake us out ("root snakes"), but before long we come across a very young western diamondback rattlesnake, which, alerted to our presence by the vibrations of the truck, darts off the road before we can admire him. Two snakes in ten minutes! A great beginning for one of our annual spring and summer snake drives—an exhilarating and safe way to enjoy the herps of the desert.

A snake drive begins just after sunset, when the temperature starts to drop. The long days of May and June are good because more light is available, although you'll have to wait longer for the temperatures to subside if the days have been well over 100°. Snakes emerge from their daytime burrows around this time and can be "caught" lounging on roads in early evening or early morning. Drive slowly and keep a sharp eye out (assign people other than the driver to this task to avoid collisions with other cars). Be careful when approaching a snake you can't identify; admire it from a distance (5 or so feet if it is docile, more if agitated). Snakes detect vibrations and movement, so move slowly and quietly.

Good snake drives include Saguaro National Park in the Tucson Mountains, especially the road to Mam-O-Gah Picnic Area; Antelope Drive in Buenos Aires National Wildlife Refuge; and Happy Valley Road (Mescal Road) east of the Rincon Mountains. Reptiles are strictly protected in all parks, and one must have a nongame hunting license to collect them on any other lands; reptiles are extremely difficult to keep alive in captivity—so enjoy seeing them in the wild and take photos for memories.

MAY SKIES

"Moon of the Bean Tree"

TRADITIONAL O'ODHAM NAME FOR MAY

Star Chart for 32°N
Mid-month, 9 pm

FEATURE CONSTELLATION

In ancient Egypt, the people greatly feared the Great Bear of the North (Ursa Major, or the Big Dipper) as it charged ceaselessly around the pole star. They found comfort in the presence of Arcturus, the Bear Watcher, a bright sun, which the Greeks later included as one of the stars of Bootes, the Bear Driver. Bootes is the bear's guardian, and it is his job to drive the Great Bear on his endless circle around the North Star.

MAY AT A GLANCE

Desertscrub

❧ Mesquites (*Prosopis* spp.) and acacias (*Acacia* spp.) put out their fuzzy tubular or ball-shaped catkins this month and next. Ocotillos (*Fouquieria splendens*) finish up blooming.

❧ Nocturnally blooming plants in the cactus family put on quite a show this month into next, including saguaros (*Carnegiea gigantea*), senitas (*C. schotii*), organ pipes (*Stenocereus thurberi*), and queens-of-the-night (*Peniocereus* spp.).

❧ Lesser long-nosed and Mexican long-tongued bats feast on the nectar and pollen of the night-blooming cactus plants, while hawkmoths dine on yucca offerings.

❧ Breeding animals include white-winged doves, roadrunners, Gambel's quail, black-throated sparrows, desert horned lizards, and desert spiny lizards. Skunks and badgers will begin to bear young this month. Gila monsters' eggs (laid 10 months ago) hatch.

❧ Kissing bugs (*Triatoma* spp.) become active—their "kiss," or bite, can be very irritating to humans, one of the many mammals on which they like to feed.

Desert Grasslands

❧ Mimosas (*Mimosa* spp.) put out their fuzzy pink or yellow catkins here and in the oak woodlands.

❧ Ocotillos (*Fouquieria splendens*) bloom this month.

❧ Soaptree yuccas (*Yucca elata*), the most common desertscrub and grassland variety, send up their tall woody flower stalks this month and next, brimming with creamy white bell-shaped flowers. Another member of the Agave family, desert spoon (*Dasylirion wheeleri*), blooms this month and next.

❧ Wild desert cotton (*Gossypium thurberi*) and coral bean (*Erythrina flabelliformis*) may begin to bloom this month. Prickly poppies (*Argemone* spp.) and New Mexico thistles (*Cirsium neomexicanum*) are in full, glorious bloom.

❧ Pronghorn antelope continue to give birth, and scaled quail begin breeding, as do Sonoran mud turtles and canyon treefrogs.

Oak Woodlands

❧ Hummingbird-adapted flowers such as coral bean (*Erythrina flabelliformis*), desert honeysuckle (*Anisacanthus thurberi*), and hummingbird trumpet (*Epilobium canum*) may flower this month.

❧ In riparian areas the Arizona grape (*Vitis arizonica*) is flourishing, and Cassin's kingbirds are nesting.

❧ Clark's spiny lizards bear live young this month, and red-spotted toads begin mating.

Pine-Oak Woodlands

❧ Early summer flowers like Fendler's globemallow (*Sphaeralcea fendleri*), with its deep pink flowers, and the lovely yellow columbine (*Aquilegia* spp.) may grace trailsides and stream banks.

❧ Singing in the tree canopies are many species of birds, including black-headed grosbeaks, painted redstarts, Scott's orioles, and American robins.

❧ Mountain spiny lizards bear live young this month and next.

Coniferous Forests

❧ Maples (*Acer* spp.), red-osier dogwoods (*Cornus stolonifera*), and aspens (*Populus* spp.) sport their new leaves, and snowberries (*Symphoricarpos oreophilus*) are just beginning to leaf out.

❧ Magnificent, blue-throated, and broad-tailed hummingbirds will arrive this month, moving up into the high country with the imminent blooming of flowers such as bouvardia (*Bouvardia glaberrima*), scarlet sage (*Stachys coccinea*), skyrocket (*Ipomopsis aggregata*), and scarlet penstemon (*Penstemon barbatus*).

❧ Black bears—perhaps females with new cubs—may be seen.

❧ Male Abert's squirrels compete vigorously for mates this month.

❧ Porcupines will bear their young this month.

Special Events

❧ **Ice Break Contest.** Tucson's Channel 4 (KVOA-TV) hosts its Ice Break Contest this month. A prize is awarded to the person who comes closest to the day, hour, and minute that Tucson's temperature reaches 100°. The gag refers to ice breaking on the Santa Cruz River, which of course is a dry wash most of the year.

❧ **Night-blooming Cereus Hotline**. Tohono Chul Park in northwest Tucson sets up a hotline. You can call daily to find out if the night-blooming cereus plants (*Cereus* spp.) are getting ready to bloom. On the "big night," the park will stay open late and provide interpretive naturalists to guide your way. See Appendix 6 for contact information.

In the Sky

❧ May 1 is May Day, the halfway point between the vernal equinox and summer solstice and, in more temperate climates, the beginning of Spring.

❧ The Big Dipper drips high in the northern sky. Look at the star from which the dipper "pours" and follow that line until you see the North Star, or Polaris.

❧ The Eta Aquarid meteor shower peaks May 3 around midnight.

See the chapter Exploring the Nature of Pima County and Southern Arizona for definitions and descriptions of communities.

june

LATE AFTERNOON. *The sun stalls on the western horizon, relentless. Heat rises in waves from the hot rocks. Barely a living thing stirs—even the broil-proof white-winged doves are quiet. A slow metallic clatter begins, building in crescendo to a nerve-piercing buzzing whine. The sound of heat: cicadas, singing down the sun, calling in the night. This is June in the desert.*

We love the staccato song of those loud green beetles, which buzz their heat-defying tunes from dawn until sunset. It epitomizes the intensity of June, a fitting soundtrack for the searing dry days. June begins where May left off: hot and dry. Days will simmer, measured in three digits, and an average of 22 days will pass without a whisper of clouds. But amazingly, June is a productive month among the desert plants and animals. Most of the legumes droop heavily with ripe seed pods: mesquite, palo verde, and coursetia trees, acacia and mimosa shrubs, and fairy duster bushes. In canyons and woodlands, coral bean plants still flower brilliant red and are setting fruit. Jojoba plants bear nuts. Organ pipe cactus blooms, as will the beautiful sacred datura if rains were generous in the spring. Atop their tall green columns, the saguaro cactus fruits burst open, carmine-red like the mouths of vampires. Bats and birds, especially doves, feast on the succulent fruit before it turns to jerky and falls to earth, prizes for the ants, mice,

Arivaca Ciénega—a lush magical wetland in the Buenos Aires National Wildlife Refuge—is filled with breeding birds in June

coyotes, and skunks. This is the most important time of year for the Tohono O'odham—"moon of the saguaro fruit," Hahshani Bahithag Mashath, *and the beginning of their year. On June 24 they will observe San Juan's Day with ceremonies to bless their seeds and fields, celebrate the new year, and call in the rains. A ceremonial wine called* nawait *is made from the saguaro cactus fruits.*

In the grasslands pronghorn antelopes continue to give birth to their fawns, which the herd fiercely protects from coyotes or golden eagles. Mule deer also will begin to give birth now through August. The summer hawks grace the rolling grasslands and riparian greenways—Swainson's in the grasslands, and rare Mississippi kites, black hawks, zone-tailed hawks, and gray hawks, in the riparian areas—just in time for a steady supply of young snakes and lizards to feed to their nestlings.

White-tailed deer in the oak woodlands begin to bear young this month, while the solitary males sport the sprouts of new antlers. Streams have retreated mostly underground now, dry but for a few pools where crowds of amphibians and invertebrates patiently wait for rain. Canyon grape vines are beginning to set their tasty fruits, but they won't ripen for a month or so. The oak woodlands seem quiet, especially after the fecund spring. Most of the birds have moved up into the higher and cooler country, waiting for the summer rains before they venture back down again.

The pine-oak woodlands and coniferous forests are bursting at the seams with life. Days are pleasantly warm, in the mid-80°s, and the nights are chilly, around 50. Gray-breasted and Steller's jays are in the midst of their busy mating season, raucously setting the tone for June in the high country. Red-faced warblers, yellow-eyed juncos, yellow warblers, and other songbirds are in full breeding mode. Huge insect blooms in the moist canyon bottoms add to the bounty for the mating birds. A few creeks still trickle in the protective shade of tall conifers, some of which may be setting their namesake cones. Abert's squirrels begin to bear young now, which will mature just in time to feast on the ponderosa pine seed crop. Mountain berry bushes, such as New

Mexican raspberry, are blooming, and summer mountain flowers like Palmer's lupine are just beginning their short show. Bracken ferns carpet the forest floors.

*In June much of the human population joins the mammals and birds in the practice of vertical migration—following the cooler temperatures up the mountains. When it hits 105° in Tucson, we head up to the top of the Santa Catalina Mountains and Rappel Rock, with the convenient excuse that we want to catch a glimpse of the peregrine falcons, which sometimes nest in the area. We also practice crepuscular behavior—becoming active in the cool hours of dawn or dusk. A favorite easy getaway is King's Canyon Wash across from the Arizona–Sonora Desert Museum. After the sun sets, the sensation of cooler, denser air rolling into the deeply in-cut wash as the day's heat rises up and away is very special. We always see lots of wildlife, especially at the small spring where a tiny bit of water sometimes is squeezed out of the dry Tucson Mountains between the sand and exposed granite. This is also a good place to enjoy most of the desert legume species as they fruit, especially the coursetia (*Coursetia glandulosa*). This plant's ripe seed pods, after drying out and heating up during June, suddenly burst open in the early evenings, sending little black seeds flying through the air, assaulting unsuspecting passersby.*

One other favorite place we visit in June, again practicing crepuscular behavior, is Arivaca Ciénega, about an hour and a half south of Tucson in the Buenos Aires National Wildlife Refuge. We arrive at dawn at the lush, magical wetlands, which in summer are filled with breeding birds: rare gray hawks, yellow-billed cuckoos, varied buntings, vermilion flycatchers, thick-billed kingbirds, and common yellowthroats. We walk the boardwalks and revel in the green and wet—sedges, cattails, reeds, thorn thickets, and cottonwoods. ❧ ❧ ❧

JUNE WEATHER

	Sunrise	Sunset	Avg. Relative Humidity/Tucson
June 1	5:18 MST	7:25 MST	5 a.m. 32%
June 30	5:21 MST	7:34 MST	5 p.m. 13%

Stations	Ajo	Tucson	Mt. Lemmon
Station Elevation	(1,800 ft.)	(2,584 ft.)	(8,800 ft.)
June Averages			
Max. temperature	99.6°F	98.5°F	78.0°F
Min. temperature	71.6°F	67.3°F	43.2°F
Precipitation	.08 in.	.24 in.	.30 in.
Snow	0 in.	0 in.	0 in.
# days 100° & over	15	13	0
# days 32° & under	0	0	0
# days precip. >.01"	1	2	1
June Extremes			
Max. temperature	115°F (1919)	111°F (1957)	91°F (1960)
Min. temperature	50°F (1921)	47°F (1955)	32°F (1982)
Max. snow/month	0 in.	0 in.	0 in.
Max. snow/1 day	0 in.	0 in.	0 in.
Max. precip./month	.79 in. (1918)	1.46 in. (1954)	3.46 in. (1984)
Max. precip./1 day	.56 in. (1958)	1.27 in. (1954)	1.22 in. (1984)

June Notes

As many as 22 days may pass in June without a cloud in the sky. If we're lucky, we may get a couple of sprinkles, but normally June is our hottest, driest month. Triple digits are common in the deserts, but the mountains stay relatively cool, usually in the low 80°s on the hottest days. By the end of the month, days will begin to feel more humid as the first of the summer monsoon clouds begin to amass to the east and south. Sometimes the rains will come early; in 1950 they began with a bang on the 22nd, with over 2 inches of rain falling over north Tucson (the data above is from south Tucson). Neighborhoods reported 3 feet of water flowing through their homes, and trees and power lines were downed by winds of up to 55 mph.

For information about data sources for these listings, see the Climate section of the chapter Exploring the Nature of Pima County and Southern Arizona.

Vertical Variations

Many animals, including humans, practice "vertical migration" to escape the heat of summer. The trip may be as short as a move from a 2,400-foot elevation desertscrub winter- or springtime home up to a 4,500-foot oak woodland summer retreat (like mule deer do), or as long as up to the top of a mountain—8,000 feet in the coniferous forest (like yellow-rumped warblers do).

Animals do this because as one moves up a mountain in southern Arizona, the total rainfall increases at a rate of about 4 or 5 inches per 1,000-foot increase, while the temperatures drop at the rate of about 3° to 4° per 1,000-foot increase. See the table below for a comparison between habitats.

Another vertical migration route is down—as in under *the ground. Many animals in the deserts, such as Harris' antelope ground squirrels, use their burrows as retreats in the daytime to cool off between bouts of foraging during midday; or they simply become nocturnal, waiting out the heat in their cool subterranean homes. A rodent's or snake's retreat just 1 foot under the surface may be as much as 60° cooler. But unlike going up a mountain, which always results in cooler and rainier conditions and thus harsher winters, going down into the ground in winter will result in warmer temperatures than on the surface because the earth is such a good insulator. See the table for more comparisons.*

Variation of Temperature and Rainfall with Elevation

	Annual Rainfall	Average May Max. Temp.
Desertscrub (2,500')	10"	88°F
Desert grassland (3,500')	12"	84°F
Oak woodland (4,500')	17"	80°F
Pine-oak woodland (5,500')	21"	76°F
Mixed coniferous forest (6,500')	26"	72°F
[Spruce-alpine fir forest] (7,500')*	34"	68°F

Variation of Temperature Underground

	Low Winter Temp.	High Summer Temp.
Ground surface	20°F	165°F
1 foot under	40°F	105°F
2 feet under	50°F	95°F
3 feet under	60°F	85°F
4 feet under	62°F	83°F

*Not a southern Arizona community. The elevations and average rainfall and temperatures are approximate, and the habitats will vary widely among the elevations. These charts were adapted from information in Charles H. Lowe, ed., *The Vertebrates of Arizona* (University of Arizona Press, Tucson, 1964); "Mean Annual Precipitation in Biotic Communities in Arizona and New Mexico," U.S. Department of Agriculture, Technical Bulletin 247 (Washgton, D.C., 1931); and from the Arizona–Sonora Desert Museum.

FLORA

The Life-giving Mesquite Tree

Grocery, pharmacy, hardware, cosmetics, building materials, sporting goods—it would take a whole mall to house all these resources under one roof. But Native Americans in the Southwest found the same resources in one tree—the mesquite.

Ethnobotanist Richard Felger has called the mesquite "an early K-Mart for desert peoples." Indeed, it is doubtful any other one plant provided so much for them. They used branches and trunks for building and fires; they made bows from the straightest limbs and baskets and medicine from the inner bark. The sap from the inner xylem provided black dye for baskets and hair, and the white gum was used as an eye medication. And of course the highly nutritious seed pods were a vital food resource—when ground into flour, they provide more protein than soybeans. The list goes on and on.

This dependent relationship toward mesquite changed with the coming of European cattle ranchers. They saw mesquite as an invader of grasslands, stealing water and nutrients from grazing country. Ironically, it is widely thought, although not proven, that cattle assisted the spread of the tree into new areas.

Some botanists believe mesquite evolved in a mutualistic relationship with the large grazing animals of the Pleistocene. The seeds of the tree are encased in a hard outer shell, surrounded by the softer pod. The animals that fed on the pods gained a rich nutrient mix from the pod, while the seeds passed through their systems intact, yet scarified enough to allow germination—aided by the nice dollop of fertilizer in which they were deposited. With the extinction of the Pleistocene megafauna, it is likely mesquite retreated to watercourses, where periodic floods tumbled the pods over rocks and scarified enough seeds to continue the species.

When European cattle were introduced, the mesquite's primary means of propagation returned, helping the tree to spread over the grasslands and deserts of the Southwest. Since then many ranchers have waged all-out war against the hardy, fast-growing tree. They have cut it down, burned it, and "chained" it—two bulldozers travel abreast dragging a huge steel chain between them to mow down trees by the dozen.

But although mesquite may no

longer figure vitally into the Native American lifestyle, it still provides food and shelter for dozens of animal species. It also serves as a "nurse tree" to more than 165 different species of plants. The full-grown mesquite provides summer shade and protection from winter freezing for seedlings that might not survive in the open during their first few years. The most famous beneficiary of this shelter is the saguaro cactus. Often one can find small saguaros under mesquite trees or see adults grown through and towering above the tree that protected them in their tender youth. Sometimes just the dead skeleton of the tree will remain beneath a vigorous saguaro.

The most common southern Arizona mesquite is the velvet mesquite (*Prosopis velutina*). It is often considered merely a variety of the honey mesquite (*Prosopis glandulosa*), a very similar tree with slightly larger, more widely spaced leaflets.

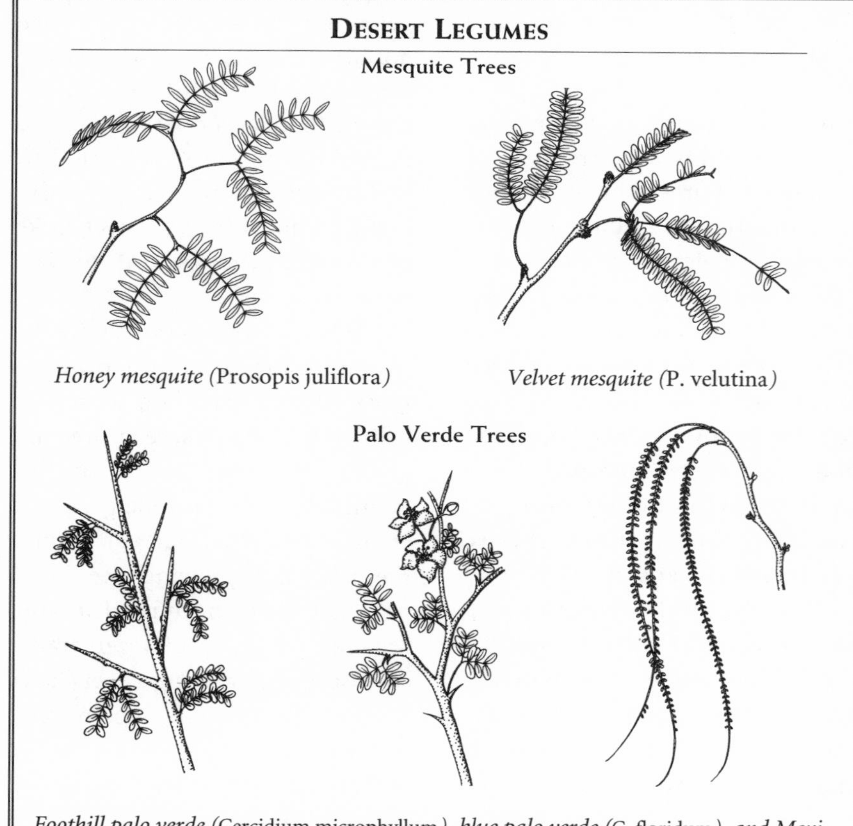

*Honey mesquite (*Prosopis juliflora*)*

*Velvet mesquite (*P. velutina*)*

*Foothill palo verde (*Cercidium microphyllum*), blue palo verde (*C. floridum*), and Mexican palo verde (*Parkinsonia aculeata*).*

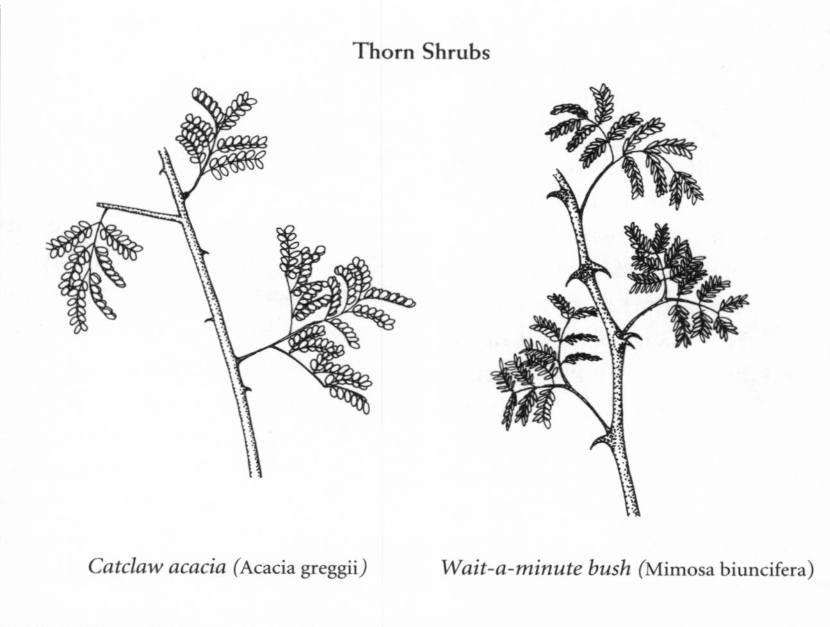

Thorn Shrubs

Catclaw acacia (Acacia greggii) *Wait-a-minute bush* (Mimosa biuncifera)

A Modern Desert Harvest

Driving down Interstate 8 between Gila Bend and Yuma just north of western Pima County, you might notice something peculiar. Flanking the highway along certain stretches are expanses of ordinary-looking desertscrub. But as you pass and look perpendicular to the road, you see that the scrub is laid out in neat rows, like so much corn or cabbage. It's a very odd effect. The shrubs are jojoba (*ho-HO-bah*), a native plant that has been "rediscovered" because of the fine oil produced from its seeds.

From close up, a jojoba (*Simmondsia chinensis*) does not look much like a desert shrub. The leaves are altogether too large compared to a creosote or acacia, and the nuts seem almost tropical. But look even closer. Those broad leaves all stand straight up, leaving very little surface area exposed to the midday sun. Most of the jojoba's photosynthesis is carried out in the morning and evening, minimizing water loss through tran-

Above, *Jojoba's vertical leaves avoid direct sun*

spiration. Also, the flowers and seeds of the plant are situated under the leaves, gaining them some shade as well.

The nuts are nearly half oil by weight. It's theorized that the oil (actually a liquid wax) helps prevent dessication, but what's known for sure is that it makes a very fine ingredient for shampoos, lotions, and soaps, qualities known to Native Americans centuries ago. As a result the jojoba has been "tamed" and farmed in locations that wouldn't support more delicate crops.

Another component in the seeds is a compound similar to cyanide, which makes them toxic to most mammals if eaten in quantity—except for the nondescript little Bailey's pocket mouse, which has developed a digestive antidote to the compound and happily munches where others fear to dine.

Jojoba is evergreen, generally 4 to 5 feet in height, with grayish green leaves that are not poisonous and are browsed by deer, bighorn sheep, and javelina. The shrub is dioecious—male plants have small yellow flowers in clusters; the female plants' flowers are single and greenish. Nuts appear in early summer on female plants.

FAUNA

But It's a Dry Heat . . .

As the hot days of May fade into the *really* hot, parched days of June, desert animals face a serious survival situation. It's likely that no rain has fallen for two or three months, streams and water holes have dried up, and the thermometer is regularly climbing above the 100° mark—often reaching 115° in the lower deserts. And 115° in the air can mean 165° on the ground.

Plants deal with such conditions by sending deep tap roots into the soil to suck up subterranean moisture, storing water in succulent tissues, dropping leaves, or existing only as tough seeds through the worst parts of the year. Obviously, animals lack most of these mechanisms, but they have their own behavioral and physiological adaptations to deal with the heat.

Mobility helps—in fact, it might be considered the chief advantage animals have over their rooted neighbors. Mobility allows many species of birds to simply migrate north to cooler regions for the summer (see March); other birds and some mammals migrate vertically up mountains to cooler elevations or retreat into burrows during daylight hours.

The Black and White of Desert Dressing

When we hike in the summertime desert, we often don light-colored clothing—khaki or white. But the funny thing is, we're the only creatures so attired. Most desert-adapted animals tend to be rather dark—even black—but never white. The reasons are surprising.

A biologist at Arizona State University studied the skin-temperature differences between male and female phainopeplas—a beautiful Sonoran Desert bird that lives here all year; the females are silky gray, and the males a shiny black. He determined that in full sun the skin-surface temperature of the male was just a tiny bit higher than the female in full sunlight, even though her feathers reflected nearly three times more sunlight. The black feathers trap most of the heat in their outer layers, where it can dissipate in the slightest wind movement. The black male will be hotter on the surface than the gray female but nearly the same temperature where it counts—on his skin.

We never see white-furred or -feathered desert animals because white allows a lot of short-wave radiation to penetrate deeply, nearly to the skin. And because much of our sunlight comprises short-wave components, a white animal would nearly roast in the hot spring and summer sun.

But sometimes just staying out of the sun isn't enough. When the humidity is 7 or 8 percent and the nighttime lows don't drop below 80°, moisture is sucked from every pore, and the animals that live on the desert floor must deal with both heat and dehydration. Over the course of millennia, many of them have evolved physiological adaptations that allow them to thrive in seemingly brutal conditions.

Sometimes that adaptation involves simple tolerance to extreme fluctuations in bodily moisture levels. For example, humans feel extreme distress when 6 to 8 percent of the body weight is lost through dehydration. At a 10 percent loss people become disoriented and possibly unable to help themselves. A 15 percent loss results in a complete shutdown of the body's cooling mechanisms; without immediate outside assistance death is imminent.

Compare this morbid countdown with the resilience of a 5-ounce white-winged dove, which can lose 20 percent of its weight in body water with no ill effects whatsoever. A Gambel's quail can lose a full 50 percent—a greater tolerance than any other vertebrate. Even the desert bighorn sheep, whose weight roughly parallels that of humans, can lose 30 percent of its weight without harm. That sheep can then drink 5 gallons of water at once to replenish itself. Imagine a 150-pound man losing 40 pounds by not drinking for four or five days, then blithely gaining it all back at once by guzzling a jerry can full of water.

Although the ability to tolerate dehydration is an advantage, avoiding it to begin with is an even better strategy. Besides perspiration, a major potential for water loss occurs during urination, a vital process for ridding the body of excess salt and nitrogenous wastes. Many desert mammals, especially the smaller ones, have kidneys that are able to concentrate both waste products much more efficiently than ours; in fact the urine of some desert mice is an almost-dry paste. Going even beyond that, birds and reptiles concentrate their nitrogen as uric acid, which can be excreted as a dry crystal.

Animals also use behavioral tricks to conserve water. Vultures urinate on their feet, gaining valuable evaporative cooling from liquid that would be lost anyway (an unsavory-sounding practice with a fancy name: urohydresis). Roadrunner fledglings void their urine and feces in membranous sacs, which are eaten by the parents; the fluid content is thus recycled.

If one had to pick the ultimate desert-adapted animal, the title would certainly go to the kangaroo rat. Although other animals tough out dehydration or gnaw on succulents to get enough water, the kangaroo rat simply manufactures its own. All animals produce minute amounts of metabolic water when protein, carbohydrates, and fat are burned in the body, releasing hydrogen, which combines with respirated oxygen. However, this water is a tiny fraction of what most animals need to survive. But members of the genus *Dipodomys* can subsist solely on this internally produced water. In fact, the diet of most kangaroo rats consists of absolutely dry seeds; they don't even bother with succulent leaves or cactus tissue. They are, without doubt, the ultimate desert rats.

CICADAS

There's no doubt about it—the sound of cicadas buzzing on a searing day is the sound of summer. But it's rare to actually see these chunky, clear-winged greenish bugs also known as cactus dodgers (Cacama valvata)*. They spend most of their lives as nymphs underground feeding on plant roots and emerge for a short time in June as adults to mate and lay eggs before* *they die. One- to 2-inches long, they crawl part way up tree trunks, shed their skins, then begin their short but loud lives (look for the pale amber ghost-like skins left stuck to tree trunks). The males are the musicians, serenading prospective loves by rapidly vibrating two plates on their bellies. Try as we might, we can never seem to find the loud Don Juans in a thick mesquite tree or hackberry shrub—our presence usually silences them before we can home in on them. Sometimes a congregation of males lets loose in a tree and the brain-numbing sound is truly impressive. Cicadas are favorite prey of birds and cicada-killer wasps (*Sphecius speciosus*), which paralyze them and feed them to their young in underground nests. Our cicadas are relatives of the "periodic" cicadas of the eastern United States (*Magicicada *spp.), which true to their name only emerge periodically, usually either in 13 or 17 years* en masse.

The Desert Sheep

The desert bighorn sheep—the one that can drink 5 gallons of water at a time—is a subspecies of the bighorn sheep that inhabits the frigid peaks of the Rocky Mountains. The desert sheep (*Ovis canadensis mexicana*) is smaller than its mountain relative—a common trait of desert subspecies—but displays no other outward signs of its vastly different lifestyle.

Perhaps the hardiest group of desert bighorns in the United States inhabit the Cabeza Prieta National Wildlife Refuge west of Ajo, in the western reaches of Pima County. One of the hottest and driest deserts in North America, the Cabeza Prieta encompasses vast, low valley floors of creosote separated by precipitous, rugged mountains that barely top 2,000 feet in elevation. Yet around 500 bighorns pursue a shadowy existence there.

Above, *desert bighorn sheep*

Each year the U.S. Fish and Wildlife Service oversees a water-hole count to help gauge the status of the bighorn population as well as that of other species in the refuge. The count is run at the end of June, the driest part of the year, when most natural water sources are dry and there is a better chance of seeing sheep at the refuge tanks (these are natural catchments in ravines, which have been augmented with cement cisterns, built-up troughs, and metal roofs). The volunteers who participate in the count sit in crude blinds in temperatures of up to 120°, noting numbers, sex, age, and condition of the sheep that show up—as well as other animals using the tanks. Many people consider the sheep count to be the ultimate rite of passage for true desert junkies.

Ironically, the Cabeza Prieta sheep are doing better than some of their relatives in more temperate ranges. The Pusch Ridge herd on the west side of the Santa Catalina Mountains north of Tucson has been faltering badly in recent years—a 1994 helicopter survey only found about a dozen animals. Disturbance from housing developments under the ridge is a possible reason for the decline, as is intrusion by hikers; another theory blames increased mountain lion predation because of brush buildup from years of fire suppression to protect homes built in the foothills. During the annual survey in 2001, no bighorns were found.

Lizard Watching

Summer is a good time for lizard watching. Even in the heat of the day, when snakes and most other animals are dozing underground, lizards can be seen dashing across scorching patches of sunny ground between sheltering clumps of vegetation or foraging in the shade of rocks or in trees. Although their small bodies heat up quickly, they can lose that heat just as readily by dumping it against a cooler surface, so many species practice an on-and-off activity schedule: they'll hunt in the open for a short time, then spread out in the shade to recuperate.

Whiptail lizards (*Cnemidophorous* spp.) of several almost indistinguishable species are common in desertscrub and desert grasslands; a long, slinky body and tail and quick, darty movements will identify one from a distance to the experienced. Zebra-tailed lizards (*Callisaurus draconoides*) are as easy to spot as their name suggests. They wave their black and white tails in a conspicuous manner that puzzles scientists—it seems like a come-and-get-me signal for predators. One theory suggests the tail-waving indicates that the lizard has seen the predator, and that pursuit would be futile. This would save energy for both animals.

The dinosaur of the desert floor is the desert spiny lizard (*Sceloporous magister*). Stout and squat, with rough, pointed scales, these lizards stomp around the scrub as if suffering from delusions of *Tyrannosaurus rex.*

In the grasslands, lesser earless lizards (*Holbrookia maculata*) are frequently seen. Although their name is descriptive (they have no external ear openings), this feature is hard to spot in the field. The beautiful chevron pattern on the back is more distinctive, and sometimes two black and blue belly markings are visible. At about the same elevation the Clark's spiny lizard (*Sceloporous clarki*) takes the place of the desert spiny. And up in the oaks and pines yet another spiny lizard, the mountain, or Yarrow's (*S. jarrovii*), basks on granite boulders, its black and gray "fishnet stocking" patterned scales glistening in the sun.

And perhaps the most ubiquitous lizard is the common collared lizard (*Crotaphytus collaris*), a medium-sized lizard that varies in color from beautiful turquoise to yellow-green, sporting a conspicuous black collar. It ranges across Pima County in rocky areas from the low west deserts to nearly 8,000 feet.

PLACES TO VISIT IN JUNE

Arivaca Ciénega

Mist swirls among the reeds and cattails of the shallow *ciénega,* a natural spring, rising up into the fingers of the cottonwood trees where it melts into the warming air. Everything around us feels heavy, wet. Exuberant birdsong fills our ears. We stroll the wooden boardwalk above the swampy soup; just ahead a small frog dives from the platform to the safety of the water with a singular *plorp!* and overhead we see the regal form of a great blue heron gliding over the rushes, its huge wings pumping with a deep *swoosh-swoosh-swoosh.* A small breeze tickles our skin, and the coolness makes our longsleeved shirts feel cozy.

June is a great time to visit Buenos Aires National Wildlife Refuge's Arivaca Ciénega, an hour and a half south of Tucson next to the little town of Arivaca. Summer birds include gray hawks, green herons, great blue herons, black-bellied whistling ducks, vermilion flycatchers, varied buntings, yellow warblers, and common yellowthroats. From the entrance just east of the mercantile and post office, you can stroll along a 2-mile loop around the ciénega. Be prepared for bugs and sun. Call the refuge for information on tours (see Appendix 6 for phone number).

King Canyon

The trick to withstanding summertime heat in the desert, to paraphrase T. E. Lawrence, is in *not minding* the heat. Try this: on a sizzling triple-digit day when the sun starts sliding down the jagged skyline of the Tucson Mountains, grit your teeth and head toward it, over Gate's Pass, to the parking lot across from the Arizona–Sonora Desert Museum. Instead of heading up the Wasson Peak trail, drop off into the wash. It will be mostly shaded by now, as the sun finishes melting into the west. As you walk up the King Canyon Wash, your boots crunching on the gravel will sound deafening. Go a ways—a quarter-mile, a half-mile—until you can't hear any traffic. Then just sit. No one comes here in summer. Cicadas, which became silent while you walked by, will begin again to drone shrilly. Close your eyes and let it sink in, the sound of heat and summer. Under you, feel the heat of the day in the soft sand. Relax and let summer and you get acquainted. Other animals will join you: coyotes, javelina, Gambel's quail, white-winged doves, curve-billed thrashers, verdins, cactus wrens, and roadrunners. Many will be on their way up-canyon another half-mile to the tiny spring seeping from under the exposed rock in the middle of the wash. We don't hang out near the spring in summer, as it keeps the animals from visiting their only source of water for miles around.

In a while, after the sun has fully relinquished the day to dusk, you will begin to notice a wonderful thing: cool air spilling over the high banks into the deep wash. This is the refreshing post-sundown summer phenomenon of cool, dense air draining into canyons as the day's heat radiates into the atmosphere. It happens surprisingly fast, and it is the secret to life in a summertime desert. In your memory, it will sustain you through the summer.

Rappel Rock and the Summit Crags

One of the most popular landforms in the Santa Catalina Mountains is Rappel Rock, so-called because it is considered one of the best places in Pima County to learn to rock climb and rappel (descend). Many times we have hiked by the great thumb of granite to hear voices filtering down from the heights: "What do I do now?" "Grab the handhold to your upper left!" "I can't—I'm gripped!" and "Relax and move slowly! And don't look down!"

Falcons also find the many cliffs around the Summit Crags, of which Rappel Rock is a part, attractive. We like to find a comfortable perch anywhere in the vicinity to sit with our binoculars and glass for the streaking forms of hunting peregrines, which have historically nested in the area. If a nest is active, Coronado National Forest officials will close off the face of Rappel Rock to climbing and restrict hiking around the base of the rocks. Before you head up, call the forest biologist (see Appendix 6 for phone number) to determine the exact closure area and rules.

Rappel Rock and the other Summit Crags rise from the shady ponderosa pine forest on the south slopes of the Catalina's highest ridge, from 8,800 feet to just over 9,000 feet. Besides peregrines, look for sharp-shinned hawks, northern goshawks, and red-tailed hawks, as well as American robins, brown creepers, red-shafted flickers, white-breasted nuthatches, and yellow warblers. Also, bears with cubs may be active, so keep an eye out.

Rappel Rock is about 30 minutes down the Lemmon Lookout Trail, starting from the parking lot at the end of the Catalina Highway (past Ski Valley), next to the observatory. Follow the signs to Lemmon Lookout; where the trail intersects a road, take the right fork (left takes you to the fire lookout at Lemmon Rock). Follow this path to Quartzite Spring (covered by a tin shed) where you head downhill to Rappel Rock. Farther along the same path are The Ravens and The Fortress, other spectacular rock formations thrusting high out of the pine forest. Technical equipment and experience are necessary to climb any of the Summit Crags.

Peregrine Recovery

In 1972 the U.S. government banned the use of DDT, which was believed to have caused severe declines in populations of raptors as well as other top-of-the-food chain predators. Peregrine falcons were among the hardest hit, and their numbers plummeted to the point they were declared an endangered species. Happily, since the 1970s, numbers of peregrines have increased steadily in the United States and in the summer of 1995 the United States Fish and Wildlife Service announced it was taking steps to remove the peregrine falcon from the endangered species list.

Arizona leads the nation in recovery for this fastest of birds—it "stoops" on its avian prey at speeds close to 200 miles per hour. The original recovery goal called for establishing 200 breeding pairs across the country; today, Arizona alone boasts as many as 250 pairs within its borders. In Pima County, the most well-known peregrines return each summer to a nest site, kept secret by biologists to help thwart nest-robbers and photographers, near the Summit Crags in the Santa Catalina Mountains. Each June the popular rock-climbing area is closed to recreational climbing while the birds rear their young.

Peregrines are found all year in Pima County, nesting in the high country on sheer cliffs in the summer and spending winters in warmer lowlands with good, high roosting areas and plenty of prey. A pair has been seen wintering in downtown Tucson, taking advantage of manmade high-rises and abundant urban pigeons.

Peregrine falcon at the Arizona–Sonora Desert Museum

JUNE SKIES

"Moon of the Saguaro Cactus Fruit"

TRADITIONAL O'ODHAM NAME FOR JUNE

NORTH

EAST

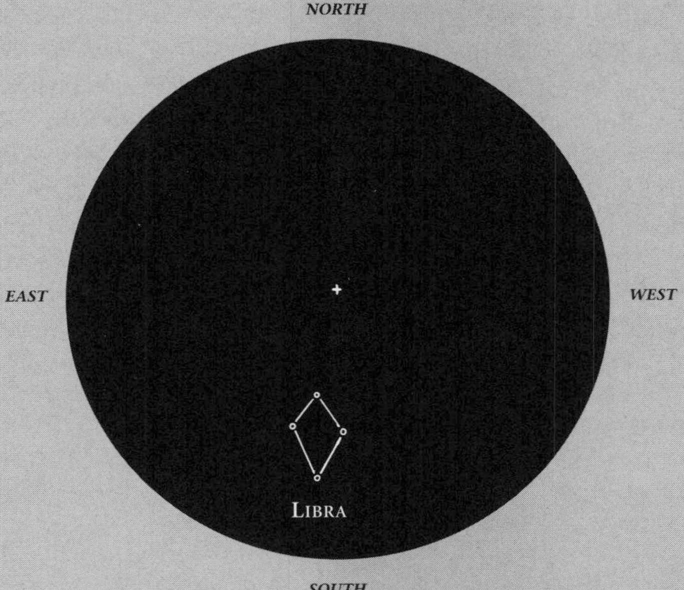

WEST

SOUTH

Star Chart for 32°N
Mid-month, 9 pm

FEATURE CONSTELLATION

Libra today is known as the Scales, but in ancient times its stars were the claws of Scorpius, the Scorpion. A vestige of its first life lies in the names of the two brightest stars: Kiffe Borealis and Kiffe Australis, Northern and Southern Claw. In the reign of Julius Caesar, the Romans cleaved the claws from Scorpius and made them into the Scales, creating the twelfth of the zodiacal signs, one for each month. At that time, the Sun was entering these stars at the beginning of the autumnal equinox, when day and night are equal—hence the adoption of their name, the Scales.

JUNE AT A GLANCE

Desertscrub

❧ Saguaro cactus (*Carnegiea gigantea*) finishes up flowering, and new fruit ripens and splits open.

❧ Blooming plants include sacred datura (*Datura wrightii*) if rains in spring were good, and organ pipe cactus (*Stenocereus thurberi*).

❧ Plants setting fruit are jojoba (*Simmondsia chinensis*), creosote (*Larrea tridentata*), palo verde (*Cercidium* spp.), mesquite (*Prosopis* spp.), catclaw acacia (*Acacia greggii*), fairy duster (*Calliandra eriophylla*), and samota (*Coursetia glandulosa*).

❧ Lesser nighthawks trill in the evenings and early mornings.

❧ Around ponds and lakes (in Pima County these occur mostly in golf courses or wastewater treatment plants), mallards (Mexican ducks) are caring for their chicks; these are the only common ducks to nest in our area.

❧ Gopher snakes and common kingsnakes (found in most habitats) lay eggs. Western diamondback rattlesnakes (up to coniferous forests) and tiger rattlesnakes (up into grassland foothills) bear live young.

❧ Large numbers of cicadas, or "cactus dodgers," emerge from underground burrows to mate; it's the males we hear buzzing so loudly, trying to attract mates.

❧ Cicada-killer wasps, which are large and colored orange and yellow, capture and paralyze cicadas to feed to their developing larvae.

Desert Grasslands

❧ Yuccas and agaves continue to bloom this month.

❧ Pronghorn and mule deer are bearing their fawns.

❧ Swainson's hawks and crested caracaras are breeding.

❧ Gray hawks, Mississippi kites, black hawks, and zone-tailed hawks breed in the riparian areas, such as the San Pedro River and Sonoita Creek.

❧ Sonoran whipsnakes lay eggs (up to pine-oak woodlands).

Oak Woodlands

❧ Coral bean (*Erythrina flabelliformis*) is setting fruit and continues to bloom.

❧ Canyon grape (*Vitus arizonica*) is beginning to set its fruit.

❧ Sonoran mountain kingsnakes (up to coniferous forests) lay eggs, while black-tailed rattlesnakes bear live young.

Madrean alligator lizards begin breeding now and into July.

Mormon metalmark, Sonoran satyr, and canyonlands satyr butterflies may be common this month.

Female white-tailed deer bear young, and the solitary males are growing their new antlers.

Pine-Oak Woodlands

Summer flowers include coral bells (*Huechera sanguinea*), alpine clematis (*Clematis pseudoalpina*), and bushy tick clover (*Desmodium batocaulon*).

Songbirds are in full breeding mode in the high country.

Twin-spotted rattlesnakes, a rare species of southeastern Arizona, bear live young.

Black bears begin their mating season in the high country.

Coniferous Forests

Mountain berry bushes are blooming, such as New Mexican raspberry (*Rubus neomexicanus*).

Some conifers, trees that bear cones, set their seeds in cones this month; pines may take two years to produce seeds.

Bracken ferns have sprouted over the forest floors.

Terloot's white butterflies emerge this month and may be seen through fall.

Abert's squirrels have their young this month.

Special Events

San Juan's Day is June 24, when native peoples bless the coming of the rains with ceremonies, as well as mark the beginning of their year. Saguaro cactus fruit wine plays an important part in these ceremonies for the Tohono O'odham. Check with the Arizona–Sonora Desert Museum, which usually offers a field trip for those who want to learn how the O'odham harvest the fruit. Also, Native Seeds/SEARCH hosts a sunrise ceremony on San Juan's Day with seed blessings, native ceremonial songs, and refreshments.

In the Sky

Summer Solstice is June 21, the day of longest daylight.

Early in the month look for the constellation Libra, the Scales, high in the sky just after evening twilight fades.

See the chapter Exploring the Nature of Pima County and Southern Arizona for definitions and descriptions of communities.

In July, pregnant clouds—like these over Bear Canyon in the Santa Catalina Mountains—build into towering thunderheads and bring drenching rains

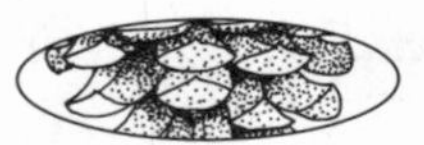

july

A SENSE OF ANTICIPATION *builds during the sultry days of early July. Among the plants, there is a great deal of preparation for something. Prickly pear cactus fruit begins to turn from tourmaline pink to ripe ruby red. Mesquites and acacias droop like weeping willows, their limbs weighted down with drying, ripe bean pods. Acorns drop from Emory oaks. Bear grass is going to seed on golden 3-foot shafts, and agaves sport towering flower stalks. What are they preparing for?*

The Tohono O'odham people who still grow traditional crops begin to prepare their fields and plant their seeds—relatives of wild beans, squash, corn, spinach, and chiles. They know the seasons of the Sonoran Desert, and they know that the winds of July will tell you what the plants and animals already know. The winds whisper with slightly moistened breath, The rains are coming. *To the O'odham, July is* Jukiabig Mashath, *"moon of the rains."*

Within a week or two into July, the late-morning and afternoon skies over the mountains bulge with pregnant clouds 20,000 feet tall with brilliant optic-white tops and brooding gray bellies. The desertscrub, grasslands, and riparian areas, though dry, suddenly break out in song and activity. Newly arrived birds like varied buntings and yellow-billed cuckoos and the summer sparrows are busy preparing for the rain—building nests, attracting mates. We call these "rainbirds," because they come with the rain and stay to breed in the verdant monsoon season.

The towering thunderheads pile up over the mountains, building, building, building, day after day, until one afternoon the trees begin to move, swaying and swaying, as though they are shivering in anticipation. A nearly forgotten smell drifts faintly on the wind, then grows more intense: wet earth. Finally, the towering clouds can no longer support their heavy cargo; they spill off the mountains, loosing black sheets of rain that sail down the slopes and across the desert floor, drenching the soil with blessed moisture and our senses with sweet relief.

Practically overnight the desertscrub and grasslands are transformed. The grasses green up, summer wildflowers germinate, shrubs like brittlebushes, ocotillos, and bursages, which remained leafless throughout the dry season now sprout bright green foliage, and the air is dense with moisture and an achingly sweet smell—the unforgettable smell of a dry spell broken, a hardship relieved.

The quiet, hot nights of summer drought are memory, replaced by coolness and a cacophony of croaks and trills from the many species of toads that begin a frenzy of mating during the short rainy season. Sonoran desert toads, formerly called Colorado River toads, hoot like weak ferry boat whistles, while spadefoot toads (there are three species common to Pima County) sing short-duration trills or bleats, and red-spotted toads sound like crickets in 5-second bursts. These ubiquitous and hardy amphibians, which are active at night, are found from desertscrub up to oak woodlands, by permanent water or ephemeral rain pools, including roadsides. Take extra care while driving rural roads at night or right after a rain.

Look for baby horned lizards, sometimes called "horny toads," although they are not amphibians. Regal horned lizards, the largest of the horned lizards, are found in desertscrub up into grassland foothills, and short-horned lizards are found in the mountains. Often in July we see silver-dollar-sized baby short-horned lizards along the trails of the pine forests. In mid-elevation canyons, the tiny western pipistrelle bat, the smallest in the United States, gives birth to up to two young—just in time to reap the bounty of rain-induced insect blooms. At lower elevations, the largest U.S. bat, the western mastiff, gives birth, as do hoary bats, high in the pine forests.

One of the most conspicuous desert insects to emerge this month with the rains is the palo verde root borer. A giant 4-inch-long oblong, dark-brown beetle, the palo verde root borer has spent the past three or so years of its life as a grub feeding on palo verde tree roots, occasionally killing its host.

In the grasslands, male Cassin's sparrows sing heartily while performing fluttery flights to attract mates, and in areas dense with ocotillos and mesquite trees, Botteri's sparrows also take up song and dance. Nights are busy, as female and juvenile nectar-feeding bats, long-tongued and lesser long-nosed, leave their summer breeding caves in the mountains of southern Arizona and begin their gradual migrations south into Mexico, where they join males for the winter. They follow the blooming of various agave plants throughout the end of the summer season; in July, the maguey and Huachuca agave plants bloom along the mountain foothills.

Around mid-month, rufous hummingbirds arrive along riparian corridors and at feeders near mountain foothills. A little later, their close relatives, Allen's hummingbirds, also arrive. The males of both species are beautiful iridescent copper and are exceptionally aggressive. They are en route to their Mexican wintering grounds. Many Anna's hummingbirds arrive back from California this month (those that left in May), the immatures before the adults, to spend the rest of the winter and early spring. Once again we can hear their delightful, squeaky songs as they mark feeding territories and their machine-gun-rattle chase calls as they chase off intruders.

Like the deserts, the high country is drenched nearly every afternoon with life-giving rain. Creeks flow full, often chocolate-milk-brown from runoff soil. Shrubs such as Fendler rose, Arizona rose, New Mexico locust, and shrubby cinquefoil present showy blossoms. Fruits begin to set from early bloomers—look for New Mexico rasp-

JULY WEATHER

	Sunrise	Sunset	Avg. Relative Humidity/Tucson
July 1	5:21 *MST*	7:34 *MST*	*5 a.m.* 57%
July 30	5:38 *MST*	7:23 *MST*	*5 p.m.* 28%

Stations	Ajo	Tucson	Mt. Lemmon
Station Elevation	(1,800 *ft.*)	(2,584 *ft.*)	(8,800 *ft.*)
July Averages			
Max. temperature	103°F	98.4°F	78.1°F
Min. temperature	77.7°F	73.6°F	48.7°F
Precipitation	1.31 *in.*	2.54 *in.*	4.04 *in.*
Snow	0 *in.*	0 *in.*	0 *in.*
# days 100° & over	24	14	0
# days 32° & under	0	0	0
# days precip.>.01"	5	11	8
July Extremes			
Max. temperature	115°F (1958)	111°F (1958)	89°F (1960)
Min. temperature	58°F (1921)	62°F (1982)	39°F (1960)
Max. snow/month	0 *in.*	0 *in.*	0 *in.*
Max. snow/1 day	0 *in.*	0 *in.*	0 *in.*
Max. precip./month	4.49 *in.* (1923)	6.17 *in.* (1981)	9.23 *in.* (1984)
Max. precip./1 day	3.17 *in.* (1923)	3.98 *in.* (1958)	2.68 *in.* (1959)

July Notes

People call the summer rains "monsoons," which is a misnomer. A "monsoon" is a tropical wind, not the rainstorms that the wind might bring. Only a third of the days in July will be clear; the rest will pile high with storm clouds. Half of those days will see thunderstorms; the other half just a bit of rain. Humidity will be high—over 50 percent at dawn—and the temperatures will climb to the high 90°s in the deserts before plummeting with the rainfall in the afternoon. Be especially aware of lightning and flashflood dangers now through the rest of the storm season.

For information about data sources for these listings, see the Climate section of the chapter Exploring the Nature of Pima County and Southern Arizona.

berries, but also look for black bears, which also look for berries. Rock squirrels are conspicuous, out teaching their new young how to forage for nuts, fruits, flowers, even insects and carrion. Songbird nestlings are fledging in the pine-oak woodlands up into coniferous forests—solitary vireos, Hutton's vireos, yellow-rumped warblers, Grace's warblers, olive warblers, and western tanagers among many others—learning to make a go of it in the short, verdant summer season.

In July, one of the best summer trails in Pima County is the Butterfly Trail, around Mount Bigelow in the Santa Catalina Mountains. Dropping off the north side of the mountain, the trail plunges into a dark, wet world that is the polar extreme of the desert world of Tucson below. Another favorite July activity, however, involves not hiking but sitting. Stormwatching is exciting, but it can be dangerous. The trick is to pick good, safe vantage points, preferably with good food on hand. For unbelievable sweeping views of the Santa Rita Mountains, we go to the dining room at Rio Rico Country Club south of Tucson and for in-the-clouds drama, one of several great cafes at the top of the Catalinas. For the best after-storm prowling around to look for spadefoot and Sonoran Desert toads, we head to one of the picnic areas in Saguaro National Park's Tucson Mountain unit.

FLORA

Spring Bonus

One of the most oft-asked questions directed at people who live in the desert by people who don't is, "Don't you miss the change of seasons?" Of course any resident of more than a year knows we have plenty of seasonal change. It may not be of the blazing-fall-colors-followed-by-six-feet-of-snow variety, but we have something better—we get two springs.

Our first spring, of course, is the protracted February-to-April spring that starts with budding cottonwoods and tapers off with blooming saguaros. After that, everything pretty much shuts down to endure the fore-summer drought and heat. The annuals have bloomed in brief glory and then died, grasses wither and yellow, plants such as ocotillo drop their leaves altogether to avoid desiccation—a survival tactic that has the ironic effect of making the plants *look* desiccated.

But something happens in July and August, with the coming of the summer thunderstorms. The desert starts to get green and fuzzy again. There are two mechanisms behind this renewed growth. Many desert plant species are opportunistic—they can take advantage of any water that comes along. Grasses will green up after even the most unseasonal rains; creosote can bloom several times a year if enough water is available. A bare ocotillo can pop a full set of leaves in as little as 72 hours after a good rain; a month later they will yellow and fall. If rain falls the next day, out comes another set of leaves, a process that may occur several times a year.

But more subtle forces are at work during the second spring. A large number of our "desert" plants are actually descended from tropical species; they originated in a hot but damp climate, and most of the rainfall occurred in summer. As the Sonoran Desert dried, these species became acclimated to less and less water—but they are still geared to a summer rainy season. A prime example are the jatrophas, or limberbushes, which only grow leaves after the summer rains. Coral bean shrubs (which grow to tree size in the tropical forests of Mexico) also remain leafless until August, when they sprout decidedly tropical-looking velvety leaves. Many other desert perennials release their seeds just before the monsoons hit in July. Saguaros and palo verdes grow only after summer rains; they will store water from winter

Flash Floods

Along with the drama and beauty of summer thunderstorms comes latent danger: flash floods. During the summer storm season it is best to avoid hiking in any water drainage, and especially ones with steep banks or walls from which there are no means of escape in high water. Even when there are escape routes, water comes on so fast it is often impossible to get out in time. It is important to remember that the absence of clouds and rain in your location does not rule out the possibility of a flash flood. An isolated storm above a drainage can send a flood flashing through a dry wash miles away—even hours after the storm has passed. And never try to walk or drive across any flooded wash. The water is often twice as deep and twice as fast as it looks; many people are swept to their deaths each summer when they try to ford swollen washes. Relax and enjoy the spectacle instead; one good thing about flash floods is that they generally subside as fast as they began.

showers and utilize it during dry spells, but this moisture does not trigger growth.

Most of the showy spring flowers are descended from northern-temperate species and would quickly bake to death if they sprouted after the summer rains. So their seeds germinate only after a prolonged period of dampness combined with cool weather. In July, after the rains come, a few summer annuals of tropical origin pop up, including summer poppies, devil's claw, and chinchweed.

Our "second spring" offers a lesson in both the adaptability and the mixed origins of the plants that thrive in the desert. (See August Flora for some common late-summer bloomers to watch for and Appendix 1: Southern Arizona Desert Plants Blooming Calendar.)

The Scented Desert

Most desertphiles agree that one of the highlights of the year is the smell of the desert after a rain, especially that first rain of the season. The feeling may be partly psychological—a buoyancy of spirit induced by the dry spell broken—but the smell is very real, a pungent, almost citrus-y perfume that dilates the nostrils and tickles the back of the throat. Everyone describes it differently, but few can actually say exactly what it is.

The source is the humble but ubiquitous creosote bush (Larrea tridentata). *More precisely, the sources are the nearly 50 volatile oils found in the resinous leaves of the creosote, among them camphor, vinyl and methyl ketones, and limonene. The creosote bush is a veritable chemical laboratory; the various oils are used by the plant to produce resins that coat the leaves and reduce loss of moisture as well as make the plant inedible to most herbivores. The intense odor of the oils is particularly strong after the first rain washes the dust from the leaves and new oils are released.*

The Ancient Pines

The dinosaurs have been extinct for 65 million years. Mankind has existed as a recognizable entity for only the past million. But the sequoias and yew trees that grow in the forests of California and Oregon are virtually identical to those whose seedlings might have been trampled by *Tyrannosaurus rex* late in the Cretaceous Period.

The class to which those trees and all our pines, firs, and junipers belong is the Coniferinae, the conifers, an ancient, primitive but still astoundingly successful group of plants that covers the temperate regions of both the Old and New Worlds with evergreen forests, so-called because the trees do not lose their leaves in winter. Conifers are considered primitive mostly because of their means of reproduction. The trees produce cones—small, fleshy male cones that produce pollen and larger, woody female cones that produce ovules (the latter are the ones we picture as "pine cones"). Pollination, which is to say fertilization, depends on wind and gravity to deposit pollen on the female cones, a somewhat inefficient system. By comparison, the flowering plants, a much younger but now larger group, have evolved mutualistic relationships with insects, birds, and mammals to ensure fertilization of their ovules.

Flowering plants are called angiosperms. Conifers, along with two other very primitive and small groups of plants—cycads and gingkos (there remains only one species of the latter)—are called gymnosperms, which means "naked seed," a reference to the lack of an ovary surrounding the ovule, such as angiosperms evolved.

At various times in the Earth's history, during pronounced climate shifts, one could have found conifers in some very odd places, including what is now Antarctica and also in the Sahara Desert. They also covered large areas in what is now Sonoran desertscrub. With our present climate, however, most conifers are restricted to temperate forests—or their equivalents at the tops of mountain ranges, such as our sky islands. Here the weather is cool and damp enough to support evergreen conifers, while frequent winter freezes preclude many broad-leaved species that might otherwise compete with them.

There is a fairly well-defined hierarchy to the order of conifer species one finds on a drive or hike up a mountain. But the borders are blurred and overlapping, and anomalies often occur, such as the junipers occasionally found along streambeds far out on the desert floor. Also, north- and south-facing slopes differ, and shaded ravines can support temperate species hundreds of feet below their normal range.

In Pima County, the normal sequence of conifers starts with alligator juniper (*Juniperus deppeana*), which begins to grow among the oaks and grasses at around 5,000 feet elevation. Next, pines such as border piñon (*Pinus discolor*), Chihuahuan (*P. leiophylla*), and Apache (*P. engelmannii*) appear. Above 6,000 feet one begins to find large, sometimes monospecific stands of ponderosa pine (*P.*

Above, *border piñon*

ponderosa), the most widespread pine in the West.

Finally, at about 7,500 feet firs begin to intersperse through the pines, becoming more prevalent as elevation increases. One of these, the Douglas fir (*Pseudotsuga menziesii*), is not really a fir at all, though its needles closely resemble those of the genus *Abies*. The genuine firs, *Abies concolor*, white fir,

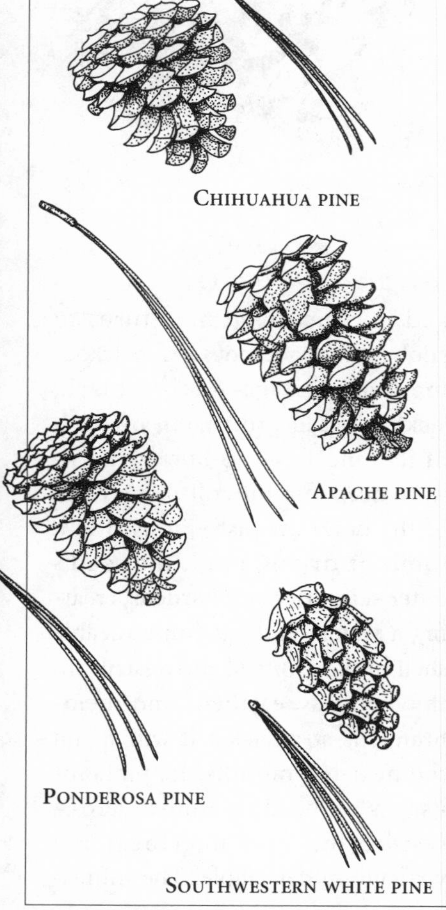

CHIHUAHUA PINE

APACHE PINE

PONDEROSA PINE

SOUTHWESTERN WHITE PINE

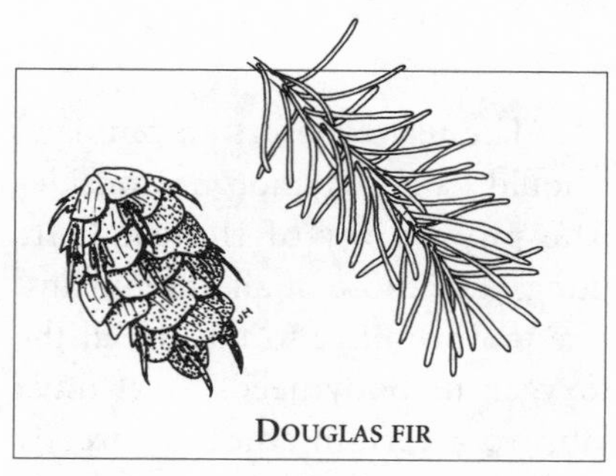

DOUGLAS FIR

and *A. lasiocarpa* var. *arizonica*, corkbark fir, range up to the highest elevations of the Santa Catalina Mountains, just over 9,000 feet.

FAUNA

Tough Toads

That lovely little toad in the road,
Croakin' out a lovely tune.
Skin as smooth as the vinyl on a
bar stool,
Eyes as bright as the moon.
Soft little hands to caress me,
Beverly was her name—
I fell in love with a pretty little toad,
And I'll never be the same. . . .

Scientists have yet to document a romantic relationship between a spadefoot toad and a raven as John Thompson whimsically relates in his song, but the toad's "lovely tune" is a signature of monsoon nights in the desert.

The term "desert amphibian" should be an oxymoron. Consider the physiology of the toad: its lungs, like those of all amphibians, are too primitive to take in all the oxygen its body needs, so it must absorb a certain amount directly through its skin. To do this the skin must be kept moist at all times. In addition, an adult toad cannot drink to replenish its fluid levels—this moisture must also be absorbed through the skin, either when the animal is submerged or lying against a wet rock. Unfortunately, in drier conditions this semi-permeable membrane allows water to evaporate just as readily—a toad loses water this way 30 times faster than a reptile. Another intrinsic amphibian requirement is that the toad must spend the first two stages of its life—egg and tadpole—entirely in the water.

So the desert would seem to be an inimical place for toads. Yet anyone who has driven down a back road at night after a good summer thunderstorm knows how hard it is to avoid squashing them by the dozens, so thickly do they carpet the lowlands. The damp night air is split by a deafening cacophony of croaks, bleats, and trills. At such times, when ephemeral rain pools turn the desert into a squishy marsh, toads seem right at home. But the summer rains last, at best, a couple of months. What happens the rest of the year?

Our desert toads, such as the Couch's spadefoot (*Scaphiopus couchi*), spend those two months of wet weather in a frenzy of feeding, calling, mating, and egg-laying. Then, as the pools begin shrinking

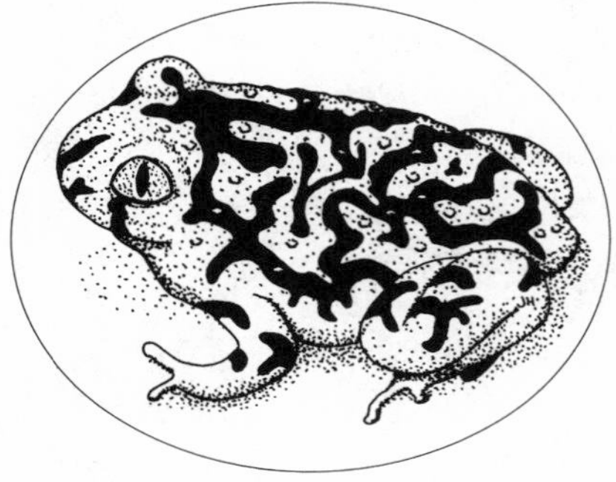

Spadefoot toad

and the uncovered mud turns to adobe, the spadefoot uses its trademark appendage—a tiny, black, sickle-shaped protrusion on each of its hind feet—to burrow backward deep into the still-damp bank of the pond or wash. Encased in a tomb of drying mud, the toad's outer skin dries and hardens, creating a water- and gas-impermeable shell broken only at the nostrils. In this lightless, earthen- and membraneous-straitjacket it will spend the next ten months. Its metabolism is reduced to almost zero—respiration and heartbeat are virtually undetectable. The minuscule amount of air that filters through the earth satisfies its oxygen needs. The toad will even cease eliminating body wastes—its urine is kept dilute enough to serve as reserve body moisture, and nitrogenous wastes are concentrated as urea to be expelled after the toad surfaces. Not until next year's heavy summer rains soak the surrounding ground will the toad awake and free itself, clawing back toward the surface to begin another frenzied cycle of life.

Even before the toad has buried itself, another miracle is happening in the puddle in which it left fertilized eggs. Those eggs face their own deadline, for the sun is relentlessly boiling off water only inches deep to start with. So the cycle of growth for the spadefoot toad has evolved to a blinding speed.

Within 24 hours—sometimes as few as 12—the eggs have hatched into tiny tadpoles, which begin feeding furiously on the algae that has grown in the pool at an even faster rate than they. Soon little hind legs form next to the tail, then front legs pop out behind the broadening head. Only eleven days after the eggs were laid, fully formed spadefoot toads emerge from the water, often just in time to put on fat reserves for a few weeks; then, as the summer rainy season ends, they respond to the same survival instincts as their parents and entomb themselves to wait for next year's thunderstorms.

. . . She's down there now,
she's sleepin,'
And for now, I've lost my friend.
But when a year rolls around
And the rains come down,
I know—she'll rise again . . .

—from John S. Thompson's
"The Lonely Raven"

When Opportunity Knocks—Nest

Diversity breeds diversity.

Southern Arizona's bi-seasonal rainfall pattern supports a second period of plant growth and blooming during July and August. This leads quickly to a new crop of seeds and a surge in insect populations, an especially noticeable phenomenon in the grasslands. As a result, many species of birds have forsaken the spring nesting season to rear their broods during summer. By doing so, they reduce competition for the spring nesting territories and foods.

Botteri's and Cassin's sparrows are notable grassland breeders. Both species build cup nests very low to the ground in shrubs or short trees. Both are able to survive without free-standing water for long periods—an important adaptation when the ephemeral rain pools dry up.

At lower elevations, in the desertscrub, black-throated sparrows utilize the same late nesting strategy, taking advantage of the jump in productivity there. And in riparian areas, varied buntings and yellow-billed cuckoos lend an exotic touch to streamside vegetation.

Small birds aren't the only ones to exploit the summer rains. Swainson's hawks feed on the burgeoning insect population and also on the many small mammals feeding on the new growth and new insects—and also on the reptiles feeding on the small mammals.

This frenzy of feeding and breeding in July and August has proven to be a successful strategy for many species. It may be 100° in the shade, but for these animals, it's a beautiful spring day.

PLACES TO VISIT IN JULY

Butterfly Trail

Five thousand feet below us on the desert floor Tucson simmers under a 105° early July afternoon. As we finally top out at Mount Bigelow—completing a 5-mile hike that took us down 2,000 feet into another world—big, sloppy-wet snowflakes catch on our eyelashes and blur our vision. Our fingers are numb and our noses running from the cold wind that is driving the storm across this 8,500-foot peak in the Santa Catalina Mountains.

The Butterfly Trail, one of the most beautiful trails in the Catalinas, is barely etched out of the steep slopes on the north side of the range, dropping dramatically into fern-choked canyons that rarely see direct sun. Unlike the south slopes' wide, dry, and rocky trails, the Butterfly is narrow and black with rich, wet soil and carpeted on either side by lush flowers and shade-loving shrubs thriving under the dense ponderosa pine canopy.

Walking slowly to take in the lush scenery and to go easy on our knees, we watched titmice gleen insects among the Gambel oaks while broad-tailed hummingbirds gathered nectar and insects from Fendler's rose and other blooming shrubs. Overhead, an olive warbler called softly its sad, slurred *Phew, phew*. At Novio Spring, as it gushes forth from a rocky outcropping and plunges beneath the trail toward the San Pedro River far below, we set off upstream to find a plane wreck rumored nearby. Among the ferns and flowers its remains lie, exploded into hundreds of pieces: on June 8, 1957, two F-86 Saberjets from Davis-Monthan Air Force Base collided above Mount Bigelow. Both pilots ejected safely while the planes plummeted into the forest. The other was cleared away, but the twisted remains of this small warplane—too remote to remove—now house small mammals, insects, and wildflowers in this magical place.

Storm-Watching

Enjoying summer thunderstorms is one of the pay-offs for enduring the seemingly endless dry heat of May and June. But safety is an important factor: in the Southwest, more people die from lightning strikes than from any other weather-related phenomenon such as tornadoes, hurricanes, or floods. Statistics show that most strike-deaths occur in open spaces—golf courses, parks, and the desert—so wisdom dictates that to enjoy storms safely, find a good indoor spot. (See lightning safety section, below.)

Thirty miles south of Tucson, in the resort-community of Rio Rico, the Rio Rico Country Club's dining room offers something almost no other place can: superb food and service with sweeping views across the Santa Cruz River valley to the Santa Rita Mountains, where spectacular thunderstorms

Lightning Safety

Most visitors to the Sonoran Desert experience trepidation about rattlesnakes, but the most powerful killer doesn't slither on the ground—it's everywhere. Lightning kills more people in the Southwest than any other weather-related event, including tornadoes, hurricanes, and floods. To stay safe, here are some good rules:

- *Don't engage in any outdoor activity during thunderstorm season if there are clouds in the sky. Very early morning is usually storm-free; afternoons nearly always have storms.*
- *If you do get caught out in an impending storm, run for shelter. Never shelter in a structure or tent in an open area; if you are near a stand of trees, take shelter beneath trees of equal height (you never want to be one of the tallest objects in an area or near solitary tall objects like trees, saguaros, telephone poles) and stay away from the trunks and roots, which conduct electricity.*

• If you are caught out in an open area with no safe shelter, squat with your knees tucked. Do not lie on the ground (this position increases your body's ability to conduct electricity).

• If you are in a vehicle, stay in it and park it away from any tall, solitary objects.

• If you are indoors during a lightning storm, stay away from doors and windows (a closed window does not stop lightning); unplug electronics and don't use the phone; and stay away from plumbing fixtures than can carry current into the building.

One final tip: lightning danger is not limited to the summer rainy season. Two workmen in Phoenix were injured one January when lightning struck the 60-foot fir tree from which they were removing Christmas ornaments.

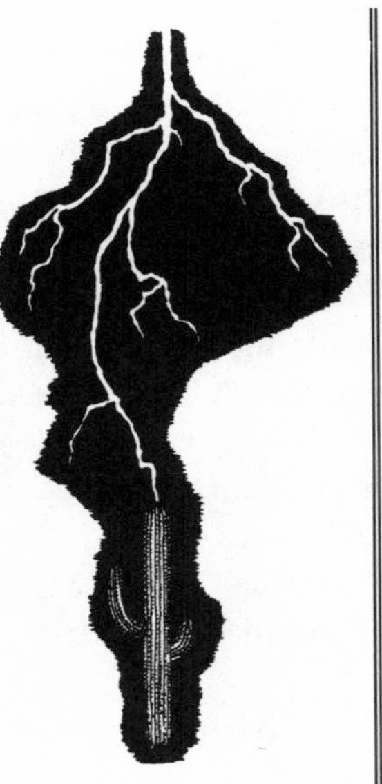

pile up nearly every afternoon. Order a bottle of wine, lunch, and sit back and enjoy the show in pampered luxury.

Another option is to head up the Santa Catalinas in late morning or early afternoon, depending on the build-up of clouds. Head all the way to the top, to the cabin community of Summerhaven, where a number of fine cafes offer lunch. Our favorite is the Mount Lemmon Cafe and its heavenly homemade pies. Although sweeping views are not part of the offerings, good food and dramatic thunder-and-lightning are sure to be had. Also try the Iron Door restaurant on the Ski Valley turnoff. A few tables have views through the trees off the southwest side of the mountain, and they have good chili and hot apple cider.

JULY SKIES

"Moon of the Rains"

TRADITIONAL O'ODHAM NAME FOR JULY

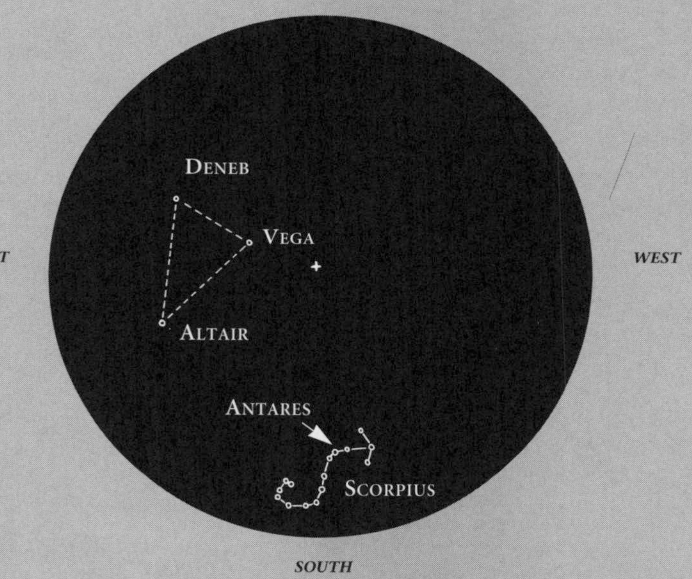

Star Chart for 32°N
Mid-month, 9 pm

Feature Constellation

When the Greek hero Orion, the Hunter, boasted that he could kill any creature on Earth, the gods sent Scorpius, the giant scorpion, to test his mettle. The contest was a draw, and the gods put them in opposite sides of the sky for all eternity, so that when one rises, the other sets, never to resume their battle. The best time to see Scorpius is in early July when it is low on the southern horizon; as a constellation it symbolized darkness to many ancient people, a sign of the waning power of the sun after the coming autumnal equinox.

JULY AT A GLANCE

Desertscrub

❧ Prickly pear cactus (*Opuntia* spp.) fruit begins to ripen.

❧ Mesquites (*Prosopis* spp.) and acacias (*Acacia* spp.) droop with drying, ripe bean pods.

❧ Within about five days of the first rains, look for blossoms on pincushion cactuses (*Mammilaria grahamii* var. *microcarpa*).

❧ Male Sonoran desert toads, red-spotted toads, and spadefoot toads (Couch's and southern) fill the nights with their songs to attract mates, from desertscrub up to oak woodlands.

❧ Regal horned lizards hatch in desertscrub up into grassland foothills.

❧ Western mastiff bats have their young.

❧ Huge palo verde root-borer beetles emerge from underground to mate and return to burrows beneath palo verde trees to lay new eggs.

❧ From the desertscrub up into the coniferous forests, look for renewed butterfly activity after the rains (see Appendix 5 for flight periods of common butterflies of our region). Bright cloudless sulphurs are very conspicuous as they move north with the summer rains.

Desert Grasslands

❧ One of the specialty flowers of the summer blooms for just a few days, right after the first good rains—the zephyr lily (*Zephranthes longifolia*), whose scientific name means "flower of the west wind."

❧ Several agaves (*Agave palmeri, A. parryi* var. *huachucensis*) bloom in conjunction with nectar-feeding bat migration.

❧ Nights are busy, as female and juvenile long-tongued and lesser long-nosed nectar-feeding bats begin their gradual migrations south into Mexico, following the blooming of various agave plants.

❧ Cassin's and Botteri's sparrows begin to breed after the rains arrive.

❧ This month and next in desertscrub and grasslands, ant colonies release thousands of winged queens and males, which will mate in huge, swirling airborne swarms. The most common and spectacular are Sonoran leaf-cutting ants (*Acromyrmex versicolor*) and large-headed seed-harvesting ants in the genus *Pogonomyrmex*. Fertile queens drop their wings, then establish new colonies in moist soil; the males die.

Oak Woodlands

❧ Acorns drop from Emory oaks (*Quercus emoryi*), and bear grass (*Nolina microcarpa*) is going to seed on golden, 3-foot stalks.

❧ Mimosa shrubs (*Mimosa* spp.) bear their seed pods.

❧ Western pipistrelle bats give birth to up to two young in mid-elevation canyons this month.

❧ Rufous, Allen's, and Anna's hummingbirds may be seen in riparian areas this month. Only Anna's will stay the winter, mostly near feeders; rufous and Allen's continue south into Mexico.

Pine-Oak Woodlands

❧ Shrubs like Fendler rose and Arizona rose (*Rosa fendleri* and *R. arizonica*), New Mexico locust (*Robinia neomexicana*), and shrubby cinquefoil (*Potentilla fruticosa*) present showy blossoms.

❧ Fruits begin to set from early bloomers—look for New Mexico raspberries, but also look for black bears, which also look for berries.

❧ Rock squirrels and their young are conspicuous.

❧ Watch for baby short-horned lizards.

Coniferous Forests

❧ Hoary bats have their young this month.

❧ Songbird nestlings are fledging in the pine-oak woodlands up into coniferous forests—solitary vireos, Hutton's vireos, yellow-rumped warblers, Grace's warbler, olive warblers, and western tanagers among many others.

Special Events

❧ Summer-monsoon season begins (July through mid-September).

❧ The Southeast Arizona Butterfly Association may be organizing summer butterfly counts this month. See Appendix 6 for contact information.

In the Sky

❧ The constellation Scorpius is low in the southeast, with the red star Antares in its center.

❧ In the east, look for three bright stars that make up the Summer Triangle.

See the chapter Exploring the Nature of Pima County and Southern Arizona for definitions and descriptions of communities.

A butterfly hunts for nectar in a clump of snakeweed

august

BRIGHT BUTTERFLIES BY *the thousands dance around the desertscrub and mountains, sipping nectar and gathering in shimmering puddle parties on damp patches of earth. White-winged doves join in large flocks and move slowly south with the sun. The first of the migrating birds trickle in to stay the winter or stop for a rest; ephemeral rain ponds echo with the unlikely calls of shorebirds resting briefly on their long flights south for the winter. Large flocks of brilliant white-throated swifts pass through briefly, gracefully. Everywhere plants are at their most lush. And so with a flurry of wingbeats and a splash of green, August settles, moist and hot, on the landscape of southern Arizona.*

Nearly every afternoon the summer monsoons continue to pour life from the sky onto the mountains, grasslands, and desertscrub, while temperatures remain high along with the humidity, although the heat is mitigated by the welcome rains. Summer flowers paint bright colors across all the communities, and grasses quickly green up and set to making seeds. The O'odham have planted their late-summer crops and tend them after the rains; to them, August is "moon of the short crops"—Shopol Eshabig Mashath.

In the rocky mountains of the low western deserts female bighorn sheep come into heat and the males respond with contests of dominance, clashing their thick horns together with violent reports. Across the desertscrub, Gila monsters, the most primitive, beautiful, and largest of our lizards, make rare shows, lumbering around as they finish up their summer breeding season. Deposited deep in burrows, their eggs remain unattended until they hatch next spring. Another conspicuous desert cruiser this month is the male tarantula spider, out looking for females who wait for prospective mates next to their burrows. The Gila woodpeckers drilling new holes in saguaro cactuses aren't getting ready to nest late in the season—they cut new holes in late summer so that by spring they will be hardened over and dry, ready for a fresh brood. Hackberry shrubs begin to put out their berries, a treat for many birds, including phainopeplas, mockingbirds, black-headed grosbeaks, and thrashers. Our summer owls of the desert, the elf owls, leave for their Mexican winter homes this month.

Along riparian areas and low mountain canyons a few new hummingbirds may stop by on their way south for the winter. Watch for the tiny Calliope or the large violet-crowned. Black-chinned, broad-billed, and Anna's hummingbirds continue to be around in large numbers, most of them going through late-summer molt; with feathers missing or sticking out at odd angles, they look like they pulled one-too-many late-nighters, and the sound of their flight is oddly muffled or blurred. Creeks that have been dry for the past three months should come up and run through at least September if the rains have been sufficient. Look along rivers and on ponds for the gregarious belted kingfishers arriving for the winter this month; an osprey might surprise you as well, as it migrates south. Mississippi kites that summered along the San Pedro River pack up and leave this month. Nights continue to be loud, full of songs of poorwills, owls, and toads.

In the grasslands Swainson's hawks might still be seen hunting for reptiles and small mammals, but red-tailed hawks are more numerous now as well. Botteri's and Cassin's sparrows are joined by lark buntings, and migrating western kingbirds seem the most common birds around as they perch on tree snags and snatch butterflies cruising by. Large flocks of white-winged doves whistle by on their way to their wintering grounds in Mexico. At night, toads and nighthawks trill, and banner-tailed kangaroo rats dart around feeding on the seeding grasses.

In the oak woodlands, the walnut trees are beginning to bear fruit, while many of the shrubs bloom and fruit, including wild cotton, lemonadeberry, birchleaf buckthorn, and seep willow. Canyon grapes are ripening; many birds gorge on them, some in preparation for upcoming migrations. Up into the pine-oak woodlands and coniferous forests, some of the early bird migrants will be taking advantage of summer's insect bounty as they move south. Olive-sided flycatchers and warblers such as hermit, orange-crowned, Nashville, Townsend's, MacGillivray's, and Wilson's may stop briefly. Williamson's sapsuckers may begin to arrive this month, but they will stay for the winter.

In August two nature "safaris" rank high for us: one for butterflies, and one for hummingbirds. For butterflies we plan a trip to the Nature Conservancy's Canelo Hills Ciénega Preserve just east of Pima County in the foothills of the Huachuca Mountains, in oak woodland with a rare wetlands. The famous monarch butterflies may be found there, as well as cloudless sulphurs, sleepy oranges, pipevine swallowtails, and variegated fritillaries, among many others. For hummingbirds, we plan a weekend around many possibilities, from the Chiricahua Mountains in the east to the Baboquivari Mountains in the west. But although birds and butterflies get a lot of our attention this month, we won't forget that down in the desertscrub prickly pear cactus fruit are at the peak of ripeness—time for a harvesting trip and a weekend of syrup-, sauce-, and jelly-making.

AUGUST WEATHER

	Sunrise	Sunset	Avg. Relative Humidity/Tucson
August 1	*5:39 MST*	*7:21 MST*	*5 a.m. 65%*
August 30	*5:58 MST*	*6:51 MST*	*5 p.m. 33%*

Stations	Ajo	Tucson	Mt. Lemmon
Station Elevation	(1,800 ft.)	(2,584 ft.)	(8,800 ft.)
August Averages			
Max. temperature	*100.8°F*	*96.2°F*	*75.3°F*
Min. temperature	*75.8°F*	*72°F*	*49.6°F*
Precipitation	*2.04 in.*	*2.03 in.*	*6.62 in.*
Snow	*0 in.*	*0 in.*	*0 in.*
# days 100° & over	*19*	*7*	*0*
# days 32° & under	*0*	*0*	*0*
# days precip.>.01"	*7*	*9*	*10*
August Extremes			
Max. temperature	*115°F (1915)*	*108°F (1950)*	*82°F (1960)*
Min. temperature	*57°F (1916)*	*61°F (1956)*	*42°F (1982)*
Max. snow/month	*0 in.*	*0 in.*	*0 in.*
Max. snow/1 day	*0 in.*	*0 in.*	*0 in.*
Max. precip./month	*5.3 in. (1947)*	*7.93 in. (1955)*	*10.54 in. (1959)*
Max. precip./1 day	*3.80 in. (1951)*	*2.48 in. (1961)*	*3.15 in. (1982)*

August Notes

August is a month of spectacular weather. Fast-moving and sometimes violent thunderstorms can drop large amounts of rain in short order, accompanied by fierce winds, lightning, and copious thunder. The strong winds are usually the most damaging feature of this month's cavalcade of storms. The soil is saturated, relative humidity is high, and most of the canyon creeks are running throughout southern Arizona. Even a short storm can send a deadly flash flood racing down streambeds, so caution is advisable this month (for lightning as well—see July for more information about lightning and flood safety).

For information about data sources for these listings, see the Climate section of the chapter Exploring the Nature of Pima County and Southern Arizona.

FLORA

Summer Bloomers

August finds us surrounded by a second explosion of flowers—bright yellows and golds, oranges and reds, creamy whites and pinks.

Along desert or grassland roadsides look for telegraph plants (*Heterotheca subaxillaris*) with small yellow blooms on Y-branching tops, big sunflowers (*Helianthus annuus*), glowing orange summer poppies (*Kallstroemia grandiflora*) low to the ground, sacred datura's (*Datura meteloides*) large white cups, and soft purple stars of ground cherries (*Solanum elaeagnifolium*). Barrel cactuses (*Ferocactus* spp.) may also be blooming, soft orange-red or yellow.

Late summer is also vine time. The yellow trumpet flowers of coyote melon (*Cucurbita digitata*) and buffalogourd (*Cucurbita foetidissima*) are less conspicuous than the baseball-sized gourds that ripen later in desertscrub and grasslands. The specific name *digitata* refers to the five-fingered leaves of the coyote melon, which distinguish it from the simple-leaved buffalo gourd. Two morning glories are evident: blue-flowered *Evolvulus arizonicus* and the tiny red trumpets of *Ipomoea cristulata*, scarlet creeper.

From the grasslands up into the pine-oak forests, look for trailing four o-clock (*Allionia incarnata*), flame-flowers (*Talinum* spp.), dakota verbena (*Glandularia bipinnatifida*), longpod senna (*Senna hirsuta* var. *glaberrima*), papalotilla (*Guardiolia platyphylla*), bouvardia (*Bouvardia ternifolia*), long-flowered four-o'clock (*Mirabilis longiflora*), and western spiderwort (*Tradescantia occidentalis*). And up into the coniferous forests, lush columbines (*Aquilegia* spp.), penstemons (*Penstemon* spp.), larkspurs (*Delphinium* spp.), cutleaf coneflowers (*Rudbeckia laciniata*), geraniums (*Geranium* spp.), primroses (*Primula* spp.), groundsels (*Senecio* spp.), goldenrods (*Solidago* spp.), silenes (*Silene* spp.), mountain thistles (*Cirsium* spp.), and indian paintbrushes (*Castilleja* spp.) really put on a show.

Butterfly Bonuses

Summer flowers mean an extra bonus: summer butterflies. Once you are even a little bit butterfly-aware, you'll be amazed at how many of these wonderful insects there are brightening the subtropical world of the summer monsoon season, as well as all year in southern Arizona.

The swallowtail family—one of the most conspicuous—is among the first you notice. Large and flashy, they trounce around on bird-like wings, visiting a variety of summer flowers, including thistles (*Cirsium pulchellum*, among others), morningglories (*Ipomoea* spp.), and milkweeds (*Asclepias* spp.). Pipevine swallowtails (*Battus philenor*) are medium-sized and blue-black; the big yellow ones with twin "tails" are two-tailed swallowtails (*Papilio multicaudatus*); and the very large, mostly black with yellow markings and a yellow abdomen are giant swallowtails (*Papilio cresphontes*). These swallowtails prefer habitats from higher desertscrub up to the coniferous forests.

Another conspicuous summer-flier family is the sulphurs, the most common in our area being the cloudless sulphur (*Phoebis sennae*), a brilliant neon yellow, large butterfly that migrates north from Mexico with the summer monsoons and prefers desertscrub habitat. Three other butterflies in the sulphur family that are common this month and into the fall are sleepy oranges (*Eurema nicippe*) and Mexican sulphurs (*E. mexicana*), which like to feed on the blossoms of the turpentine bush (*Ericameria laricifolia*), and southern dogfaces, all found from desertscrub up into the coniferous forests. The latter are bright yellow with black markings that, like an inkblot psychological test, resemble the face of a perky poodle in profile if stared at from just the right angle. Once you see the face, you won't miss it. Dogfaces, like so many of this season's butterflies, favor the blossoms of desert broom (*Baccharis sarothroides*).

Buckeyes (*Junonia coenia*), Texas crescentspots (*Anthanassa texana*), American painted ladies (*Vanessa virginiensis*), variegated fritillaries (*Euptoieta claudia*), and Lacinia checkerspots (*Chlosyne lacinia*) are all nectar-loving fliers of the brush-footed butterfly family, which take advantage of the summer flowers such as verbena, lantana, senecio, and desert broom, in nearly all Pima County's habitats. Two other brush-foots out and about in quantity this month and into the fall are the hackberry butterflies—the Leilia hackberry butterfly (*Asterocampa leilia*) and the mountain hackberry butterfly (*A. celtis*). Both depend on plants of the genus *Celtis* for food (sap) and for depositing eggs; the Leilia favors desertscrub and the desert hackberry along dry washes (*C. pallida*) and the mountain form is found along mid- to high-elevation riparian canyons where netleaf hackberry trees grow (*C. reticu-*

lata). Most brush-footed butterflies are small- to medium-sized with brownish or orange backgrounds and fairly strong patterns.

We could go on listing butterflies but must end with one of the most famous. Monarch butterflies (*Danaus plexippus*), of the milkweed butterfly family, are the great North American migrators, traveling from Mexico to California in huge numbers in late summer. Southern Arizona boasts a population of monarchs that breeds around the rich ciénegas of Canelo Hills, just east of Pima County on the western slopes of the Huachuca Mountains. August is one of the best times to see this large, classically patterned orange-and-black butterfly with a loop-dee-loop flight and a nose for milkweeds (*Asclepias* spp.), on which it lays its eggs. (See Appendix 5, Common Southern Arizona Butterflies, for more information about our area's butterflies, their habitats, nectar plants, and flight seasons.)

FAUNA

The Lizard That Ate Tucson

Many B-movies of the fifties featured dressed up lizards with glued-on spines and frills that were enlarged to look like prehistoric monsters. But when Hollywood made *The Giant Gila Monster* in 1959, no such artifice was needed. An unadorned, 100-foot-long Gila monster was terrifying enough.

Even a life-sized Gila monster, all 15 or so inches of it, has a startlingly primitive appearance. Its beaded skin gives the impression of flexible armor—which indeed it is. The thick body, massive head, and lumbering gait add to the antediluvian impression, as does the knowledge that the Gila monster is one of only two venomous lizards in the world (the other is the closely related, but larger, Mexican beaded lizard found farther south).

Gila monster

The real life of *Heloderma suspectum*, though, belies its ferocious image. That slow gait restricts it to a diet of small, helpless mammals, baby birds, or eggs. And the venom, while fairly potent, is delivered inefficiently along grooved teeth in the lower jaw instead of being injected through hollow fangs as in rattlesnakes. David E. Brown and Neil Carmony, in their whimsical but authoritative book *Gila Monster: Facts and Folklore of America's Aztec Lizard*, concluded from extensive review that not a single human death has ever been attributed to a Gila monster bite. In fact, biologists are not really sure why the Gila monster *has* venom. It is not needed for subduing the lizard's usual prey, and when biting defensively, the Gila monster must hang on ferociously and chew to deliver any venom at all—not a wise tactic for a defensive bite. Virtually all bites on humans have occurred due to careless handling, and with a few exceptions result in nothing more than intense pain and swelling for a few days.

The range of the Gila monster extends throughout western Mexico, but in the United States about 90 percent of its range is in Arizona. Small populations are also found in California, Nevada, Utah, and New Mexico. Even in the heart of the Sonoran Desert, however, they are very rarely seen, even by scientists who study them. The infrequent sightings may be due to their sparse—and probably declining—population, but a good measure results from their activity patterns. Radio tracking has revealed that Gila monsters spend about 99 percent of their lives underground, either resting, hibernating, or hunting for the dens of small mammals from which to steal young. Further proof of this secretive nature is revealed by the fact that no one has ever reported finding a Gila monster nest in the wild or observed wild eggs hatching.

From captive observations and extrapolations from wild sightings, it is known that Gila monsters mate in the spring, shortly after emerging from hibernation. Using anal glands, males leave scent markings on rocks to mark their territories; they fight with each other for dominance. After mating, the pair splits, and the female lays three to seven (sometimes two to twelve) eggs in July or August. Although under captive conditions hatchlings emerge in November or December, in the wild they do not appear until the following spring. Whether hatching is delayed in the wild or the young stay in the hidden nest until warm weather arrives is not known. When the young do appear, they are virtual carbon copies of the adults—right down to miniature venom glands and tiny grooved teeth. Their subsequent life span in the wild is unknown, but captives have lived for 30 years.

Gila monsters have few, if any,

natural predators, but they face great danger from two types of human. The first is the ignorant, scared, or just plain cruel individual who will kill them on sight—a pathetically easy task. The second, and probably more dangerous, is the illegal collector. Gila monsters have been protected in Arizona since 1952 (the first venomous reptile ever granted official protection in the United States). But poachers still seek them for unscrupulous collectors who don't care about their status in the wild—in fact, the value goes up as populations decrease. Foreign collectors have paid well over $1,000 for a single specimen. Suffice to say that it is illegal anywhere in the United States or Mexico to capture, keep, or sell Gila monsters. If you are lucky enough to spot an individual in the wild, you should watch from a distance and count yourself among the very lucky to have seen such an elusive and beautiful desert animal.

LAND OF THE AMAZONS

The sex of some lizards is almost impossible to determine externally; for most others you need to capture the individual and examine it closely. But if you're hiking with friends and chance to spot a Sonoran spotted whiptail lizard, or any of several other whiptail species in the genus Cnemidophorous, *you can authoritatively state that it is a female. No clue or examination is needed because the individuals of these species are all female.*

Most higher plants and animals reproduce sexually. The male and female each produce gametes (sperm and egg, for example), each of which contains half the chromosomes present in the adult. When the gametes join, the offspring gets a full set of chromosomes—and a combination of features of the parents. The variation produced helps facilitate natural selection.

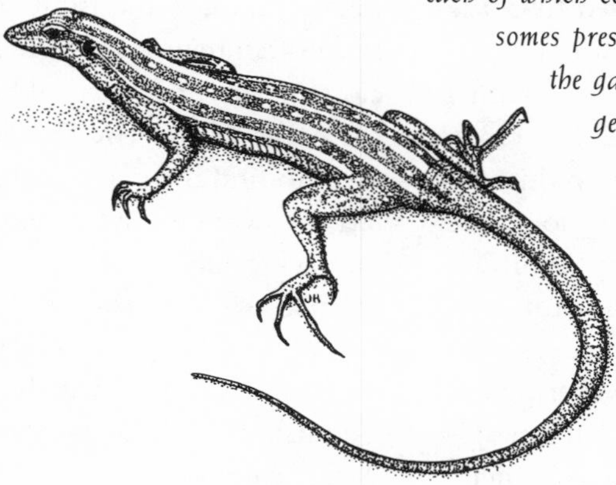

*But sexual reproduction can be chancy and time-consuming. The Sonoran spotted whiptail (*C. sonorae*) has circumvented these disadvantages through a process called parthenogenesis. The eggs produced in her ovaries develop with a full set of chromosomes, so no male is needed to fertilize them. The offspring are all female and genetically identical to their mother—essentially clones of her.*

Parthenogenesis is advantageous in certain situations—for example, when a new habitat must be colonized quickly, ahead of competition. One theory regarding the origins of parthenogenetic whiptails is that they proliferated within the past 200 years, after cattle were introduced to the Southwest and drastically altered the landscape. The resulting habitat suited whiptails, and unisexual reproduction allowed them to rapidly expand their range. A single female could move into an area and immediately begin producing offspring without having to find a male first.

There is, however, a disadvantage to this strategy. Because variation in these whiptails is virtually nonexistent, changes in their environment would find them unable to evolve to survive in the new conditions, and theoretically they could become extinct.

Or the Spider That Devoured Benson

The tarantula, another Sonoran Desert B-movie star, has appeared in more evil roles than one could count. Yet, if anything, its reputation is more undeserved than the Gila monster's. Like all spiders, tarantulas have chelicerae (fangs) and can bite—but they very rarely do; if one is goaded into biting, the result could be mistaken for a bee sting. The only danger tarantulas pose is to various grasshoppers, beetles, and other insects that make up their prey. Nevertheless, to someone afraid of garden spiders the sight of a 4-inch-diameter tarantula must be terrifying. If you can get over the arachniphobia, you'll notice they look more like eight-legged mice than spiders (of course if you're afraid of mice this imagery is no help).

Tarantulas are most often seen in late summer, and those seen are most often males. The females stay close to the small, vertical burrows they dig, while the males sally forth to find them and mate, regularly showing up in our headlights on back roads in August and September. After mating, the female lays up to 300 eggs at once in the burrow. Males can usually be distinguished from females by their darker coloration.

Tarantulas periodically shed their skin. They do this in the entirety, like snakes—the old skin is left in a complete, dried-out tarantula shape, with an obvious "hatch" near the front where the spider extracted itself.

Although there are over two dozen species of tarantula in Arizona, they are very similar; the most commonly seen near Tucson is *Aphonopelma chalcodes.* Other species extend across the Southwest and into Mexico and Central and South America. All of them are notably long-lived—sexual maturity isn't reached for eight or nine years, and although the male dies only a year later, females can live for another fifteen.

Many myths persist regarding tarantulas, chiefly their supposed jumping abilities. Although they can dart very quickly for short distances when alarmed, they can't jump. Their bodies are far too heavy for their legs; in fact they are rather fragile and can be easily killed if dropped.

Tarantulas do have an interesting means of defense, however. On their abdomens are loose, barbed hairs which they can kick off into the face of attackers, including coyotes, skunks, and coatimundis. The hairs are extremely irritating if they become lodged in the nasal passages. They also sometimes come off on the hands of humans who are handling the spiders and can prickle sensitive skin.

Above, *the tarantula has an undeserved evil reputation*

Desert Compasses

They say you can tell direction in a forest by looking for the moss that grows on the north sides of trees. There's some truth in this bit of folklore, as there is in the desert equivalent: barrel cactuses tend to lean south. But there's another desert orienteering tip that may be more accurate than either: resting jackrabbits point north.

Obviously the jackrabbit's enormous ears give it acute hearing. But in hot weather they serve an even more important function as very efficient radiators. The surface of each ear is highly

vascularized—that is, covered with blood vessels. These vessels bring blood from the animal's body core right to the surface, where it is cooled by radiation to the air, thus significantly lowering the entire body temperature.

Furthermore, jackrabbits have learned to optimize this function by resting in depressions on the north side of shrubs or trees and orienting their ears at a spot about 30° above the northern horizon. This spot has the lowest radiant temperature in the sky, so the heat loss is maximized.

PLACES TO VISIT IN AUGUST

Sticky Harvest, Sweet Rewards

Across the hillsides of the desertscrub this month, fruits of the prickly pear cactus are ruby-red and ripe. Javelinas, coyotes, foxes, squirrels, and ants are among the many animals to partake of their sweet juiciness. We join them most every summer, heading out in early morning, usually late in the month, armed with plenty of plastic shopping bags and metal tongs, and dressed in old clothes. (Hint: make sure they're long-sleeved and thorn-resistant, too.) Roadsides are the best bet for collecting; for one, it's convenient, but also, it's illegal to collect in any national park or monument, or on private property without permission.

Fill about six bags if you can (don't pick all the fruits from one cactus; save some for animals) to yield maybe a half-gallon or gallon of juice. Use tongs to handle the fruits, which are covered with tiny soft stickers called glochids; pick the soft, deep red ones. When you get back home, the real fun begins. De-sticker by holding each fruit under running water (with tongs) and scrubbing well with a stiff brush. Slice, remove seeds, and place into a large kettle with no more than an inch of water; then steam until tender (keep water replenished as necessary). Mash fruits with a potato masher, then pour the juice out through several layers of cheesecloth, repeating if necessary. You will need to do several batches.

With the prepared juice, which has a flavor reminiscent of strawberries, you can produce all sorts of delicacies: jelly (follow a standard recipe and add 1/2 c. lemon juice to each 3 c. of prickly pear

Above, *prickly pear pads and fruit*

juice), fruit ice (again, follow a standard recipe and add a little lemon or lime juice), prickly pear-lemonade, prickly-pear margaritas, syrup—just use your imagination!

Bug Season Health Tips

Bugged by bugs? Mosquitos, chiggers, biting gnats and other winged critters are out in force following summer rains, feasting on any available warm-blooded creatures. But beware of bug repellents: the most powerful ones, those containing 40 percent or more of the chemical DEET (N,N-diethyl-meta-toluamide), can cause serious health problems if used too frequently or applied too heavily, especially on children. DEET is absorbed into the bloodstream and can lead to neurological problems. In one extreme case, DEET was applied every day to six girls at a camp for weeks; three of the girls developed toxic encephalopathy, or swelling of the brain, which resulted in seizures, disorientation, and death. Other symptoms reported with prolonged use of DEET are confusion, irritability, and insomnia.

Some options are to (1) use DEET-based products with nonabsorbent agents such as Skedaddle and DEET-Plus; (2) use non-DEET repellents such as Green Ban, Natrapel, Bygone Bugs, and Buzz Away; (3) apply repellents to clothing such as bandanas, collars or cuffs (natural fabrics only; synthetics are damaged by chemicals such as DEET); or (4) wear long-sleeved shirts, long pants, and a hat.

Kingdom of the Monarch

Rich green swales of water-loving plants roll before us. Bright flowers dot the green, and all around butterflies bounce color from plant to sky to plant. In late summer, the Nature Conservancy's Canelo Hills Ciénega Preserve, 65 miles southeast of Tucson on the western slopes of the Huachuca Mountains, is a perfect destination for butterfly lovers.

A short path, about a mile or so, winds through the natural ciénega, or spring—a truly endangered habitat in Arizona. Canelo Hills' ciénega is perhaps the best preserved. The spring feeds O'Donnell Creek, which supports small populations of endangered native fishes and the rare Canelo Hills ladies' tresses orchid. Late-summer blooms, especially the milkweeds, attract butterflies by the bushel. Look for famous monarchs, cloudless sulphurs, dogface, painted ladies, several species of swallowtails, among many others.

History buffs will enjoy the beautiful restored adobe ranch house on the property, one of the oldest still standing in the state.

See Appendix 6 for contact information (phone before visiting, and we recommend becoming a Nature Conservancy member if you visit their preserves often, since they do not charge entrance fees).

Abuzz with Hummingbirds

August is one of the best hummingbird-watching months, and southern Arizona happens to be one of the best hummingbird-watching regions because it lies on one of their major flyways from northern breeding grounds to southern wintering grounds. Established feeders are usually the best places to see hummingbirds because they may return year after year during migration. If you prefer to see them sipping wild flower nectar, it's a little tougher but if you know where to start, it's very rewarding. Below are some of the common species and good places to see them (because they are so crowded with people, we've not included Ramsey or Madera canyons):

Broad-billed: A common riparian woodland species, especially closer to the Mexican border. Try Sycamore Canyon west of Nogales or Sabino Canyon northeast of Tucson. Feeders in Patagonia would be a good bet.

Blue-throated and **magnificent**: You have to go high to see these largest of our species. Try Marshall Gulch in the Santa Catalina Mountains or feeders in Summerhaven, also in the Catalinas.

Broad-tailed: Found in the same highlands as the above two species, the broad-tailed is smaller, but the males have a particular trill associated with their outer wing feathers.

Black-chinned: The most common summer hummingbird, the black-chinned is found in lower and middle elevation woodlands like Sabino and Romero canyons in the Catalinas. Feeders in Brown Canyon on the Buenos Aires NWR also attract many of this species.

Anna's: Just arrived back from summer in California, this squeaky bird is common nearly everywhere: canyons and backyard feeders, from desertscrub up to middle elevations.

Calliope: Though not particularly common, this smallest of our hummingbirds is worth seeing as it passes through on migration this month. The best bet are the feeders in Portal in the Chiricahua Mountains.

Rufous: This fiesty, fiery-colored hummingbird is conspicuous at feeders and around flowers along mountain foothills and in canyons. Rufous can be seen at the Nature Conservancy's Muleshoe Ranch, Brown Canyon, and Sabino Canyon.

Above, *a broad-tailed hummingbird recovers from a collision with a window*

AUGUST SKIES

"Moon of the Short Crops"

TRADITIONAL O'ODHAM NAME FOR AUGUST

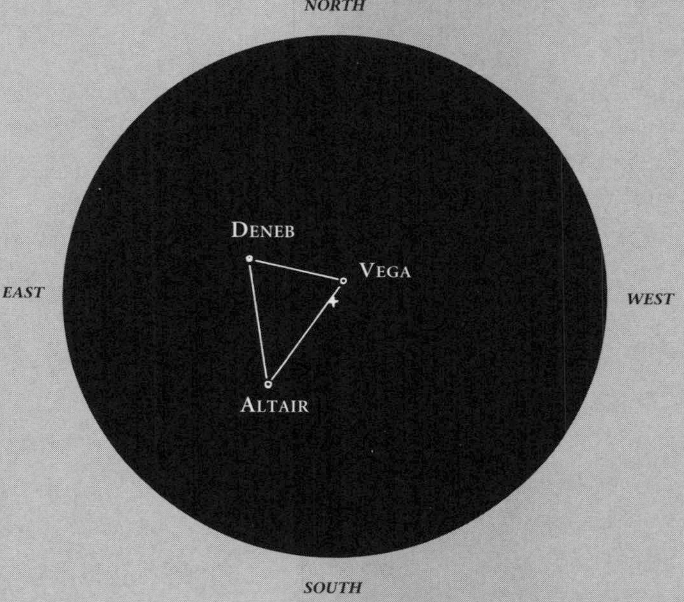

Star Chart for 32°N
Mid-month, 9 pm

FEATURE CONSTELLATION

The beautiful Summer Triangle once had a more macabre association. Called the Stymphalian Flock, Vega (vulture), Deneb (swan), and Altair (eagle) were monster-birds that prowled the woods of Greece and fed on the flesh of humans. Hercules dispatched the flock as his sixth labor, and now they reside for eternity in our heavens.

AUGUST AT A GLANCE

Desertscrub

❧ Flowers include telegraph plants (*Heterotheca subaxillaris*), summer poppies (*Kallstroemia grandiflora*), barrel cactuses (*Ferocactus* spp.), asters (*Machaeranthera* spp.), trailing four-o'clock (*Allionia incarnata*), buffalo gourds (*Cucurbita foetidissima*), devil's claw (*Proboscidea* spp.), morning glories (*Ipomoea* spp.), sacred datura (*Datura wrightii*), and ground cherries (*Solanum elaeagnifolium*), which will bloom across the desertscrub and up into the grasslands.

❧ Desert hackberry shrubs (*Celtis spinosa*) are fruiting; look for Leila hackberry butterflies flitting around the foliage.

❧ This month and next are the best for butterfly watching, from desertscrub up to coniferous forests. See Flora section in this chapter, and Appendix 5. Snouts, monarchs, and painted ladies are especially common in most communities.

❧ Throughout the communities gnats, both benign and biting varieties, chiggers, and mosquitos can plague mammalian visitors.

Desert Grasslands

❧ Trailing four-o'clock (*Allionia incarnata*), wiry lotus (*Lotus rigidus*), flameflowers (*Talinum aurantiacum* and *T. pulchellum*), dakota verbena (*Glandularia bipinnatifida*), jatropha (*Jatropha macrorhiza*), and longpod senna (*Senna hirsuta* var. *glaberrima*) will be flowering.

❧ Variegated and gulf fritillaries are common butterflies this month.

❧ Lark buntings settle in the grasslands for the coming fall and winter.

Oak Woodlands

❧ Papalotilla (*Guardiolia platyphylla*), bouvardia (*Bouvardia* spp.), long-flowered four-o'clock (*Mirabilis longiflora*), and western spiderwort (*Tradescantia occidentalis*) present flowers in moist, shady areas.

❧ Manzanitas (*Arctostaphylos pungens*) droop with their namesakes—little red "apples" the size of peas, and canyon grapes (*Vitus arizonica*) are ripening.

❧ Nabokov's satyr butterflies emerge this month and may be seen through October.

Pine-Oak Woodlands

❧ Flowering plants include columbines (*Aquilegia chrysantha*), penstemons (*Penstemon* spp.), and gilias (*Ipomopsis* spp.).

Small trees and shrubs are putting out their berries, including birchleaf buckthorns (*Rhamnus betulaefolia*) and lemonadeberry (*Rhus aromatica*).

The bark of ponderosa pines (*Pinus ponderosa*) smells strongly of butterscotch or vanilla this month (volatile oils in the sap smell most strongly in warm weather).

Coniferous Forests

This month is the peak for flowers in the high country: indian paintbrush (*Castilleja* spp.), mountain thistle (*Cirsium pulchellum* and *C. wheeleri*), aspen fleabane (*Erigeron macranthus*), goldenrod (*Solidago* spp.), senecio (*Senecio* spp.), beardlip penstemon (*Penstemon barbatus*), pinks (*Silene* spp.), Hooker evening primrose (*Oenothera hookeri*), cutleaf coneflower (*Rudbeckia laciniata*), and Richardson's and purple geranium (*Geranium richardsonii* and *G. caespitosum*).

Some odd-looking plants are conspicuous this month, especially along trails or roads, including flannel mullein (*Verbascum thapsus*) with its fuzzy foliage and wand-like flower stalk; false heliobore (*Veratrum californicum*), which looks like a prehistoric plant with its huge cabbage-like leaves; and green gentian (*Swertia radiata*), which looks like mullein without the fuzzies.

Masses of ladybugs (*Hippodamia convergens*), also called convergent lady beetles, cover rocks and shrubs in the high country, especially in August. They are not breeding or feeding much—they're just "hanging out" (called diapause). Ladybugs descend to the lowlands in early spring to mate and lay eggs.

Special Events

August 12, the Perseid Meteor Shower (see below).

In the Sky

August 1 marks the midpoint between summer solstice and autumnal equinox, traditionally called Lammas. In more temperate climates, Lammas was the beginning of the harvest.

The Summer Triangle (Vega, Deneb, and Altair) is overhead.

High in the northeast, look for the spectacular Perseid Meteor Shower on August 12 around 11 p.m. to midnight if the sky is clear of clouds.

See the chapter Exploring the Nature of Pima County and Southern Arizona for definitions and descriptions of communities.

Near Miller Creek in the Rincon Mountains, many species of bats may gather on September evenings

september

RESTLESSNESS MOVES WITH *September into the landscapes of southern Arizona. As summer rains taper off, the breeding and growing of animals and plants wane, and preparations begin for migrations and the coming of fall drought and winter cold. Days dawn bright and hot. Only the barest trace of coolness may waft in early morning breezes for a day or two, teasing us with thoughts of fall—but the sun won't relinquish its hold on the desert for over a month, and even then it may sneak back in with some over-90° days.*

Yellow seems to be the color of September: snakeweed, turpentinebush, goldeneyes, asters, and telegraph plants bloom across the desertscrub and grasslands. And one of our favorite September bloomers are sunflowers, gracing miles of roadside with stands 6 and 7 feet high. Migrating western kingbirds, with lemony yellow underbody washes flashing as they fly, are among the most common birds of the southern grasslands. Pale lemon-and-cream western meadowlarks, with cadet-like caps, return later this month to the grasslands where they will gather in small flocks throughout the winter, and the pronghorn antelopes will breed this month and next. By the end of the month the grasslands will be mostly dry, the seed heads of the grasses waving golden in the soft fall light. To the O'odham, September is Washai Gakithag Mashath, *"moon of the dry grass."*

Along creeks and washes in desertscrub up into oak woodlands, seep willows, which are in the genus Baccharis *and are not true willows, open their unremarkable sprays of tiny white flowers. But like busy neighborhood markets, the bushes hum and buzz with hundreds of bees, wasps, butterflies, and flies shopping for nectar and pollen. Rocky hillsides and mountain foothills near the Mexican border are awash in the soft pink of mimosa blossoms, called* gatuño *in Spanish.*

In nearly all the communities, two of our favorite fliers are tanking up for their migrations south. Bat and hummingbird numbers increase during the month, as individuals that spent the summer farther north move into Pima County for refueling. Homeowners around the foothills of the taller mountains will notice a lot more activity at their nectar feeders both in daytime and at night. Broad-billed, rufous, Allen's, black-chinned, and Anna's are all possible hummingbird visitors (the Anna's may stay for the winter). And nectar-feeding bats, the Mexican long-tongued and lesser long-nosed, have recently learned of the freebie feeding stations and will drain a full feeder by morning. In September, the fliers are mostly females with their new juvenile offspring, gaining strength for migrations south to join the males in Mexico. Other bats moving through on their way south include insect-eaters such as the Mexican freetail, hoary, and red bats, and arriving for the winter are silver-haired bats.

Deer may begin to adjust their seasonal ranges this month, and the males will be sloughing off the remaining velvet on newly grown antlers. The velvet is a blood-rich membrane that dries up once the horn is fully developed and males may be seen with bits and scraps of it hanging untidily off their bright new racks. They will polish the horn on trees and shrubs in preparation for winter's "rut," or breeding season. In southern Arizona mule deer may spend the summer ranging up into the oak woodlands or above and move down to desertscrub and grassland foothills this month, while some white-tailed deer, a mountain-woodland species, are more likely to congregate in the lower oak woodlands for the winter.

In the high coniferous forests, plants like mountain spray and snowberry go to seed, and butterflies still flutter about finishing their life cycles among late bloomers. Pine-oak woodlands offer flowers such as Arizona trumpets to the butterflies and migrating hummingbirds, and beautiful Lemmon's marigolds brighten the forest floor. Across the oak woodlands you'll see bright gold bushes aflame on the hillsides and creekbottoms; these are the coral bean shrubs, about to lose their leaves until next summer. Up close you'll see their 6-inch bean pods ripening. Other golden highlights are the flowers of senecio, telegraph plants, and goldenrod. Many oaks will be producing acorns, and the manzanita shrubs will have mostly dropped their little fruits.

Day by day, as October approaches, fall will work its way down the mountains. Summer's creeks recede, their voices softening in the cooling, drying air. Leaves dry out and rustle in fitful breezes. Evenings quiet down, as the nightjars migrate south or down to the low deserts for winter, and owls either leave or call less frequently. The canyons fill with cool air that flows out into the deserts before dawn to tease us with a promise of relief from summer's heat.

September draws out our peregrination urges—like the restless animals, we head out on a few favorite excursions. We like to go down to the northern foothills of the Santa Rita Mountains for a Sunday drive through the beautiful grassland and oak woodland hills of Greaterville Road. A hike down the Box Camp Trail to look for rufous hummingbirds in the conifer forests of the Santa Catalinas is a perfect September excursion. For a nice overnight trip, we go to Happy Valley on the eastern side of the Rincon Mountains and watch bats. ❧ ❧ ❧

SEPTEMBER WEATHER

	Sunrise	Sunset	Avg. Relative Humidity/Tucson
September 1	*5:59 MST*	*6:49 MST*	*5 a.m. 55%*
Spetember 30	*6:17 MST*	*6:11 MST*	*5 p.m. 27%*

Stations	Ajo	Tucson	Mt. Lemmon
Station Elevation	(*1,800 ft.*)	(*2,584 ft.*)	(*8,800 ft.*)
September Averages			
Max. temperature	*97.3°F*	*93.5°F*	*72.4°F*
Min. temperature	*71.9°F*	*67.3°F*	*44.2°F*
Precipitation	*.85 in.*	*1.34 in.*	*2.78 in.*
Snow	*0 in.*	*0 in.*	*0 in.*
# days 100° & over	*12*	*4*	*0*
# days 32° & under	*0*	*0*	*0*
# days precip.>.01"	*3*	*4*	*4*
September Extremes			
Max. temperature	*113°F (1950)*	*107°F (1948)*	*81°F (1959)*
Min. temperature	*49°F (1965)*	*44°F (1965)*	*32°F (1982)*
Max. snow/month	*0 in.*	*0 in.*	*0 in.*
Max. snow/1 day	*0 in.*	*0 in.*	*0 in.*
Max. precip./month	*5.68 in. (1946)*	*5.11 in. (1964)*	*5.73 in. (1962)*
Max. precip./1 day	*4.15 in. (1946)*	*2.85 in. (1964)*	*1.35 in. (1982)*

September Notes

Early September will continue to see some rain, but by the end of the month hot and dry is the norm. Expect some over-100° days even up to the end of the month—it's still summer in the desert. The mountains will be slightly cooler, with highs in the mid-70°s, and a little wetter.

For information about data sources for these listings, see the Climate section of the chapter Exploring the Nature of Pima County and Southern Arizona.

FLORA

Hitchin' a Ride

A hiker in the desert, cursing because a cholla cactus segment has just embedded itself in a bare shin, takes little time to contemplate the situation. Out comes a comb or pocketknife; the offending joint is carefully pried out of the flesh and flung vengefully as far as possible with an extra curse thrown after it.

If the cholla segment, and the parent plant from which it so easily dislodged, could talk, they would say, "Thanks very much!" For the hiker has unwittingly done just what the plant intended—the flung joint will swiftly sprout roots and grow into a new cholla, a genetically identical descendant of the original cactus.

Dispersal is a key element in the survival strategy of plants. The farther a plant can disperse its offspring—seeds or viable sections of itself—the greater the probability that some of them will survive events in the immediate environment, such as fires or browsing animals. Of course some seeds wind up in hostile spots—on rocks, in flood-prone wash beds, even in the ocean—but presumably enough survive to ensure the continuation of the plant's genes.

The simplest, and probably most ancient, way to disperse seeds is on the wind. Small seeds, such as those of some flowers and grasses, accomplish this easily, by growing filaments or hairs into various forms of "parachutes" that catch the slightest breeze and waft along, sometimes for miles. But some trees—ashes and maples, for example—have evolved a way to loft a heavier seed. Their seeds form propeller-like appendages called samaras, either singly or in pairs, that whirl in the wind like helicopter blades, providing enough lift to deposit the seeds many yards from the parent tree.

Other plants, such as cholla, take advantage of passing animals to disperse their offspring. The hitchhiking strategy can take two forms: external and internal. The cholla's aggressive external approach is effective, if painful, for the unwitting vehicle. Foxtails, the barbed seeds of red brome grass, stick unpleasantly in socks and dangerously in a dog's fur—if they happen to lodge in an ear they can work their way down the canal and puncture the eardrum, which can even cause death if the owner is unaware of the problem. Red brome grows in winter and the foxtails are dry and dangerous by

May. Burrs also tangle miserably in a dog's fur but usually pose no health hazard. The large curved hooks on the seed pod of the devil's claw attach themselves unerringly to boots and legs. Many species of forbs and grasses have sticky coatings or hairs on their seeds that adhere to fur and fabric.

A more subtle, and evolutionarily complex, method of hitchhiking is the internal route: an animal eats the seed because it has some sort of attractive nutritional coating; the seed survives the trip through the animal's digestive system and is expelled. The mesquite, for example, has been spread throughout the Southwest with the considerable help of cattle, who eat the bean pods, digest the nutritious casing, and poop out the seeds with a nice dollop of fertilizer. The seeds have a hard coating that resists the acids in the cow's system but becomes scarified enough so that the seeds germinate after deposition.

In the fall, the wild chile plant, or chiltepine (*Capsicum annuum* var. *aviculare*), produces bright red berries that are unpalatable to mammals because of their fiery capsaicin (although many humans have developed a masochistic attraction to this chemical, which they indulge with hot salsas and other chile foods). But the color of the berries is a clue to their intended customers: most mammals can't see red, but most birds can. Birds like cardinals, mockingbirds, and thrashers are attracted to those red berries—and are completely unaffected by the capsaicin content. The chiltepine is known as the *pajaro pequeño* chile in Mexico, the "little bird pepper." Because birds often perch in bushes or trees when they defecate, the seeds of chiltepine and other desert shrubs like hackberry are deposited right where they need to be: under "nurse plants," which will protect them from frosts and dessicating sun. So the mutualistic relationship is well suited to both the chile and the bird. (See October's Flora section for more on the chiltepine.)

September is a good time to enjoy—and curse—the inventiveness of plants as many species begin to put out their seed wares in case the right dispersal agent will pass by.

A Grove of Aspen Tree

No, it's not a misprint. On the highest northern slopes of southern Arizona's sky island mountain

Aspen leaves

ranges such as the Santa Catalinas, you'll find isolated stands of aspen trees. These are genuine cold-weather trees that can only survive in a few such spots at our latitude.

Aspens are easily distinguished by their fluttery, bright green, round leaves, which tremble in the slightest breeze and turn yellow-gold in autumn. The long, straight trunks are white-barked. Aspen groves form delightful contrasting patches within a coniferous forest. But recent research into the nature of aspen reproduction has uncovered some new facets to their ecology.

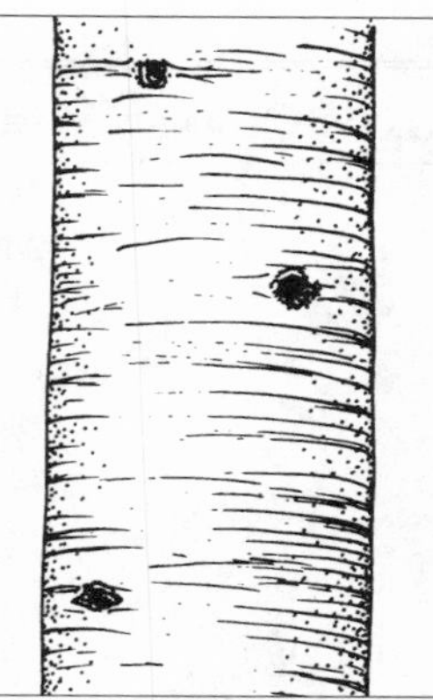

Aspen trunk

Aspens have the ability to produce offspring through flowers and seeds, just like other flowering plants. More often, though, they reproduce by sending out underground shoots, called rhizomes, that form new trunks. This technique, known as vegetative reproduction, is used by many plants. The process results in a "new" plant that is genetically identical to the parent and in most cases remains attached to it by the root system. Often the parent eventually dies, leaving the vegetative shoot or shoots still vigorous.

Botanists studying aspens made the startling discovery within the past decade that some entire groves of aspens are genetically identical, meaning they all sprang from one ancestor tree and might, with a little argument, be considered one gigantic organism. Support for this theory came from an investigation into the root systems that connect the trunks of the grove. It was found that the roots of trunks growing in a wet area could send moisture through the system to trunks growing in a dry area; in return, those trunks could reciprocate with minerals not found in the damp location. So the grove functions as a single living being. Since aspens are dioecious—male and female flowers are borne on different plants—the cloned groves are either female or male.

If we accept the premise that these groves are single organisms, then they are very large organisms indeed. One male grove in southern Utah, whimsically named Pando (a Latin word roughly translated as "I spread"), consists of about 45,000 trunks and weighs, conservatively, 13 million pounds. This would make it the largest living thing on the planet.

Nature's Corner Markets

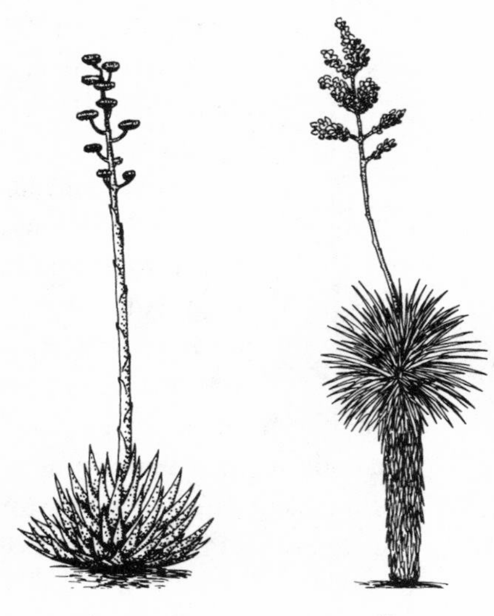

Agave Yucca

Mesquite trees have been called "K-Marts" for early peoples because they provided so many of their living needs, from food to building materials to cosmetics to medicines. Similarly, southwestern plants in the family Agavaceae—agaves and yuccas—could be called the corner markets, providing soap, basketry material, liquor, and "fast food." Agaves are one of the West's signature plants. There are about 40 species in the Sonoran Desert region, and all have long, sharp-ended succulent leaves arranged around a short stem, rosette-style. Most will produce but one 5- to 10-foot-tall bloom stalk after the plant reaches 10 to 30 years of age and then die. This habit gave rise to the popular name given most species, the "century plant," because folklore holds that they did not bloom until age 100.

Native peoples used agaves for liquor, food, fiber, and medicine. The stems or "hearts" of certain species were cut out just prior to blooming, when the sugar content is highest, then roasted in pits, fermented, mashed, and distilled into mescal and tequila. The leaves yield strong fibers, which were woven into rope, and leaves and roots were used in various medicinal tonics.

*Yuccas are also members of the Agavaceae family but are more tree-like with similar spikey leaves that drape down the tall stalks like hula-dancer skirts. The common soaptree yucca (*Yucca elata*) is often 6 to 15 feet tall, with one to several branches. Yucca flower stalks are tall, making showy stands across desertscrub and grasslands in May, and the creamy flowers are pollinated by the yucca moth (*Tegeticula *spp.). Native people harvested the flower buds as a quick food source, and leaf fibers were made into rope and baskets. Its roots are saponaceous, or soapy, and chunks were swished in water and used as laundry, hair, and body soap.* *(See Birds, Bees, and . . . Bats? in May's flora section for a discussion of Agavaceae and their relationships with bats, moths, and hummingbirds as pollinators.)*

FAUNA

Bats, Bugs, and Birdfeeders

One of the most relaxing things to do on a late-summer evening is sit out at dusk and watch the bats swoop and dive in the failing light. The knowledge that they are aiding our comfort by eating hundreds of irksome bugs each just adds to the pleasure.

A female Mexican free-tailed bat (*Tadarida brasiliensis mexicana*) with a nursing offspring (in spring and early summer) can eat nearly her own weight in mosquitoes, moths, and other insects each night. For a very small colony of about 5,000 individuals—about the number that roosts in the University of Arizona football stadium—that adds up to over 50 pounds. An impressive total, until you consider the 20 million bats of Bracken Cave in Texas, who nightly consume 100 tons of flying bugs.

These bats locate and capture their prey, often in complete darkness, using echolocation, or sonar—a rapid series of high-frequency oral clicks that bounce off objects and return to the bat's sensitive ears. So accurate is this system that bats placed in dark rooms strung with nylon fishing line easily avoid the obstacles. So selective is it that they have no trouble negotiating narrow cave entrances through which thousands of other bats are flying, each emitting its own sonar clicks up to 200 times per second.

It was originally thought that bats caught insects in their mouths. Only with the advent of high-speed photography did we learn that they scoop them up with their wings and the membrane between the feet and tail (called the interfemoral membrane), then lean down and eat them in mid-air.

There are 28 species of bats found in Arizona; the more common insectivorous bats of southern Arizona include big brown (*Eptesicus fuscus*), the California myotis (*Myotis californicus*), and the tiny western pipistrelle (*Pipistrellus hesperus*), the smallest bat in the United States—at 3 grams it is no bigger than a hummingbird. Our largest bat is the western mastiff bat, a relative giant at 60 grams with a 21-inch wingspan. The pallid bat (*Antrozous pallidus*) distinguishes itself by hunting on the ground, using its huge ears to hear the movements of its prey, which includes grasshoppers and scorpions.

Not all bats are insectivorous. Two that enter southern Arizona, the lesser long-nosed (*Leptonycteris curasoae*) and Mexican long-

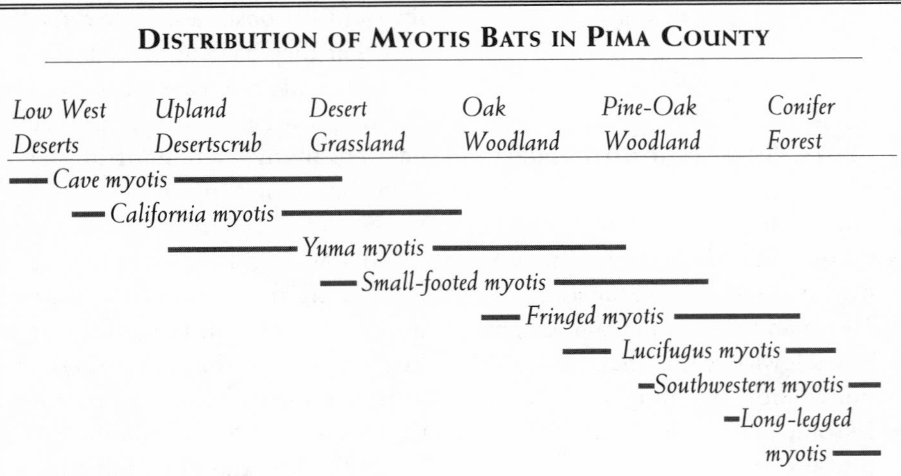

The distribution of eight species of *Myotis* (little brown) bats in Pima County's communities shows how many species can share a region if each specializes in a different area. Note: Graph is approximation only, to show relationships. For specific distribution, see Donald A. Hoffmeister, *Mammals of Arizona* (University of Arizona Press, Tucson, 1986), p. 67, from which this graph is adapted.

tongued (*Choeronycteris mexicana*) subsist on the nectar and pollen of certain agave and columnar cactus, occasionally eating ripe fruit as well. They are physiologically well-adapted to this diet: their snouts are elongated, tongues long and hummingbird-like. In spring, these two species follow the blooming cycle of cardón, organ pipe, and saguaro cactuses up into southern Arizona from Mexico. In fall they return south, feeding largely on agave blooms. The bats serve as vital pollinators for these plants.

Nectar-feeding bats will also visit hummingbird feeders, especially at houses near mountain canyons. They can be voracious and very sloppy: at our house, during peak months, including September, they can go through a half-gallon of food a night in several feeders—a lot of it ending up spattered on the porch. One study at a feeder in the foothills of the Santa Catalina Mountains counted 305 "hits" at the feeder in a 5-minute period.

Most bats migrate or hibernate in winter, but a few, such as the California leaf-nosed bat (*Macro-*

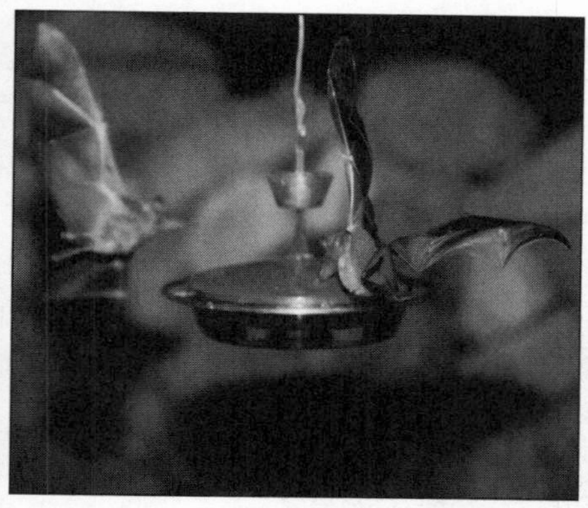

tus californicus) remain active all year. Others hibernate but emerge on warm evenings to feed, like the western pipistrelles. September is the peak time for bats on the move from north to south or from high elevations to lower elevations, in preparation for winter.

Much hysteria has been propagated regarding bats and rabies. It is undeniable that bats can contract rabies—just like any other mammal. But consider a couple of statistics. In the forty years between 1952 and 1992, a total of 16 people in the United States died of bat-induced rabies. In the past ten years, automobile accidents have claimed 450,000 lives. The incidence of rabies in bats is normally no higher on a percentage basis than in any other mammalian population. When bats get the disease, they sicken and die just like any other mammal. If a bat is seen in unusual circumstances—perched in the open or lying on the ground, for example—there is certainly a higher possibility that it is sick in some way, so it should simply be left alone. Rabid bats do not fly around attacking people.

Above, *Mexican long-tongued bats at a hummingbird feeder*

Bats are in far more danger from us than we are from them. Insectivorous bats are susceptible to the insecticides sprayed on crops; these poisons accumulate in the animals' fatty tissues, which they utilize during hibernation. Ironically, if farmers did more to attract bats they might not need insecticides in the first place. In one study, corn borer damage was reduced by 50 percent—simply by broadcasting the sound of bats over a cornfield.

Desert Pigs

Several years ago a woman who lived in the desert west of Tucson began feeding the herd of javelinas that frequently passed through her yard. The javelinas quickly became accustomed to regular free food and would show up each evening like clockwork for their handout. Several months later the woman took a trip and did not arrange for someone to continue feeding the javelinas while she was gone.

The evening of her return, she opened the sliding glass door to take out her offering and about 15 *very* disgruntled javelinas stormed into the house and, once they realized they were trapped, proceeded to panic and demolish the place while the woman stood on a counter screaming for the sheriff over the telephone. After a half hour of utter chaos, the javelinas found their way back out the door.

The moral of the story—well, the moral of the story should be obvious. But it points out the adaptability and boldness of *Tayassu tajacu*, the collared peccary, or javelina. This small pig-like animal can become quite accustomed to human presence and is sometimes seen wandering unconcernedly down the streets of outlying subdivisions in herds of 10 to 20.

Javelinas, which weigh between 30 and 50 pounds, typically inhabit desertscrub between about 2,000 feet and 6,500 feet. They prefer heavy cover and are often flushed out of wash bottoms where they rest. They seem to be very short-sighted and will often stop and peer myopically at an intruder after running a few yards. Javelinas grunt and snort rather comically to each other whether alarmed or just feeding, and group recognition is reinforced by smell—a gland along the javelina's flanks produces a musky odor, and herd members rub each other to exchange the scent.

In addition to table scraps, javelinas will eat grass, bulbs, seeds, agaves, cactus, and cactus fruit—reportedly even small animals and carrion. Sometimes hikers happen across a clump of prickly pear that looks as if someone had tossed a hand grenade into it—a sure giveaway of javelina herd activity; they obviously enjoy rowdy communal buffets. Even if a single animal has been feeding, the individual pads will be shredded (neat little semicircles bitten out of the pads usually indicates rodent foraging).

Javelinas give birth throughout the year, with a peak during the summer months, so September is a good month to see them. Litter size is almost always one or two, very occasionally three. The young are reddish in color, in contrast to the gray-black adults, and sport a dark racing stripe down the back.

Above, *a javelina enjoys its preferred meal—a prickly pear cactus*

Ancient Rhythms

Ancient rhythms call to the bird populations of the world, and in September the wave of feathery flights peaks. In the communities of southern Arizona's wildlands, you may notice a lot of unfamiliar birds, welcome back some winter visitors, and say farewell to spring and summer breeders. Below is a rough list of who's passing through, leaving, and arriving in September and early October. (For a thorough treatment, see *Davis and Russell's Finding Birds in Southeast Arizona* published by Tucson Audubon Society.)

Passing through: eared grebes, blue-winged and cinnamon teals, white-faced ibises, marbled godwits, western sandpipers, long-billed dowitchers, and Wilson's phalaropes; Hammond's, dusky, and Pacific-slope flycatchers; warbling vireos; and MacGillivray's, Wilson's, hermit, Townsend's, and Nashville warblers.

Leaving: gray, Swainson's, zone-tailed, and black hawks, and Mississippi kites; flammulated owls; whip-poor-wills, buff-collared nightjars, common nighthawks and lesser nighthawks; poorwills become less common; northern rough-winged, bank, cliff, barn, tree, and violet-green swallows and purple martins; western wood-pewee; dusky-capped, brown-crested, and sulphur-bellied flycatchers (ash-throated flycatchers may move into the west deserts as well as move south); tropical, Cassin's, thick-billed, and western kingbirds; gray and Bell's vireos; yellow-breasted chats, and olive, red-faced, Grace's, Lucy's, Virginia's, and yellow warblers; tanagers, orioles, and trogons; Botteri's sparrows; buntings and grosbeaks.

Arriving: green-winged teals, mallards, northern pintails, northern shovelers, American wigeons, redheads, ring-necked ducks, and lesser scaups; great blue herons become more numerous; American pipits; kestrels become more numerous; northern harriers and sharp-shinned hawks; gray flycatchers; yellow-headed and Brewer's blackbirds; green-tailed towhees; chipping, clay-colored, savannah, and Baird's sparrows, and chestnut-collared longspurs; Brewer's, vesper, and sage sparrows, and lark buntings; golden-crowned, white-crowned, and Harris' sparrows form flocks; fox, Lincoln's, swamp, and white-throated sparrows.

FLIGHT COMPANIONS

A familiar sight in September are flocks of turkey vultures cruising the thermals, slowly working their way south as the temperatures drop. Look closely at the groups, and sometimes you might detect a slight variation in one of the vultures. Does it have a barred tail and a fully feathered head? It's probably a zone-tailed hawk, which when soaring looks suspiciously like a vulture in shape. Enough so, in fact, that it probably fools a lot of the hawks' prey—rodents, birds, lizards—into thinking it's a harmless vulture until it is too late to flee. No one knows for sure, though, and the relationship between vultures and zone-tailed hawks remains a mystery. Near where we live is a zone-tailed hawk nest, and on most spring and summer evenings six to a dozen turkey vultures roost in the nest-tree—a surprising phenomenon given the zone-tails' extreme intolerance of the presence of any other bird or mammal within 100 feet of the nest.

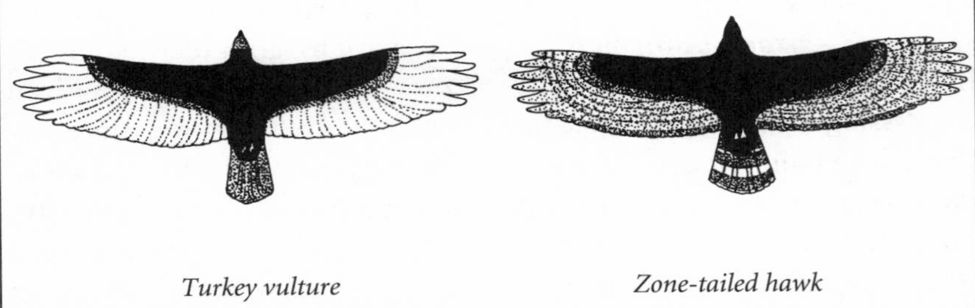

Turkey vulture *Zone-tailed hawk*

PLACES TO VISIT IN SEPTEMBER

Happy Valley Bats

Dusk was settling on the mountain above us and the air cooled perceptibly. Lying on a smooth rock slab in Miller Canyon, still warm from the late-summer sun, we watched the small pools below. Just as our eyes adjusted to the murky light they came: fluttering like butterflies down from the mountain, delicate puttering of soft wings in the gray light. One by one they dipped down to the pool and so quickly did they drink we would not have known except for the tiny spreading ripple rings where their quick tongues lapped the surface. By their size we could only guess which species—too big for western pipistrelles, so perhaps little brown bats. There could be a dozen species in this valley this month.

Happy Valley on the eastern side of the Rincon Mountains is a wonderful retreat in late summer and early fall, which is a good time to see bats before many head south for winter or hole up somewhere nearby. Blooming agaves tempt the nectar-feeding bats—lesser long-nosed and Mexican long-tongued—and there are also many insect eaters such as western "pips" and hoary bats.

Take Interstate 10 east to the Mescal Road exit and head north on this washboardy dirt lane into the valley between the Rincon and Little Rincon mountains (you pass the western town movie set of Mescal on your way in, a strange apparition rising from the high desert grassland). The road enters the small valley amid oaks and junipers in Coronado National Forest, winding back and forth across Ash Creek, which will most likely be dry this month. The road ends at a locked gate just past the Miller Canyon Trail. This is cattle country. There are numerous primitive campsites and parking areas.

We head up Miller Canyon Trail until we can see late-summer pools still languishing in rocky Miller Creek on the right side of the trail. Then we hop down and find a spot above and away from one of the pools to watch the evening bat runs. Dusk is a good time for many species, but even more will come after dark. Bring a red-lensed light if you want to continue watching after dark (don't blind the bats with un-shaded flashlights). An alternative is to hang out at a cattle pond, another favorite bat drinking source, but the sights and smells are less appealing than the canyons above. Don't camp within a quarter-mile of any water—it keeps the animals from coming in to much-needed water.

Abuzz and Ablaze at Box Camp

Early one September we headed down the Box Camp Trail just after a morning rainstorm. The sky was just-washed blue, a few puffy white clouds scudded by barely above the glistening wet ponderosa pine tops, and our boots sloshed in an inch or two of runoff flowing down the ruts of the trail. About a mile down the trail we came upon several small fields of flowers that looked almost cultivated—honeysuckles, thistles, Indian paintbrushes, and penstemons. A general din suddenly reached our ears, a surprisingly loud fuss and buzz and fury in the usually quiet pine forest. What was making all the racket?

In September, mountain meadows are aflame with flowers and abuzz with activity—dozens of hummingbirds, butterflies, and bees take advantage of the last gasp of flowering before the first fall freeze, perhaps as early as next month. Look especially for feisty rufous hummingbirds, small rusty-red hummers that migrate through this month on their way south for the winter.

The Box Camp Trail in the Santa Catalina Mountains offers a relaxing stroll through a few small mountain meadows with nice bird and butterfly viewing opportunities. The trailhead is near the top of the mountain, on the left just past the turnoff to Spencer Canyon. In 1.8 miles the trail reaches a spur that heads down (steeply) to Box Spring, a lovely lunch spot and the headwaters of Sabino Creek. Just beyond this spur the trail reaches a promontory that overlooks part of the city far below; a large fire ring indicates this is a popular camping spot. From here the trail drops 5.3 miles very steeply and roughly to Sabino Basin and the Sabino Canyon network of trails (7,600 feet to 3,800 feet). The land agency is Coronado National Forest.

Sunday Drive to the Santa Rita Mountains

By late September the waning of summer and the commencement of fall spark our urge to wander—a road trip is the only cure. The northern flanks of the Santa Rita Mountains offer a rugged but interesting drive through beautiful desert grassland and oak woodland. Plan on a day-long trip with a picnic.

We usually head south down Interstate 19 to the Continental Road turnoff. Follow the signs to Madera Canyon, but at the fork to Greaterville, take the left fork, a dirt road. This road curves up into high desert grassland and into the woodlands of the northern slopes of the Santa Rita Mountains. Parts are narrow and have sharp hairpin turns, so go slowly and stop well off the road to enjoy views. About halfway, the oak woodland is nice and thick, making a good picnic stop. Check out the oaks to see if any have ripe acorns, and gather a few to roast for pesto or snacks.

Greaterville Road (Forest Road 62) hooks up with paved Highway 83 a few miles north of Sonoita. It's worth making the drive back to Tucson on this lovely highway in late-afternoon light. Coronado National Forest is the land agency.

SEPTEMBER SKIES

"Moon of the Dry Grass"

TRADITIONAL O'ODHAM NAME FOR SEPTEMBER

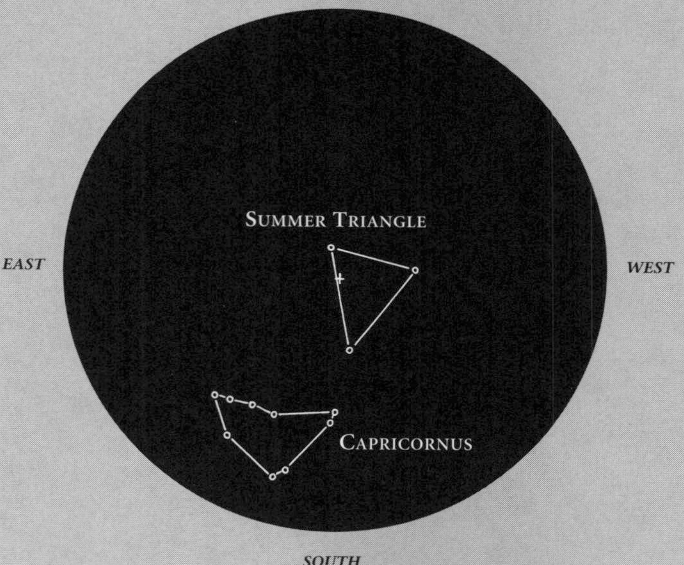

Star Chart for 32°N
Mid-month, 9 pm

FEATURE CONSTELLATION

Capricornus has long been known as the Seagoat, often depicted with the head of a goat and the tail of a fish. He resides in the area of the sky known as The Sea, alongside Pisces, the fishes, and Aquarius, the water-bearer. Thousands of years ago, goats were sacrificed in rituals to ensure the return of the sun at the winter solstice.

SEPTEMBER AT A GLANCE

Desertscrub

❧ Snakeweed (*Gutierrezia sarothrae*), turpentinebush (*Ericameria laricifolia*), goldeneyes (*Viguiera multiflora*), desert asters (*Machaeranthera* spp.), common sunflowers (*Helianthus annuus*), and telegraph plants (*Heterotheca subaxillaris*) bloom around the desertscrub and grasslands, especially along roads.

❧ Along creeks and washes in desertscrub and grasslands, seep willows (*Baccharis salicifolia*—not true willows) bloom, and canyon ragweed (*Ambrosia ambrosoides*) offers its sticky burrs to human socks or mammal fur.

❧ Bird migrations are at their peak; see Fauna section for details.

❧ Butterflies continue to be abundant from desertscrub into the coniferous forests; in desertscrub look for snouts, common gray and great purple hairstreaks, funereal duskwings, and American painted ladies.

❧ Desert bighorn sheep continue breeding.

❧ Bats and hummingbirds are preparing for migrations in early October, so their numbers and activity increase this month. Both groups include first-year juveniles, which must gain strength for their first long flights to wintering grounds.

Desert Grasslands

❧ Migrating western kingbirds are one of the most common birds of the southern grasslands, and western meadowlarks return later this month to the grasslands where they will gather in small flocks throughout the winter.

❧ Look for flocks of migrating Swainson's hawks, especially in fallow fields or recently burned grasslands where they gorge on grasshoppers, other insects, and rodents.

❧ Pronghorn antelopes breed this month and next.

❧ Bird migrations are at their peak; see Fauna section for details.

❧ Variegated fritillary butterflies fly in grasslands in the fall.

Oak Woodlands

❧ Coral bean (*Erythrina flabelliformis*) shrubs have woody bean pods 6 or more inches long and their foliage turns golden yellow.

❧ Oak trees may be setting acorns.

❧ Flowers include senecio, telegraph plant (*Heterotheca subaxillaris*), and goldenrod (*Solidago sparsiflora*).

❧ *Gatuño* (*Mimosa dysocarpa*) sports delicate pink catkins, washing whole woodland hillsides a glowing pink in southern Arizona.

❧ Bird migrations are at their peak; see Fauna section for details.
❧ Mule deer and some white-tailed deer may begin to move downward in elevation for the winter; males shed their antler velvet.
❧ Butterflies to look for include Nabokov's satyrs, Mormon metalmarks, and Elada and Dymas checkerspots, as well as pipevine swallowtails, cloudless sulphurs, painted ladies, and snouts.

Pine-Oak Woodlands

❧ Flowers still grace trailsides and forest floors, including Lemmon's marigolds (*Tagetes lemmonii*), Arizona trumpets (*Zauschneria latifolia*), and bushy tick clover (*Desmodium* spp.).
❧ Common deerbrush (*Ceanothus* spp.) will bloom this month.
❧ Bird migrations are at their peak; see Fauna section for details.
❧ Look for Patrobas satyr butterflies this month.

Coniferous Forests

❧ Most shrubs have gone to seed, including mountain spray (*Holodiscus dumosus*) and snowberry (*Symphoricarpos* spp.).
❧ A few stoic flowers bloom on, such as indian paintbrush (*Castilleja* spp.), primrose (*Oenothera* spp.), and fleabane (*Erigeron* spp.).
❧ Bird migrations are at their peak; see Fauna section for details.
❧ Terloot's white butterflies make a fall flight beginning this month, and American painted ladies are common among the waning thistle stands.

Special Events

❧ Bird migrations are at their peak; the Tucson Audubon Society will host many free or inexpensive outings this month. See Appendix 6 for contact information.

In the Sky

❧ September 23 is the autumnal equinox, when the sun passes directly over the equator. Day and night lengths are approximately equal.
❧ The Harvest Moon, the full moon nearest the autumnal equinox, occurs late this month or early October. For several days the moon will rise soon after sunset; the extra light helped farmers complete their harvests, thus the name.

❧ The constellation Capricornus is best viewed in mid-month in the southeast.
❧ The Summer Triangle moves high overhead.
❧ Moonless nights are perfect for viewing the wonder of the Milky Way, stretching from the northeast to the southwest.

See the chapter Exploring the Nature of Pima County and Southern Arizona for definitions and descriptions of communities.

october

BRIGHT ORANGE FRUITS *like tiny pumpkins dangle from hackberry bushes. Ocotillos have shed their leaves and stand bare in the warm October sun. Dryness marks the days once again; dust moves in the air like mist. The land looks dust-coated, not quite brown, a kind of un-green color. Young red-tailed hawks test their wings high over the desertscrub, and from the tops of shrubs and bunch grasses we hear the sound we've been patiently anticipating through the months of summer, the sound of fall:* Tweeee-tweedeldee-DEE-DEE-dee! *Sweet, exuberant, hopeful after the weeks of heat and drought—the white-crowned sparrows arrive early this month in high desertscrub and grasslands, and remind us that cool weather—and rain—is surely just around the corner.*

Fall, regardless of its hot, dusty cloak, is nonetheless a fruitful time of year in southern Arizona. Plants in all communities are putting out loads of berries, nuts, or beans: in desertscrub and grasslands, deep red fruits still cling to pads of prickly pear cactuses and miniature pineapple-like fruits crown barrel cactuses; in shady canyons, purple canyon grapes still hang temptingly, wild beans dangle pale little seed pods, and the fiery wild chiles, the little chiltepines, glow like Christmas lights; and in moist woodlands, wild cotton offers its fiberless bolls, black walnuts and acorns ripen and fall, and pale lilac-frosted berries

Fruits, like these pods of the coral bean plant, are plentiful in the fall

hide in the soft green foliage of junipers. Birds, rodents, coyotes, foxes, bears, and others gorge on the bounty, stashing as much away in caches or fat as they can, to get them through late winter when the land is cooler but less giving. In the O'odham language, this is Wi'i-hanig Mashath, *"harvest moon."*

By month's end, we will feel our first "real" cold mornings, although always they are followed by a few more days of heat just to remind us that this IS a desert, after all. By the end of the month we will notice the shortening of the days, and a few clouds will begin to show up; it may even rain if late-season hurricanes continue in the Gulf of Mexico or off the Pacific coast of Mexico. Most of our wintering birds will be amassed and the land is again filled with birdsong and activity, not intense and frenetic like spring or after the summer rains but soft and contented, with a feeling of comfortable settling-in.

In the desertscrub, cactus wrens may begin to build winter roosting nests in cholla cactus or other cactus or spiny shrubs and line them with feathers to keep them warm. The most common hummingbird will be the hardy and adaptable Anna's. On cool mornings, look for roadrunners standing with their backs to the sun, their head feathers raised like mohawks; they are exposing their dark skin to the warmth of the rays. White-throated woodrats, or packrats, scurry about during the nights or early mornings gathering prickly pear and other fruits, which they stash away in their large, messy stick-nests. Other rodents, like pocket mice, may begin hibernation this month. Snakes slow down as well, though warm days will still find them out looking for that last meal before hibernation.

Female harrier hawks precede their mates into the grasslands this month, hunting gracefully and low over rolling hills, scaring up small rodents or insects, such as the giant horse lubber grasshoppers that move languidly around this month, occasionally flaring their bright pink hindwings. Other hawks arrive as well: strong, thick-winged buteos like rough-legged hawks and ferruginous hawks. Kestrels become more numerous, and if you're lucky you may see a merlin or prairie falcon migrating into our area from northern summer grounds.

Ravens band together into noisy groups, quorking *loudly as they cruise for food in open areas. The grasses are setting their seeds atop tall panicles that wave and sparkle in the low fall light.*

Along higher watercourses, deciduous trees may begin to drop their leaves. Soft golds and coppers touch walnut and sycamore, cottonwood and alder trees. Lower riparian corridors and canyons are full of high-mountain birds down for the winter, including ruby-crowned kinglets, orange-crowned warblers, yellow-rumped warblers, gray-breasted jays, white-breasted nuthatches, and solitary vireos. Lots of woodpeckers and sapsuckers join them—Williamson's and red-naped sapsuckers, Lewis' and acorn woodpeckers. Look for the knobby pinkish berries of the soapberry trees this month as well; native peoples swished them in water to produce suds for washing.

In the oak woodlands band-tailed pigeons gather in large flocks, wandering up into the higher forests and back looking for acorns and other foods. Dark-eyed juncos return from the north for the winter. White-tailed deer range down from the high country looking for water and escaping the cold. Black bears are preparing for their hibernation, perhaps later this month or next, by gorging on the fruits and nuts of fall. The forests are quiet, cold; aspens and maples begin to turn gold and rusty red later this month. Summer's annuals have died and shriveled, composting into the ground to help nourish next year's seeds. The first dusting of snow, probably later this month, is patiently awaited.

October finds us heading up high to watch the maples and dogwoods turn red in Bear Wallow in the Santa Catalina Mountains. We also head south to the Tumacacori Mountains to the Wild Chile Reserve to see the wild chiles ripen and watch the many birds that come in to eat them. And if the fall is wet, in an El Niño year when we get wave after wave of unseasonable October rain from the southwest, we hurry out to Aguirre Lake to witness the wonder of waterfowl in the desert grasslands of the Buenos Aires National Wildlife Refuge.

OCTOBER WEATHER

	Sunrise	Sunset	Avg. Relative Humidity/Tucson
October 1	*6:18 MST*	*6:10 MST*	*5 a.m. 53%*
October 30	*6:39 MST*	*5:36 MST*	*5 p.m. 25%*

Stations	Ajo	Tucson	Mt. Lemmon
Station Elevation	*(1,800 ft.)*	*(2,584 ft.)*	*(8,800 ft.)*
October Averages			
Max. temperature	*87.1°F*	*84.1°F*	*64.2°F*
Min. temperature	*61.2°F*	*56.5°F*	*35.9°F*
Precipitation	*.55 in.*	*.79 in.*	*1.92 in.*
Snow	*0 in.*	*0 in.*	*2.93 in.*
# days 100° & over	*1*	*0*	*0*
# days 32° & under	*0*	*0*	*9*
# days precip.>.01"	*2*	*3*	*3*
October Extremes			
Max. temperature	*107°F (1980)*	*101°F (1955)*	*76°F (1982)*
Min. temperature	*32°F (1971)*	*26°F (1971)*	*20°F (1959)*
Max. snow/month	*0 in.*	*0 in.*	*20.0 in. (1961)*
Max. snow/1 day	*0 in.*	*0 in.*	*15.0 in. (1961)*
Max. precip./month	*3.41 in. (1941)*	*4.98 in. (1983)*	*9.65 in. (1983)*
Max. precip./1 day	*1.89 in. (1940)*	*2.96 in. (1983)*	*5.10 in. (1983)*

October Notes

The beginning of the month remains dry and warm, even hot, with at least eight or nine days over 90°F. Over twenty days will be clear, and the chance for rain is slight, though usually we will see about three days of rain. On occasion, tropical storms or weather anomalies will produce deluges of unseasonable rain; in 1983 torrential rains and flooding displaced 10,000 people, killed 13, destroyed crops, bridges, and roads. It will freeze and snow in the high mountains this month, but we probably won't see a freeze in the deserts. By the end of the month the days will be noticeably cooler and shorter.

For information about data sources for these listings, see the Climate section of the chapter Exploring the Nature of Pima County and Southern Arizona.

FLORA

Bounty of the Wild

It was warm as we carefully picked our way around the boulders and thornshrubs that choke the small canyons of the Tumacacori Mountains foothills, about 50 miles south of Tucson. Emory oaks jockey for space with mesquite trees around the canyon rims, and prickly pear cactus grow next to clumps of bear grass—a classic convergent vegetation zone of desertscrub, grassland, and oak woodland, between 3,600 and 4,500 feet in elevation.

Sweat wetted our shirts, and our jackets, necessary in the early morning but now tied around our waists, caught in the prickly plants. We were with Gary Paul Nabhan, world-renowned ethnobotanist and founder of Tucson's Native Seeds/SEARCH, looking for the now-rare wild chile plants, known as *chiltepínes* in Spanish. After poking around for a few minutes, we found a large, rangey plant tucked under the protective shoulder of a granite boulder. Its small heart-shaped leaves were crackly dry, but there were dozens of dark red, pea-sized berries sitting erect atop thin stems.

Nabhan and Native Seeds worked with Coronado National Forest officials to establish the first *in situ,* or on-sight, botanical reserve for wild crop relatives in the United States. This area of the Tumacacori Mountains, just west of the Spanish mission of Tumacacori, nurtures the northernmost populations of the chiltepine (*Capsicum annuum* var. *aviculare*), the genetic grandmother of nearly all cultivated chile pepper plants, from bell peppers to jalapeños. Also found here are wild squash, cotton, beans, a relative of manioc, agaves, walnuts, ground tomatoes, and grapes. Fall, when most of these plants go to seed, is a good time to find and appreciate wild crop relatives (see Places to Visit section). It is important to preserve wild crop relatives in their native communities rather than in herbariums' seed vaults because, as Nabhan explained, "You can't just preserve the plant—you have to protect all the species in the ecosystem. Each has unique characteristics because of its interactions" with other plants, as well as birds, insects and mammals (see September's Fauna section for more on bird-chile relationships). Wild crop relatives are naturally resistant to diseases and pests as well.

Above, *chiltepine leaves and fruit*

Nabhan explained that genetic material from wild Arizona canyon grape plants was used to boost the sickly, disease-prone cultivated grape orchards of France. Similar genetic engineering using wild cotton plants might also produce more disease-resistant commercial cotton plants that would need fewer pesticides to produce usable cotton. Chiles, of course, as a crop are worth millions of dollars to southwestern agrarian economies, so preserving wild chiles in the wild has never been so important to the success of a crop plant. But wild chiles are especially endangered now because of over-harvesting of wild populations in Mexico. Spice agents pay a lot of money for the fiery little chiles, which are marketed all over the world. Land clearing for cattle grazing is also harming wild chile plant populations.

Native Seeds/SEARCH research scientists are working with the Forest Service to develop a plan for managing the 6,000-acre reserve.

Color the World Red

If you're out walking in areas with a lot of prickly pear cactus, especially suburban neighborhoods where they are often planted as ornamentals, and you see groups of them spattered with a white spitwad-like substance, it isn't the work of bored juveniles. It is the waxy protective coating of an insect called the cochineal (Dactylopius confusus), *a member of the scale insect family, which is small and flat and which sucks the plant's juices through a long beak.*

*If you carefully scratch away the white waxy coating, you may find a quarter-inch red bug, the female (males are not sedentary, having wings with which to fly about looking for the stationary females). The red pigment—*cochineal *is Spanish for scarlet-colored—is a chemical called anthraquinone that protects the insect from most predators. Usually cochineal colonies don't kill the host cactus.*

When Cortéz conquered the Aztecs, he also usurped their well-organized textile industry. The prize of the lot was the scarlet fabrics, colored with a dye made from the dried bodies of an insect the Aztecs called nochezli, *the cochineal. Cortéz sent bags of the dried insects back to Europe, where they became highly prized for their brilliant dye. Michelangelo used it in his paintings, and Hungarian Hussars and Turkish noblemen wore breeches and fezzes dyed with it. When American colonialists cried, "The redcoats are coming!" they could thank the cochineal. And Betsy Ross reportedly used fabric dyed with cochineal to sew our first flag.*

Today cochineal is produced commercially for fabric dye in Oaxaca, Mexico, and in Algeria and the Canary Islands.

FAUNA

Elusive Felines

Bobcats (even this one at the Arizona–Sonora Desert Museum) rest during the heat of the day

Our dog was raised in the city with cats as companions; his experiences with wildlife were limited to backyard birds, so we expected some adjustments after moving to a house in a remote desert canyon. We got an idea of how much he had to learn just a few days after settling in. We were in the living room early one morning and heard him in the bedroom, making the same friendly cooing noises he made at the neighborhood cats in town. We went in to find him standing on the bed, looking out the window, and wagging his tail at a large bobcat that was glaring at him from a rock ledge about 5 feet away. As we watched, the dog seemed to realize that something was different about this kitty, and his tail slowly wagged to a halt. His coo faded away and a low, *uh-oh* sort of growl replaced it, as the bobcat casually loped up the hill and away.

The bobcat was a lucky sighting, but the two mountain lions we saw a few weeks later barely a hundred yards from the house made us feel really fortunate. Although neither species is endangered, both are very secretive, and most of us spend a lifetime hiking through the territory where they live and hunt without catching a glimpse of one.

With the notable exception of African lions, cats are solitary creatures except when breeding. This plus their tendency toward nocturnal activity adds to the difficulty of spotting them—few people realize, for example, that bobcats (*Felis rufus*) are actually fairly common in canyon desertscrub communities and often live close to human habitation. Occasionally, however, they display boldness, such as the mother bobcat that strolled nonchalantly across a neighbor's back porch in broad daylight, with two kittens bouncing along behind her.

Bobcats' looks can be deceiving. They appear quite large, and indeed can range to about 3 feet long—but their weight seldom exceeds 20 pounds. Long legs add to the impression of size. Stand a desert bobcat next to a cousin from the north woods and it appears lean as a greyhound—a typical contrast among species that inhabitat both hot and cold climates.

Bobcats hunt within a home range of about a 2-mile radius, from a den in a rock crevice or under a boulder or fallen log. Their prey consists almost exclusively of small mammals, about half rabbits, the rest mice and wood rats. Sometimes birds, reptiles, and carrion augment the diet.

Most litters are produced in spring; however, reproduction has been documented in every month of the year. The average litter size is two to three.

A much bigger cat, and more difficult to see, is the mountain lion (*Felis concolor*), males of which might weigh 150 pounds, although the average is about 125. Mountain lions—also called pumas or cougars—frequent rugged, mountainous terrain and need fairly large home ranges, since their chief prey consists of deer. Unlike that of many other predators, the lion's reputation as a stock killer is sometimes deserved—when deer populations are low or cattle are allowed to calve in remote areas, a lion will happily dine on domestic beef. Harley Shaw, a research biologist for the Arizona Game and Fish Department and author of *Soul Among Lions,* believes that keeping calves out of lion country until they are near their adult weight would minimize such losses.

Mountain lions can breed at any time of the year, which presents a problem for a solitary animal—without a regular breeding season, such as deer and coyotes have, male lions have no way of knowing when a female has come into heat. It is thought the females signal their readiness by urinating on top of male scratch marks and, possibly, by calling, though neither theory has been confirmed.

After a three-month gestation period, two to five kittens are born. These kittens will stay with their mother for up to two years—well into adulthood—before dispersing to find their own territories. Such an extensive development is helpful for learning to take down large prey. Sometimes after splitting off from their mother the young will hunt together for a while, but eventually they make their solitary way in the world.

If the bobcat and mountain lion are elusive, another southern

Arizona cat is nearly a ghost. The magnificent jaguar (*Felis onca*) was probably never common this far north, but because of unrelenting eradication efforts over the past 100 years north and south of the border, we are now lucky if one verified sighting is recorded in a decade. It is possible the few animals that make it to southern Arizona are immature males on far-flung searches for new territory; these animals might have traveled hundreds of miles from the thorn forests of central Mexico, where a small population of jaguars still exists.

An Ashamed Insect

At the beginning of time, according to the Southwest's Cochiti people, Pinacate Beetle was given the important task of placing all the stars in their proper places in the sky. But he became careless and dropped his burden of stars, spilling them across the sky like milk. This is how the Milky Way came to be, and this is why Pinacate Beetle always hides his face in the dirt when anyone approaches—he's too ashamed to face them.

*This is a good month to find the shiny black Pinacate beetles (*Eleodes *spp.), crossing roads and trails, with their rear ends raised up higher than the front like roadsters. Sure enough, when you approach, they stop and stick their heads down and hind ends even higher up. But the scientific reason is not that they're ashamed. Pinacate beetles, of which there are many species, all black and about an inch or so long, have glands on the tips of their abdomens that emit a nasty smelling and tasting substance. Most birds and mammals steer clear of Pinacate beetles, except grasshopper mice, which have learned to grab the beetles and stuff their offending ends down into the dirt while they eat them from the head back. Look around and you'll find the half-eaten beetle bodies.*

Pinacate beetles feed on decaying plant material and are found throughout the desertscrub. They are active most of the year, day and night, although in winter they prefer warmer days.

Bird Clans

One early fall day, on a leisurely hike up the pine- and oak-lined Green Mountain Trail in the Santa Catalinas, we noticed a flurry of movement up a side drainage. Two

Arizona gray squirrels were moving around with apparent purpose on a 50-foot-tall, long-dead pine snag. We knew this to be a well-used acorn woodpecker "granary," a tree in which the birds drill holes into which they stuff acorns to last them through the winter. The woodpeckers defend their granaries fiercely, so we sat back with our binoculars to watch the upcoming fight we knew the squirrels would provoke.

But the woodpeckers who were in charge of granary defense seemed to have taken the day off. The squirrels were intent on both stealing as many acorns as possible and trying to compete with each other. Eventually one squirrel ran the other off, and the winner continued to fill his cheeks with nuts. Finally, about 15 minutes later, two acorn woodpeckers showed up and, calling their ratchety alarm call, attempted to dive-bomb the offending squirrel. The squirrel was tenacious, but after one apparent direct-hit from a diving woodpecker, the squirrel, cheeks full, scampered down the tree and ran off.

Acorn woodpeckers are unusual among birds in that they form complex social societies, or clans. There are typically about 15 or 16 clan members and they all cooperate to raise the young of one nest. But unlike Harris' hawks, which practice cooperative breeding but almost always have only 1 breeding male and female, acorn woodpecker clans might include 4 or so breeding males, several breeding females, and support staff of up to 10 nonbreeding offspring from previous broods. In scientific terms, an acorn woodpecker clan could be monogamous (1 breeding male and female), polygynous (1 breeding male and 2 females), polyandrous (1 breeding female and multiple males), or polygynandrous (multiple breeding males and females). But regardless of the number of breeding individuals, one nest, usually in a tree cavity, is provided for at a time, and a feeding territory and food warehouse, a granary, are also maintained and defended.

The granary is the mainstay of the clan; without a well-stocked food warehouse to last the winter or beyond a bad crop year, which is not uncommon among oaks and piñons, the clan would not fare well. So the ultimate size and reproductive success of the group depends on the birds that maintain an adequate granary, which is usually located in a dead tree or in thick bark of a live tree. In the fall, the woodpeckers gather acorns and piñon nuts directly from the trees and fill as many granary holes as they can; the nuts are kept dry and fresh for up to a year, and usually rodents and other birds, lacking the specialized woodpecker bill, cannot pry them out. Granaries have been found containing as many as 50,000 acorns, but a couple of thousand is typical. We have a 10x3-inch piece of oak with 25 3/8-inch holes drilled in it, several still filled with acorns.

The granary will support the entire clan throughout the lean months of winter in the high country, when other animals must hibernate or move downslope to find food. In early spring the adult acorn woodpeckers can get a head start on rearing young by continuing to use their food stores; nestlings are fed a more protein-rich diet of insects. If a granary or nut crop is inadequate to support the clan, pairs have been known to strike off on their own to look for new territories and start new clans.

One issue that might come up regarding reproductive success of a bird clan is inbreeding. Acorn woodpeckers within a clan are related but only males-to-males and females-to-females. Thus male offspring never become breeders in a clan where their mother, sisters, or aunts are breeders—to breed, they must join other clans, as would young females.

Another communally breeding bird species common to southern Arizona, and in similar oak woodland territory as the acorn woodpecker, is the gray-breasted jay (scrub jays are known to breed communally but only in Florida). Noisy and conspicuous, a gray-breasted jay clan comprises 8 to 18 individuals. Slightly less harmonious than acorn woodpecker clans, a gray-breasted jay clan may have 2 or 3 breeding pairs nesting separately but simultaneously each season, creating some conflict, mainly in the form of nest-material robbing but occasionally a competing female will destroy the eggs of a rival nest. The nesting females are fed by their monogamous mates and by helpers, as are the nestlings.

The "why do they do it" question posed by cooperative breeding and bird clans continues to elude biologists. Originally thought to be based on kin selection (reproductive success based on genetic ties), it is now thought that environmental constraints—shortage of new territories or reliable food—may force birds into breeding groups because opportunities for younger birds to breed successfully are limited, particularly in the arid Southwest where gray-breasted jays and acorn woodpeckers are found. Similar cooperative bird clans in arid and semiarid regions of Africa and Australia support the environmental theory.

Sticky Abodes

Early one spring we watched a cactus wren pair build a nest in a cholla cactus for a spring brood. Pretty soon the female was holed up incubating eggs inside the snug, football-sized pouch nest. The male, however, kept busy building another nest in a nearby palo verde tree—wrens often build second nests just for roosting. But this bird went right on building nests—three, four, then five! He was quite the real estate tycoon.

Cactus wrens, Arizona's state bird, are the largest of the nine North American wrens, about 7" to 9" long. This month, you may see more nest-building activity, as they get ready for the winter with cozy feather-lined roosting nests. Usually cactus wrens—as their name suggests—build their nests in the spiny branches of cholla cactus, or, rarely, in spiny shrubs or trees. The reason became clear to us one spring when we helped a researcher survey nests: trying to reach through the branches and navigate a light and mirror for counting eggs, we came away with more wounds than data.

Anders and Anne Anderson spent nearly 38 years, off and on, studying the behavior of cactus wren pairs around Tucson. They determined that cactus wrens are very resident: once a breeding-roosting territory is established, on average about 10 acres, they pretty much stick to it unless food sources change or a more desirable territory becomes available. Pairs will tolerate juveniles, usually their own fledged broods, in their territories. Each wren enters its own roosting nest each night, so one group's territory may have many nests. More mature birds generally pick the better-quality nests, leaving the run-down real estate for the immature birds. Curve-billed thrashers can be pesky—they often destroy wren nests, so in areas where both live, the wrens are kept busy all year building and repairing nests.

Late October and November is the "dormant" period for cactus wrens, a short vacation before breeding begins again in December.

PLACES TO VISIT IN OCTOBER

Waterfowl Wonder

Good things come to those who wait, says the axiom. For those of us who prefer to see wild ducks, geese, herons, and other water birds in wild settings rather than on sewage ponds or golf course water hazards, if we wait patiently some Octobers will produce inches of unseasonable rain and fill the great Aguirre Lake on the Buenos Aires National Wildlife Refuge.

When this happens we bundle up in warm clothes (unseasonable rain can also mean lower temperatures) and head down Sasabe Road (Highway 286) to the refuge headquarters 45 miles south of Robles Junction at Ajo Way, southwest of Tucson. The 100-acre lake was carved out of desert grassland in the 1880s by Pedro Aguirre, when he owned the vast Buenos Aires Ranch. Aguirre attracted scores of waterfowl to this lake and also scores of duck hunters; he also used the lake to water his stock and grain fields. Wind courses across the grasslands, tousling the hair, making noses run, and carrying aloft the bugling calls of waterfowl; it is cold, but it feels like *fall.*

In good years, when the lake is full, we have seen pied-billed grebes, great blue herons, snowy egrets, green herons, green-winged and cinnamon teals, mallards, gadwalls, American wigeons, American avocets, killdeer, least and western sandpipers, and Wilson's phalaropes. There are about 130 smaller ponds on the 116,000-acre refuge as well. Call ahead to check on water levels and hours before heading down. (See Appendix 6 for phone number.)

Last of the Red-Hot Chiles

October is the month of the harvest—many plants are putting out seeds in the form of nuts and berries, including oaks (acorns), canyon grape, ground cherries, wild cotton, beans, walnuts, hackberries, and wild chiles. One of the best places to see southern Arizona's wild bounty is in the Tumacacori Mountains, 50 miles south of Tucson, across from the Spanish mission of the same name (see Flora section, above). It is best to park on the west side of the freeway about a quarter of a mile up the road and walk, unless you have a sturdy four-wheel-drive.

Once you're up in the oak woodland country, about 3 miles, stay on the established paths; if you happen upon a chile plant, don't pick any fruit—these rare plants need all the reproductive chances we can give them. If you want to sample chiltepines, you can buy them from Native Seeds/SEARCH or grow your own from the seeds they sell.

Serendipitously, the headquarters for the Santa Cruz Chile & Spice Company, which grows chiles and herbs along the Santa Cruz River, is in Tumacacori, across from the old mission (follow the highway signs to the Tumacacori National Monument from Interstate 19 south of Tucson). In the visitor center and gift shop, look for an interpretive sign that explains the purpose of the wild crop research and the reserve. In the shop, you can buy commercial chile powder, salsas, other chile products, and gifts.

Leaf Shows

Where can you find good fall color near Tucson this month? Try Bear Wallow in the Santa Catalina Mountains, at milepost 22.2. Down in the draw, you'll see the beautiful red of bigtooth maple and red-osier dogwood. On the hillsides, look for golden aspens, Gambel oak, and box elders. Higher up the mountain you'll find more aspens turning, especially along the road between Sykes Knob and Loma Linda, and on the road past Ski Valley. Here you'll also see Rocky Mountain maple. Take a picnic lunch and a jacket, and savor the season. Good hiking trails include the Butterfly Trail, Green Mountain Trail, and Aspen Loop Trail. If you want to hit fall color at its peak, keep an eye on the newspaper. The *Arizona Daily Star* usually runs a "fall colors alert" box, which is updated daily so you won't miss the show.

Slip Slide and Away

One of the best fall and winter hikes is the steep but quick ascent of Wasson Peak, the high point of the Tucson Mountains. From its top you can scan a large portion of Pima County: the great Baboquivari Peak standing watch over the vast grasslands and desertscrub of the west and south; the Sierrita and Santa Rita mountains rising to the south and east; the blue hummock of the Rincon Mountains directly east; and the raggedy tops of the Santa Catalina Mountains to the north and east.

But consider this: 70 million years ago, Wasson Peak was situated 20 miles to the northeast—on top *of the Santa Catalinas.*

The Tucson Mountains formed more than 70 million years ago when a great volcano erupted—perhaps 1,000 times more explosive than Mount St. Helens—where the Catalinas stand today. The eruption subsided over time into a caldera, like a soufflé collapsing when it cools. Over the next 40 million years, the huge granite mass of the Catalinas rose beneath the caldera until, between 30 and 17 million years ago, the entire volcanic complex slowly slid off *the mountain, spilling and stretching southwestward for 20 miles to its present location. Eventually the land between the two ranges subsided, forming the Tucson basin.*

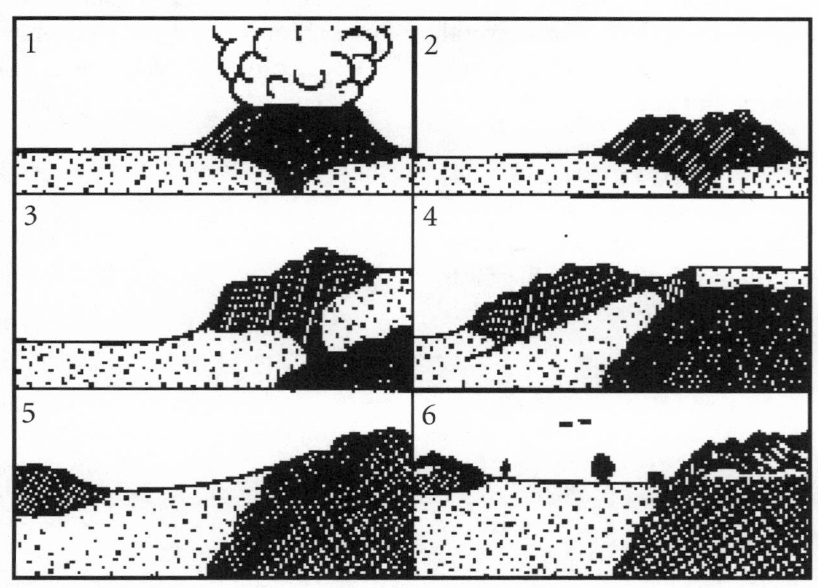

OCTOBER SKIES

"Harvest Moon"

TRADITIONAL O'ODHAM NAME FOR OCTOBER

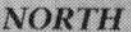

Star Chart for 32°N
Mid-month, 9 pm

FEATURE CONSTELLATION

Four bright stars form the constellation Pegasus, the Winged Horse. Perseus, the slayer of Medusa, rode Pegasus. The northeast corner star of the constellation is called Alpheratz, or "the horse's navel." Near each of the southern corner stars and also between them are three mysterious "quasars," or "quasi-stellar radio sources." Astronomers believe they are not single stars but intense sources of radio energy that may be billions of light-years distant—created when the universe was very young, indeed.

OCTOBER AT A GLANCE

Desertscrub

❧ Desert broom (*Baccharis sarothroides*) blooms this month; this oft-disparaged colonizer shrub is a favorite of hundreds of butterflies, bees, wasps, beetles, and flies, all of which partake of its sweet, tiny white blooms. Look especially for great purple hairstreak and snout butterflies.

❧ Prickly pear (*Opuntia* spp.) and barrel cactuses (*Ferocactus* spp.) continue to fruit this month.

❧ In desertscrub and grasslands, snakeweed (*Gutierrezia sarathrae*) and turpentine bush (*Ericameria laricifolia*) flower golden yellow.

❧ Along watercourses, soapberry trees (*Sapindus saponaria*) may set their knobby fruits (they produce suds when swished in water).

❧ Gulf fritillary butterflies have a fall hatch later this month.

❧ Sage thrashers return to winter in the lower deserts, especially in the west.

❧ Cactus wrens may begin to build winter roosting nests in cholla cactus.

❧ The most common hummingbird will be the hardy and adaptable Anna's.

❧ White-throated woodrats, or packrats, gather prickly pear and other fruits, which they stash away in their large, messy middens. Other rodents, like pocket mice, may begin hibernation this month.

❧ Snakes slow down as the temperatures drop, though warm days will still find them out looking for that last meal before hibernation.

❧ Rosy boas, however, live in the warmer west deserts and will give birth this month and next.

Desert Grasslands

❧ Most of the grasses have set their seeds atop panicles that wave and sparkle in the low fall light; Lehman's lovegrass (an alien) is common, but look for natives like Arizona cottontop (*Trichachne californica*), cane beardgrass (*Andropogon barbinodis*), and the gramas (*Bouteloua spp.*).

❧ Barrel and prickly pear cactuses still produce fruit.

❧ Variegated fritillary butterflies may be out this month in grasslands.

❧ Winter's hawks arrive this month: female harrier hawks precede their mates into the grasslands, joining rough-legged hawks and ferruginous hawks; kestrels become more numerous, and merlins and prairie falcons migrate into our area from northern summer grounds.

❧ Ravens may band together into noisy flocks, *quorking* loudly as they cruise for food in open areas.

❧ Horse lubbers (*Taeniopoda eques*) are the very large (2-4") grasshoppers seen squashed all over roads this month (they have yellow and orange stripes, green-veined wings with pink hindwings).

Oak Woodlands

❧ Trees such as walnuts (*Juglans major*), sycamores (*Platanus wrightii*), cottonwoods (*Populus* spp.), and alders (*Alnus* spp.) may begin to turn golden and copper in higher elevations later in the month.

❧ American painted lady butterflies have a fall hatch late this month.

❧ Many birds move down to this elevation to wait out the cold winter above. These include ruby-crowned kinglets, orange-crowned warblers, yellow-rumped warblers, gray-breasted jays, white-breasted nuthatches, and solitary vireos.

❧ Williamson's and red-naped sapsuckers, Lewis' and acorn woodpeckers are arriving, especially along riparian corridors.

❧ White-tailed deer range down from the highlands looking for water and escaping the cold.

Pine-Oak Woodlands

❧ Deciduous trees such as Gambel's oak (*Quercus gambelii*), alders, boxelders (*Acer negundo*), walnuts, and cottonwoods will drop their leaves this month, following freezing temperatures.

❧ Black bears are gorging on nuts and fruits and other foods to put on fat for winter hibernation.

❧ Abert's squirrels begin to build their pine-bough nests high in ponderosa pine trees throughout the woodlands and higher forests.

Coniferous Forests

❧ Trees such as golden aspens (*Populus tremuloides aurea*) and maples (*Acer* spp.), as well as shrubs like red-osier dogwood (*Cornus stolonifera*), will begin to turn gold and red later this month.

❧ Most other shrubs and trees will drop their leaves after the first freeze this month.

❧ Band-tailed pigeons may be seen in large flocks throughout the mountains.
❧ Dark-eyed juncos return from the north for the winter.

Special Events

❧ Watch for announcements of the Tucson Botanical Garden's annual Chile Fiesta, usually held the third weekend—it's a lively event of fiery delights.
❧ Fall colors begin in the mountains; check the *Arizona Daily Star*'s "fall colors alert" each day for an updated listing of good spots.

In the Sky

❧ The Orionid Meteor Shower appears around October 19–22.
❧ Look for the constellation Pegasus, four stars in the east.

See the chapter Exploring the Nature of Pima County and Southern Arizona for definitions and descriptions of communities.

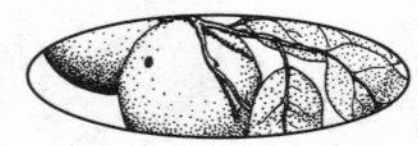

november

CLOUDS OF FLUFFY *desert broom seeds swirl in gentle breezes. Light the color of melted butter pours over rolling fields of lovegrass and cottontops that are setting their seeds. Red-tailed hawks sketch circles in the sky as they ride air pockets warmed by the balmy sun.*

November is soft. The hot edges of October are gone, and the sharp cold of January and February is still a distant threat. The Tohono O'odham people call this Kehg S-hehpijig Mashath, *the "moon of the fair-cold." We may see a little snow in the mountains, a little rain in the lower deserts, and possibly a freeze, too.*

Just as spring begins in the lowlands and creeps up the mountainside, so does fall take its time working its way down to the desert. Freezing temperatures have already visited the mountain habitats, signaling deciduous plants to shed their leaves and focus on surviving the winter. In the lowlands, signature desert trees such as mesquite are still fully leafed. But if a hard freeze comes to the desertscrub and grasslands, which happens infrequently, mesquites and catclaw acacias may begin to drop their leaves in a quiet desert version of fall. Look for industrious leaf-cutter ants, of which there are two species in the Sonoran Desert, carting off the bounty into their nearby burrows where they will compost the leaves in order to eat the nutrient-rich

A walk along Bear Creek in Sabino Canyon is a lovely Thanksgiving outing

mold. The trees will continue to shed until they are mostly bare, usually by February, but in mild years you may still see trees with the majority of their leaves.

In desert riparian areas, such as Sabino and Madera canyons, deciduous trees will already be turning color because colder, denser air drains into the lower channels of the waterways at night, bringing freezing temperatures sooner to these areas than to the surrounding deserts. These trees may include velvet ash, walnut, netleaf hackberry, Arizona sycamore, and Frémont cottonwood.

But even if it does freeze, daytime temperatures in the lowlands will hover in the 70°s and often the 80°s, making for great outdoor exploration weather. As kids we would bundle up in bulky coats and scarves and mittens to play in our mesquite treehouses in the mornings; by afternoon layers of our clothing lay scattered like fallen leaves, and we'd be hot and sweaty.

It rarely rains in November—just a few days if at all. Warm rain from the southwest means that El Niño is acting up. This phenomenon occurs when warm Pacific Ocean currents off South America move farther north than normal, sending a tropical storm up into our region. We may also see the edges of an early winter storm sliding in from the Pacific Northwest and Alaska, bringing snow to the mountains and on very rare occasions to the deserts.

In November, the animals are finishing up vertical migrations—following fair weather down the mountains—or preparing their winter burrows. Small groups of mule deer move down into the desertscrub and grasslands; the groups usually comprise all females, while the males continue their solitary roaming in the foothills, anticipating the rut. Most of the reptiles and very small rodents are entering their winter hibernation, mostly underground in burrows, although arboreal lizards find winter homes under the peely bark of mesquite trees. Some desert-dwelling mammals such as kangaroo rats, packrats, kit foxes, and coyotes will remain active throughout the cold season. In the warmest parts of the desert, out near Organ Pipe Cactus National Monument for example, Merriam's kangaroo rats will sometimes produce a winter brood.

NOVEMBER WEATHER

	Sunrise	Sunset	Avg. Relative Humidity/Tucson
November 1	*6:41 MST*	*5:35 MST*	*5 a.m. 54%*
November 30	*7:06 MST*	*5:19 MST*	*5 p.m. 28%*

Stations	Ajo	Tucson	Mt. Lemmon
Station Elevation	(1,800 ft.)	(2,584 ft.)	(8,800 ft.)
November Averages			
Max. temperature	74.3°F	72.5°F	59.3°F
Min. temperature	49.7°F	45.2°F	30.0°F
Precipitation	.63 in.	.59 in.	1.39 in.
Snow	.02 in.	.19 in.	6.54 in.
# days 100° & over	0	0	0
# days 32° & under	0	1	19
# days precip.>.01"	2	3	2
November Extremes			
Max. temperature	95°f (1915)	89°f (1980)	71°f (1962)
Min. temperature	30°f (1919)	24°f (1958)	4°f (1958)
Max. snow/month	1.0 in. (1964)	6.4 in. (1958)	22.0 in. (1958)
Max. snow/1 day	1.0 in. (1964)	6.4 in. (1958)	22.0 in. (1958)
Max. precip./month	3.51 in. (1923)	1.90 in. (1952)	2.77 in. (1981)
Max. precip./1 day	1.81 in. (1965)	1.57 in. (1968)	2.70 in. (1981)

November Notes

November is a time of moderations in weather for the deserts and grasslands; daytime temperatures are usually balmy, around 70°, and for a few days it might drop to below freezing at night, but on average only one or two times. Rain is only a slight possibility for all elevations, averaging a day or so with a trace. November is notorious in Arizona's drought history; not a trace of rain was recorded anywhere in the state for November in 1894 and 1903 (with 57 stations reporting). But in 1958, 6.4 inches of snow fell in Tucson, pretty much paralyzing the desert town; sadly, three Boy Scouts died after becoming stranded in the Santa Rita Mountains south of Tucson. This month, the mountains will see about half a foot of snow and nearly two-thirds of the nights will dip to freezing or below.

For information about data sources for these listings, see the Climate section of the chapter Exploring the Nature of Pima County and Southern Arizona.

In the oak woodlands, white-tailed deer, which live their whole lives in home ranges of a few square miles, are still separated by sex—the females congregate in small groups; males are off by themselves gaining strength for the exhausting rut season of December and January. The mountaintops seem quieter; summer migrants are long gone, and residents like acorn woodpeckers and Abert's squirrels are busy tucking away food for the coming winter.

In November, we like to head to the southwestern grasslands, where the soft, low light of impending winter softens the hard edges of the jagged mountain ranges that line the plains. There is something wonderful about basking in the sun for the first time in six months, rather than hiding from its intensity. Later in the month, we may enjoy a first dusting of snow up in the mountains and spend a day looking for mammal tracks. Thanksgiving usually finds us boulder-hopping along one of the gently trickling creeks in Sabino Canyon. ❧ ❧ ❧

FLORA

Desert Snow

It was a sunny day in mid-November, and we were driving through a neighborhood on Tucson's northeast side. Emerald fairways smooth as felt twisted artfully through token swaths of desertscrub habitat; bloated saguaros stood next to well-watered putting greens. The desert that remained seemed as carefully tended as the grass—the mesquites were trimmed into elegant shapes and even the cholla looked suspiciously symmetrical. While "environmentally sensitive," this community was obviously intent on keeping Nature in its place.

The neighborhood seemed to have as many landscapers as residents, and as we drove slowly along, a flatbed Chevy pulled out in front of us from a golf course service road. The guys had been clearing out the latest crop of the fast-growing curse of desert developments: desert broom. A succession plant, desert broom thrives in disturbed ground and pops up everywhere land has been under the blade of bulldozers. The landscapers had done their job well—the truck bed was piled high with broom.

They had made just one mistake: timing. For as we followed behind them, our car was engulfed in a swirling snowstorm of fluffy white desert broom seeds, blown off the cut plants by the bushel.

THE LAST CONQUISTADOR

A new conqueror is invading the Sonoran Desert, silently, without much notice, and with terrible consequences. A species of nonnative range grass called buffel (Cenchrus ciliaris) *is spreading north from Mexico, where cattle ranchers are bulldozing huge tracts of Sonoran Desert and replanting with this prolific grass to feed their cattle, which in turn feed American and Mexican consumers. Some Arizona ranchers are considering planting buffel. The problem with buffel is that it alters the natural ecosystem by creating a drastically reduced biological diversity. Native plant species, and in turn the native insects, birds, and mammals that rely on them, are replaced by this voracious plant. Initially scientists believed buffel would not spread very far north of the border because the climate is too cool; it has since been found in Tucson. As yet there is no way to control its spread. Experts fear that the face of the Sonoran Desert could be altered forever.*

Drifts of it piled on our hood and swept off in our wake, twisting in a graceful twin vortex and settling on the freshly graded sides of the road—a perfect desert broom nursery.

Because of its affinity for urban surroundings, many people think desert broom (*Baccharis sarothroides*) must be an introduced species like that other famous "western" plant, the tumbleweed (which is properly called Russian thistle and was not brought to the United States until the nineteenth century). But desert broom is indeed a native, adapted to swiftly colonize disturbed ground, whether of natural origin, such as landslides and floods, or artificial, like roadsides and vacant lots. Plants that have evolved to fill this niche are known as succession plants because they are eventually displaced by more permanent but slower-growing residents.

The broom's windborne seeds are ideal for colonizing new territory. Of course, only a tiny fraction find themselves in their preferred habitat, but those that do grow quickly, their deep roots helping to stabilize the disturbed ground against erosion. Although it grows to well over head-height, desert broom only lives about 20 years—just about the time it takes for permanent resident shrubs and trees to establish themselves and begin to erase the raw look of the disturbed plot.

The stems of desert broom contain chlorophyll and can carry on photosynthesis, so the plant doesn't need large leaves that waste water and take time to grow. The broom can be dormant during a drought, yet immediately take advantage of rains—or golf course

Wasp Galls

Some look like tiny gourds, an inch across at most. Others resemble minuscule balls of pink cotton candy. A couple could be mistaken for undersized sea anemones, and one giant is nothing more than an amorphous blob of misshapen plant tissue—a tennis-ball-sized carbuncle weighing down the stem on which it has formed.

They are oak galls, numbering over 500 distinct varieties in the United States, and at least a couple hundred in Arizona. They are formed entirely from the mutated cells of the host oak tree, but the spark of their creation comes from an insect.

A tiny cynipid wasp, no larger than the nib of a ballpoint pen, lays her egg in newly forming tissue on an oak tree. Compounds secreted by the larva induce the tree to form the gall, which then provides protection and food for the developing larva until it emerges as a fully formed adult. Each of the wasp species that prey on oak trees produces a unique gall and only on a specific part of one kind of tree; the galls don't harm the tree, and they dry up and disintegrate after the young emerge. Galls may be found on many other plants; each is produced by a specific insect that only lays its eggs on a specific plant.

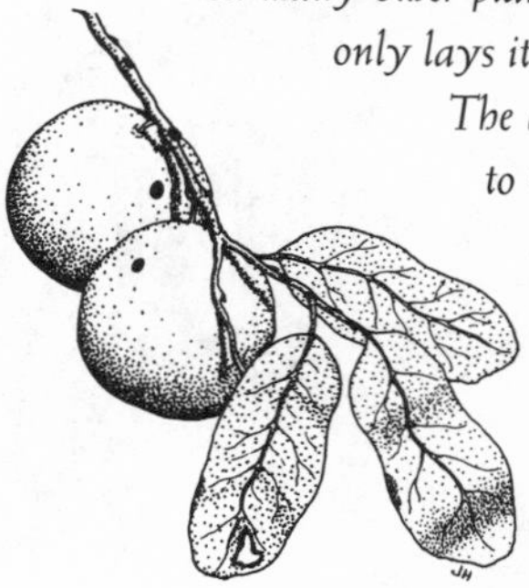

The diversity of gall forms is probably a response to the eternal arms race waged between predator and prey. One type of gall exudes a sticky sweet substance that attracts ants, whose presence helps deter egg robbers. The fuzz on the cotton candy gall may confuse the antennae of wasp-egg parasites seeking the proper spot to insert their eggs.

There are about 100 named species of oak gall wasps in Arizona, but there might be at least that many more not yet described. The best time to look for oak galls in Arizona is in the fall and winter, since most cynipids lay their eggs in summer. Look especially at new leaves and stems. A close examination might reveal a tiny hole where the adult wasp has already emerged or where a parasite has entered.

sprinklers—to produce new growth or flowers.

FAUNA

Where Have All the Reptiles Gone?

As temperatures begin to drop, the chances of seeing snakes and large lizards decrease, but small lizards are still evident. This discrepancy seems contrary to logic—shouldn't the little ones be more susceptible to cold? The answer is yes, they are generally more susceptible, but they also warm up more quickly. Their small body mass absorbs enough heat on a tepid day to get them out and moving. The larger reptiles need a higher average ambient temperature to keep their metabolisms up in the operating range. Once they cool off, they tend to stay cooled off.

In early November, before any "cold snaps" have hit, you can still see snakes out during the day. Come a week of 50° nights, and the snakes head for burrows and rock crevices, and sink into torpor. Unless an exceptionally long warm spell occurs, they are likely to stay there for the remainder of the winter.

Common wisdom says you don't need to watch for rattlesnakes during the winter months. Statistically, this is true, but given a long enough warm spell, you never know. We've seen rattlesnakes out in every month of the year.

Small lizards also head for cover when it gets cool, even if it's only under a rock or a piece of bark on a tree. But one warm day can penetrate their shelter with enough heat to arouse them, and out they pop. You'll see tree lizards basking on limbs and walls in town, side-blotched lizards on rocks in the desert, and lesser earless lizards in the grasslands.

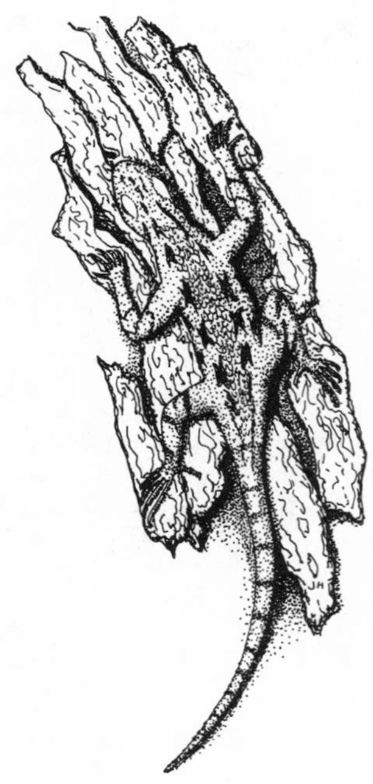

Above, *a tree lizard blends in on a mesquite tree trunk*

Other Hibernators

True hibernation is defined as a long-term period of dormancy and greatly reduced metabolism. The body temperature of a hibernating animal will drop far below normal; its respiration and pulse rate will slow dramatically as well. Many years ago we raised a round-tailed ground squirrel that had been rescued from a cat when only days old. He grew up tame as a dog and would follow us around the house and beg for treats at the refrigerator. His cage was in the unheated kitchen, and one November morning when we opened the top the squirrel didn't respond. When we picked him up from his shaved-cedar nest we were horrified to find him cold and curled up, stiff as a little board. We were heartbroken and sat on the couch holding him and wondering how he had died so suddenly, when he stirred slightly. The warmth from our hands had roused him, and he gradually came around, although very grumpy at having his hibernation so rudely disturbed.

Even though temperatures in the low desert rarely drop below freezing, a few small mammals hibernate. These include silky pocket mice and rock pocket mice, and several species of bats, such as the California myotis, spotted bat, and pallid bat. Round-tailed ground squirrels hibernate but sometimes emerge during warm spells. And rock squirrels spend the cold months in their dens.

Most other low-desert mammals remain active all year. Kangaroo rats, packrats, harvest mice, deer mice, and grasshopper mice all brave the cold season, as do the larger mammals such as kit foxes, badgers, skunks, and coyotes. In the higher country, black bears den for the winter, but they don't truly hibernate. The metabolism of a denning black bear remains close to normal, and it can easily be awakened—a good point to remember.

Grassland Raptors

Driving down Highway 286 through the Buenos Aires National

Right, kestrel at the Arizona–Sonora Desert Museum

Wildlife Refuge, you'll see many mourning doves on the telephone wires, sitting at about a 45-degree angle from vertical. If you see a bird about the size of a dove, but sitting very erect, take a look through your binoculars. A miniaturized falcon shape, rusty back, and two black stripes down a white face will identify a kestrel *(Falco sparverius)*, our smallest falcon and a common resident of open country. The 11-inch-long kestrel feeds on insects, reptiles, birds, and any mammal small enough to subdue with its 4-ounce mass: mice and sometimes bats (kestrels used to be called sparrow hawks, a double misnomer since they are not hawks and do not often prey on sparrows).

The kestrel's hunting pattern is distinctive. It flies with very rapid wingbeats, then hovers over a spot if it spies possible prey, swooping down to pounce if something shows itself or flushes. It will also dive directly from a perch if it sees food. Kestrels, though they like open grassland, can become quite urbanized. One spring an enterprising female set up a hunting station on a light pole opposite the University of Arizona football stadium, in which lives a sizeable colony of Mexican free-tailed bats. Each sunset, when thousands of bats emerged from several crevasses *en masse* to forage for the night, the kestrel would dive straight through the densest part of the cloud, apparently connecting more through statistical probability than skill. The bird would carry its prize back to the light pole and happily munch away.

Buteo

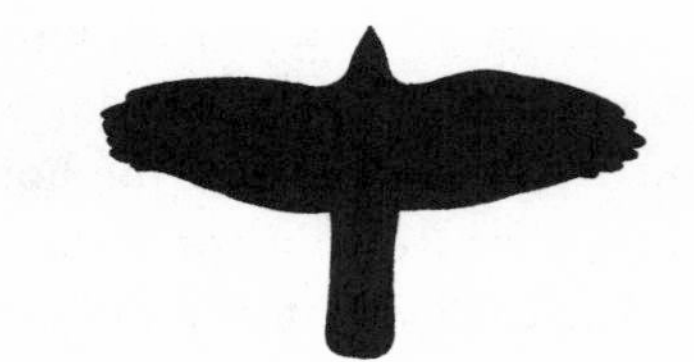

Accipiter

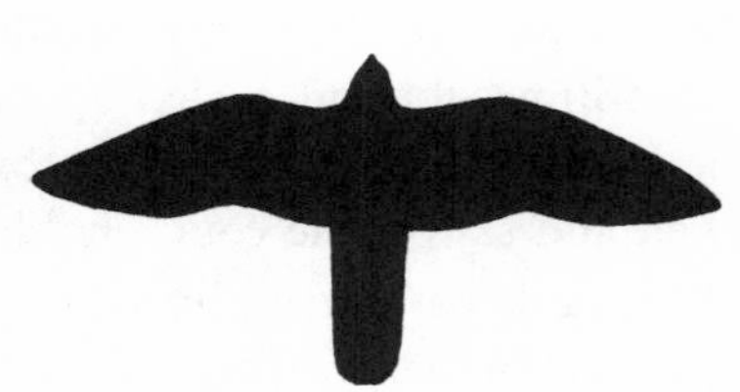

Falcon

Driving down the back roads of the Buenos Aires National

Wildlife Refuge or other grassland habitats in the winter, you might see a lovely raptor flying and gliding slowly along only ten or twenty feet above the ground, looking like a stealth jet-fighter. Look for wings held in a noticeable V, called a dihedral, to identify a northern harrier *(Circus cyaneus)*. Females of this species have rufous breasts and dark backs, but the males are a beautiful gray on the back, with black wing tips and light breasts. Both sexes have a white rump and, if you can get close enough to see, a barn owl–like facial disk. It is thought that—as with the barn owl—this disk might help funnel faint sound waves to the bird's ears.

Harriers use their low-flying technique to flush prey into the open where they can drop on it. Prey can include mice, lizards and small snakes, and large insects like grasshoppers. Arthur Bent, who published exhaustive research on raptors in the 1930s, reported harriers hovering in front of prairie fires, scooping up luckless fleeing rodents.

Much higher in the sky over the grassland, you might see the familiar shape of a soaring buteo—a genus of hawks with broad, blunt-tipped wings and short tails held in a fan shape as they fly. The most common is the red-tailed hawk *(Buteo jamaicensis)*, its rich chestnut upper tail flashing in the sun as the bird circles, wings rarely flapping, on thermals of warm air rising from the ground (keep in mind that immature red-tails are all buffy and brown streaked, with a dark brown bar on the leading wing edge, and no red tail band).

Possibly the most stirring sight over the grasslands is the rapier silhouette of a long-winged falcon—either a prairie falcon *(Falco mexicanus)* or the rarer peregrine *(Falco peregrinus)*. The long, slim wings of these birds allow fast flight and 100-mph dives on fleeing prey.

The eyesight of the hawk family (and raptors in general) is thought to be the keenest of any species on earth. Imagine being able to read the classified ads from 50 feet away; this will give some sense of the vision of a hawk that can spot a mouse from 1,000 feet up. The eyes of the hawk don't *magnify* the object; it is simply sharper. The microscopic photosensitive cells in the back of the eye (the retina) of both man and hawk are of two types. The rods are light gatherers—they are responsible for low-light vision. The cones control visual acuity and color perception in bright light. The density and ratio of these cells in the *area centralis*, the region of the retina where central images are directed, determines the quality and sensitivity of vision. Humans have around 200,000 receptor cells per square millimeter; hawks up to 1 million. Our view of the world is a muddy dot-matrix image compared to the hawk's laser print.

PLACES TO VISIT IN NOVEMBER

Mustang Trail, Buenos Aires National Wildlife Refuge

This trail is a remnant of one forged by wild mustang horses nearly two centuries ago. Some people believe that the horses are descended from Spanish mustangs that once belonged to Father Eusebio Kino, a famous Jesuit explorer who founded many southwestern missions in the 1700s. The trail's namesakes are gone now, but you can easily imagine them galloping across the rocky hills.

The Mustang Trail is on the southeast portion of the 116,000-acre Buenos Aires National Wildlife Refuge near the town of Arivaca in south-central Pima County. It begins in the thick mesquite bosque and cottonwood groves of Arivaca Creek and winds up-country for about 2 miles to the top of El Cerro ("The Hill"). Along the creek, which may be dry if there has not been fall rain, look for brilliant red male vermilion flycatchers and elegant black phoebes. If you're out early you might be lucky and spot a troop of raccoon-like coatimundis.

Once you climb out of the large trees you'll enter desertscrub and grassland—rocky slopes covered with grasses, ocotillos, prickly pear cactuses, sotol, shrubby mesquites, palo verdes, and creosote. You'll see sparrows—most common are the chittery, active white-crowned—and this is prime time to watch hawks. (See Fauna section, this month.)

From the top of El Cerro you can see to the northwest the huge obelisk of Baboquivari Peak, home of the legendary Tohono O'odham creator, I'itoi. To the east is Atascosa Peak and the Santa Rita Mountains.

Seven Falls Trail, Sabino Canyon

Every Thanksgiving we spend a few hours before dinner revving up our stomachs with a walk along Bear Creek. The trail begins at the end of the tram road for lower Bear Canyon. You can pay to take the tram to the trailhead from the Sabino Canyon Visitor Center parking lot or walk the extra couple of miles.

The Arizona sycamores, velvet ash, and a few remaining Frémont cottonwoods (many very old and large specimens were knocked out in huge floods that raged through the canyon in 1983 and 1993) are golden and copper, and leaves swirl in the amber-colored pools of the creek. The amber color is caused by minerals dissolved into the water as it makes its way through the rocky upper canyons of the Santa Catalina Mountains.

The hillsides around us are surprisingly noisy: cactus wrens and Gila woodpeckers keep up a general racket as they forage and defend territories. Verdins announce their presence vociferously as they hop through shrubs and trees in search of insects. The water trickles melodiously over the boulders that we hop as we move slowly upstream.

On our return, as the sun sets behind the low hills on the other side of lower Sabino Creek, flaring through the golden leaves of the deciduous trees, a chorus of coyotes almost always bids us a good night.

Green Mountain Trail, Santa Catalina Mountains

At least once in November a quick cold front will move in and drop a dusting of snow over the mountains, like powdered sugar over a pound cake. The Green Mountain Trail is a good place to walk beautiful upper Bear Canyon and examine fresh animal tracks. If the snow is heavy, consider taking snowshoes. The trail begins along the creek near the parking lot for General Hitchcock Campground off Catalina Highway, at milepost 12.

It winds upstream beside Bear Creek amid a lush pine-oak woodland, climbing for a couple of miles to a saddle and the headwaters of the creek. If you plan a car shuttle, the trail ends up climbing around Green Mountain another couple of miles to the San Pedro Vista parking lot on the highway.

After an early, light snow, a naturalist friend once followed mountain lion tracks from this area into the surrounding hills for a couple of miles. He never saw the cat, but was not sure he wasn't being watched as well.

NOVEMBER SKIES

"Moon of the Fair-Cold"

TRADITIONAL O'ODHAM NAME FOR NOVEMBER

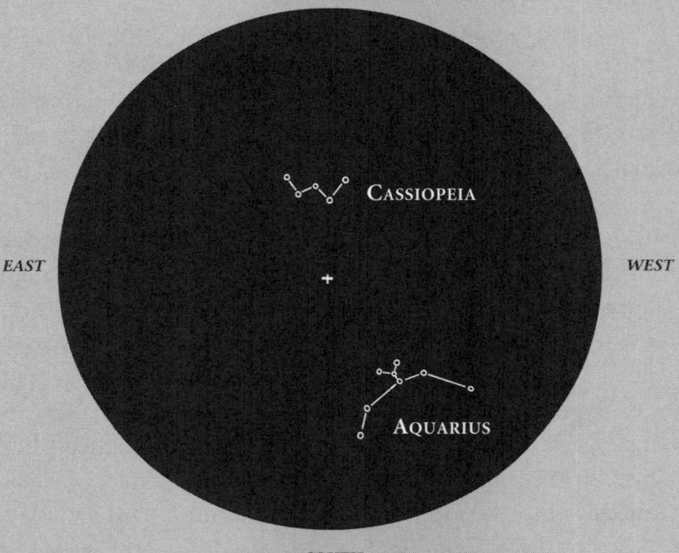

SOUTH

Star Chart for 32°N
Mid-month, 9 pm

FEATURE CONSTELLATION

You'll find Aquarius in a region of the sky called The Sea, the dwelling place of the ancient water-signs such as Capricornus, the sea goat; Delphinus, the dolphin; Pisces, the fishes; and Cetus, the sea monster. Aquarius is the water-carrier, hauling his huge urn across the night sky. He is best seen in early November. When Zeus became disgusted with the human race, he ordered Aquarius to empty his urn over the earth and drown the inhabitants. Pyrrha and Deucalion, son of the god Prometheus, were the only to survive, having been saved by riding out the deluge in a great chest, which came to rest on Mount Parnassus.

NOVEMBER AT A GLANCE

Desertscrub

❧ In riparian areas, the leaves of deciduous trees such as velvet ash (*Fraxinus velutina*), Frémont cottonwood (*Populus fremontii*), and Arizona sycamore (*Platanus wrightii*) will be turning golden and copper, and dropping. If a hard freeze hits, the leaves of desert trees may start dying and dropping.

❧ Desert broom (*Baccharis sarothroides*) are releasing clouds of snowy seeds.

❧ Branch-ends of mesquite trees in desertscrub and grasslands may brown up and die. Look for signs of the female mesquite twig girdler (*Oncideres rhodiosticta*), a small beetle that eats a deep channel through the bark, which cuts off the life-giving sap to the twig end. She then lays her eggs in the dead part (look for little slits), where they develop without getting drowned by sap.

❧ Reptiles in all communities will hibernate, although you may see smaller ones darting around after a couple of warm days.

❧ Large, dark gray mesquite buck moths (*Hemileuca juno*) are common fliers this month; the males may be seen in daytime, the females mostly at night.

❧ Some desert mammals, such as silky pocket mice and rock pocket mice, hibernate in burrows for the winter, though most small low-desert mammals remain active; look for signs of kangaroo rats, packrats, deer mice, and grasshopper mice.

❧ Larger mammals such as kit foxes, badgers, skunks, and coyotes remain active throughout the cold season.

❧ Male phainopeplas, beautiful black birds with elegant crests, arrive back from summering in the west or north; they perch conspicuously atop desert trees. The gray females follow soon.

❧ Anna's hummingbirds are conspicuous now, establishing their winter territories. They are the most common hummers at backyard feeders. You will also see and hear the squeaky songs of this ubiquitous bird up into the oak woodlands.

Desert Grasslands

❧ California myotis, spotted, and pallid bats will be returning to rock caves or crevasses to hibernate for the winter.

❧ Harriers are very common on the Buenos Aires National Wildlife Refuge, near Sasabe, as well as in Tucson's surrounding grasslands and fields.

❧ Flocks of white-crowned sparrows may be seen in grasslands and desertscrub.

Oak Woodlands

❧ Desert spoon *(Dasylirion wheeleri)* is dropping its seed from tall, delicate spikes.

❧ In canyon bottoms, Arizona walnut trees *(Juglans major)* may be dropping their fruit.

❧ Arizona sister butterflies have a fall hatch this month.

❧ Female white-tailed deer are congregating in small groups; males are off by themselves gaining strength for the exhausting rut season of December and January.

Pine-Oak Woodlands

❧ Abert's squirrels are building their stick nests high in the pine trees, padding them for the coming winter with warm grass.

Coniferous Forests

❧ The first dusting of snow may fall this month.

❧ Early in the month, small Terloot's white butterflies may be seen in the tops of pines.

In the Sky

❧ November is a good month for meteor showers: the Leonid peaks around the 14th, the Andromedid between the 17th and 27th, and the Orionid around the 19th.

❧ Constellation hunters will find Pegasus directly overhead, and Cassiopeia paints an "M" in the northern sky. Orion appears over the eastern horizon in the late evening. Early in the month, look for Aquarius pouring his great water urn about 20° southwest of Pegasus.

❧ The Pleiades, an open star cluster containing around 3,000 stars—only 7 of which are visible to the naked eye—is found northwest of Orion.

❧ On dark nights away from city lights the Andromeda Galaxy is visible as a faint patch of light almost directly overhead.

See the chapter Exploring the Nature of Pima County and Southern Arizona for definitions and descriptions of communities.

december

SUN AND RAIN. *Growth and decay. Hibernation and procreation. December is a time of contrast in southern Arizona.*

The first winter rains have come, bringing with them change. For some plants, cold and rain signal a time to drop expendable leaves and focus on root growth deep in the earth where the soil is still warm and newly moistened. For others, it means a time to burst forth with new leaves and take advantage of the abundant moisture to produce stored sugars for future growth. Some animals lie swaddled in the warm earth, deep in their winter sleeps, while others warm up with some hot-blooded courtship displays and territory marking. And throughout December's quietly schizophrenic biological activity, days of gentle sun alternate with days of cloudiness, cold, wind, and rain, as the year winds down to the winter solstice, the shortest day of the year. The Tohono O'odham call this month Eda Wa'ugath Mashath, *"moon of the backbone," when the year is divided in half by the sun.*

In the desertscrub in December, some of the desert legumes such as mesquites and acacias are commencing to shed their small leaves, which began to die in late November; now they are pelted to the ground by the cold rain. Higher in the foothills, many trees stand nearly bare, beautiful in their twisted, spreading forms. Elegant and bizarre ocotillos, spraying forth from the rocky desert floor like frozen

December weather is perfect for hiking in the front range of the Santa Catalina Mountains

spiked fountains in a surrealist painting, have been leafless throughout the months of drought. Throughout the winter in the higher desert elevations they will remain leafless, but in the west deserts a few days of rain, a few days of sunshine, and suddenly they are fuzzy with hundreds of small, bright green oval leaves. They will for a month or so take advantage of moist winter conditions to manufacture sugars; then, the leaves will wither and die. An ocotillo may go through this cycle many times a year.

Other plants that react as quickly to winter rains as shoppers to a close-out sale are brittlebush, which passed the previous months dust-covered and dead-looking, and creosote bush, the drought-time leaves of which may not look entirely dead, just brown and sickly. Both these plants will respond to rains this month with bursts of new, shiny-bright leaves, the brittlebush a blue-gray and the creosote a neon green, lending the wintertime desert a soothing, verdant cast. Nowhere as in the Sonoran Desert is there such variety in shades of green, so many as to be nameless: the nearly black mosses that spread like velvet frosting over north-facing hills, the blue succulence of desert prickly pear cactuses suggesting the color of the ocean over a white sandy bottom, or the neon leaves of the creosote as though sprayed from the same can of paint as the hottest new mountain bike.

Among the amazing array of greens displayed by the wintertime desert, you'll see a few bright surprises: the fire-engine-red fruit of the desert Christmas cactus, which can be found under sheltering trees such as palo verdes or mesquites, and the rich pink-red fruits of the desert mistletoe, seen in their canopies. The blossoms of the mistletoe, inconspicuous and pale green in color, have a glorious honey-apple fragrance that hangs in the air and catches your attention as you wander down a trail, because at first glance you will see no apparent source of such delight.

Many resident desert birds are revving up their reproductive hormones by establishing territories, anticipating mating in a month or so. The black-crested birds perched so conspicuously on the highest tree limbs or phone poles, so glossy they look wetted down and ready for a night on the town, are male phainopeplas. In December these insect-eating "silky flycatchers" build up their strength for the impending breeding season by gorging on ripe desert mistletoe or pyracantha fruits in urban areas. Curve-billed thrashers are also conspicuous now, not because of their striking plummage but for their intense, melodious territory songs, which continue into January. And male Anna's hummingbirds can be heard belting out their squeaky territory songs and seen swooping in daredevil dives as they seek out mates.

In the grasslands, wintering sparrows fill the rolling hills with their endearing song and dance: bursts of music, a flurry of flight, as a dozen or so of the drab little birds tumble across the landscape from bush to bush to bush in a never-ending bird waltz. Cassin's, chipping, vesper, savannah, sage, Brewer's, Lincoln's, and white-crowned sparrows all enliven the winter landscape in southern Arizona's grasslands. Later this month, mule deer will begin to rut, that violent-looking but seldom injurious combat in which males engage to win over females to their "harems" for mating.

Yellow-eyed juncos and black-chinned sparrows forage among the evergreen oaks, manzanitas, and grasses of the oak woodlands, where small canyon-bottom creeks burble happily after the rains visit. Shindagger yuccas that bloomed in the summer and fall are now brown, tilted over and dying, having given their all for one great burst of seed production on 6-foot-tall woody stalks, a strategy called semelparity (or sometimes "big bang" reproduction).

Up in the pine forests, the ground freezes almost every night, but during the day the mercury will climb into the low 50°s, high enough to partially melt each night's ice. The results in areas where the ground is very wet, in creek bottoms and near springs, are beautiful prismatic ice sculptures, sheets of ice comprising hundreds of multisided towers created by repetitive melting and re-freezing. Understories are bare, divested of their freeze-prone leaves—red-osier dogwood, raspberry, snowberry, New Mexican locust—and here and there are patches of crusty snow early in the month, and if enough Pacific moisture has passed our way by later in the month, as much as a foot of snow will

DECEMBER WEATHER

	Sunrise	Sunset	Avg. Relative Humidity/Tucson
December 1	7:07 MST	5:19 MST	5 a.m. 61%
December 30	7:24 MST	5:29 MST	5 p.m. 34%

Stations	Ajo	Tucson	Mt. Lemmon
Station Elevation	(1,800 ft.)	(2,584 ft.)	(8,800 ft.)
December Averages			
Max. temperature	66.1°F	65.2°F	52.2°F
Min. temperature	43.3°F	39.0°F	23.5°F
Precipitation	.84 in.	.91 in.	2.29 in.
Snow	.11 in.	.30 in.	15.20 in.
# days 100° & over	0	0	0
# days 32° & under	1	5	30
# days precip.>.01"	3	4	3
December Extremes			
Max. temperature	86°F (1958)	84°F (1954)	65°F (1958)
Min. temperature	22°F (1954)	16°F (1974)	4°F (1960)
Max. snow/month	3.0 in. (1960)	6.8 in. (1971)	65.0 in. (1961)
Max. snow/1 day	3.0 in. (1960)	6.8 in. (1971)	12.0 in. (1961)
Max. precip./month	3.94 in. (1965)	5.02 in. (1965)	10.01 in. (1961)
Max. precip./1 day	1.53 in. (1941)	1.22 in. (1967)	2.60 in. (1961)

December Notes

After several months of weather that turns the skin to jerky, we welcome gentle, penetrating rains, about four to five days' worth in normal years for the deserts, a little less for the mountains because moisture is falling as snow—about 15 inches for December. And although every night falls below freezing among the pines, among the desertscrub we'll endure about five nights of below-freezing temperatures. Occasionally strong winds whip things up in December; in 1947 a small tornado was sighted south of Phoenix, and in 1949 60-mph winds stirred up Tucson. Although July and August are on average our months of greatest rainfall, December can throw a wrench in the data. In 1965, the University of Arizona reported 7.27 inches for December (annual rainfall is 11.13 inches).

For information about data sources for these listings, see the Climate section of the chapter Exploring the Nature of Pima County and Southern Arizona.

carpet the earth beneath the evergreen ponderosa and white pines, Douglas and white firs. Cloud-colored forest accipiters, such as northern goshawks, streak through the winter landscape in search of squirrels or small birds.

In December we might head out to the far western deserts of Pima County to look for glimpses of the rare Sonoran pronghorn antelopes, which forage among the galleta and gama grasses, creosote and bursage bushes. During days of gentle rain, we don rain gear and walk the trails of the western Catalina Mountains foothills and canyons. And on those clear days when the sun warms the skin but the air burns the nose with cold, days when you can't possibly stay inside, we head to Saguaro National Park and breathe in the many colors of winter green for which there are no names and absorb the sweet songs of desert resident birds. ❧ ❧ ❧

FLORA

December Showers Bring March Flowers

In the desert, it's not only the amount of rain but the timing and nature of it that determines the crop of spring wildflowers.

The summer and winter rainy seasons often drop about the same amount of precipitation. But the summer thunderstorms are brief and violent, and much of the water runs off into washes and out of the area. The gentler and longer-duration fall-winter rains allow a higher percentage of water to soak into the ground. It is this moisture that spurs the germination and growth of dozens of species of annuals. If rains are generous from October through January, the result is a brilliant blanket of color over much of the desert floor come February and March. However, if rains cease or a long cold snap hits after these annuals have sprouted, the bloom may be curtailed.

In the 1950s, an ecologist attempted to replicate a Sonoran spring bloom using sprinklers and well water in place of winter rains. His results were intriguing: it took more than four times as much well water to even approach the fecundity generated by the real thing. Chemically the well and rain water were virtually identical, so some other force had to be at work:

either the actual physical impact of the falling rain triggered something in the seeds or some unfathomable variable made the difference. One is tempted to wonder whether desert annuals could have a sense of aesthetics regarding their water supply.

There are many spring-bloom snobs who will pooh-pooh any spring show that wasn't preceded by 10 inches of rain and a 70° January and February. Don't believe them. There are always wonderful wildflower displays around; sometimes they are just a bit harder to find. During "soft" years, ask around—wildflower lovers always share their finds—and watch the *Arizona Daily Star* for its "wildflower report" in March.

Cactus Watching

One of the wonderful things about a desert winter is the constancy of cactus. Other plants may drop leaves, dry up, die back, or die altogether, but the cactuses just *are*, standing stolidly through gray skies and chilly winds, seemingly unperturbed even under a rare cap of snow. Only a noticeable increase in girth after the rains betrays their reaction to the world around them.

The Sonoran Desert of postcards and westerns is defined by but a few of the larger and more photogenic cactuses. Although there are more than 100 species of Cactaceae in southern Arizona, the most common dozen or so are easy to learn.

Two species of columnar cactus in southern Arizona can be easy to confuse with similar species that occur in Mexico. Our saguaro (*Carnegiea gigantea*) looks a lot like the cardón (*Pachycereus pringlei*)—they are among the largest cactuses in the world (saguaros grow up to 50 feet tall, and cardóns as much as 70 feet), and they share a tall profile with upcurving arms. But the epidermis of the saguaro has more grooves, or "pleats," and its arms rarely branch out lower than 6 or 7 feet off the ground. The cardón's pleats are deeper and fewer, and it often branches nearly at ground level, giving the effect of numerous main trunks. The cardón does not occur north of the Arizona-Mexico border.

A similar distinction differentiates the organ pipe cactus and the senita. Both are medium-sized (10–20 feet tall) and multitrunked, resembling candelabras. But the organ pipe (*Stenocereus thurberi*) has the finer pleats, and the tops of the senita's (*Lophocereus schottii*) trunks are usually bearded with a fuzz of long, gray spines—thus its Spanish name, which means "old one." Organ pipe is

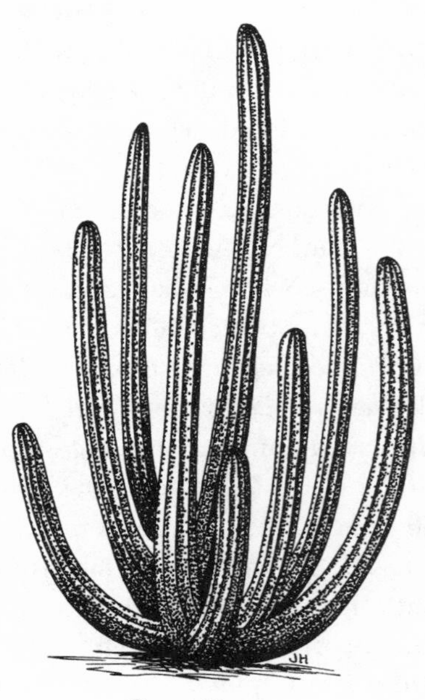

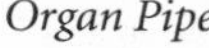

Organ Pipe

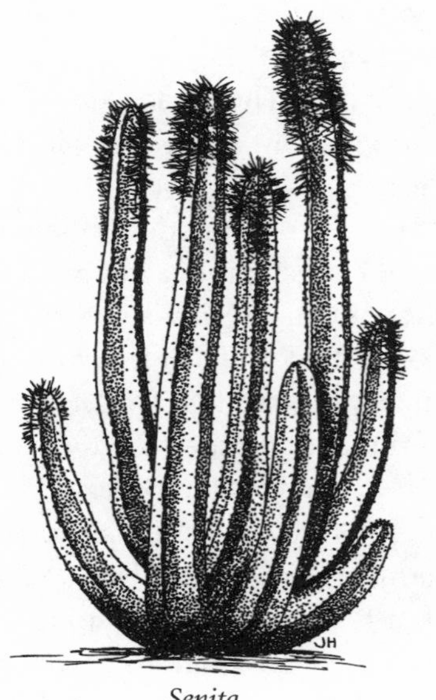

Senita

common in western Pima County, but only a few senitas grow north of the border, in Organ Pipe Cactus National Monument in southwestern Pima County.

If saguaros are the most famous, then chollas (pronounced *CHOY-ahs*) are certainly the most *infamous* of our cactuses. These are the ones that seem to launch their spiny sections through thin air to embed themselves excrutiatingly in one's shin, earning the species the nickname "jumping cactus." But cholla doesn't really jump; sections of several species are merely attached so lightly to the plant that they come loose at the slightest nudge. Though this experience is painful for the victim, it is great for the plant: dislodged sections fall to the ground and take root, producing new cactuses. The three most common species of cholla in Pima County are teddy bear, chainfruit (also called "jumping"), and staghorn. Most of the chollas bloom in late April and May.

The teddy bear (*Opuntia bigelovii*) looks like its namesake—from a distance. It appears to be covered in a perfectly huggable downy white fuzz; it is only from up close that the fuzz resolves into a wicked covering of spines, noticeably denser than other chollas. The trunk of the teddy bear is dark, often festooned with old, shriveled

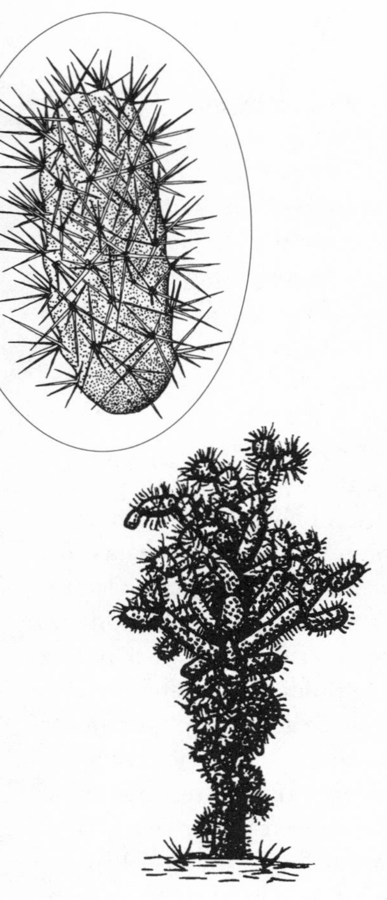

Teddy bear cholla

sections of stem. The teddy bear can grow to a height of about 7 feet (but usually is about 5 feet) and is most common on the lowest, dry deserts where it forms nearly impenetrable thickets. Packrats (white-throated wood rats) use the fallen chunks of teddy bear stems and other cactuses to armor their dens against marauding coyotes.

The chainfruit cholla (*Opuntia fulgida*) is taller (up to 12 feet, commonly 6 feet), and often multi-trunked. It is from the woody skeletons of these cactuses that lamps and other *objets de touriste* have been made. Not so luxuriously spined as the teddy bear, the chainfruit gets its name from the long strings of fruit—sometimes 15 or 20—that dangle from the plant, offering juicy browse to deer and javelina. These fruits are usually sterile, so when they finally fall or are knocked from the cactus, the entire fruit simply grows roots and forms a new plant.

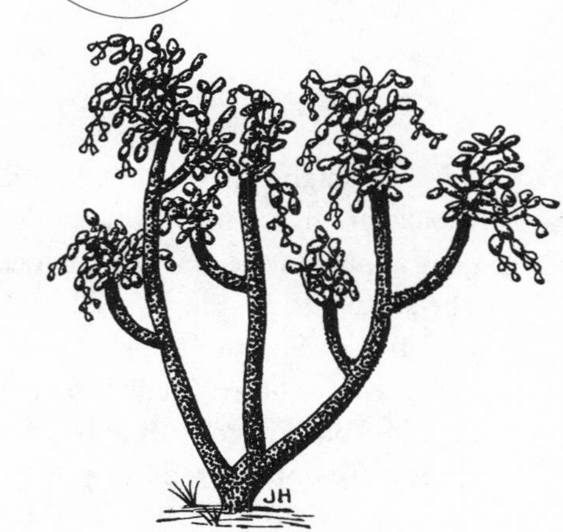

Chainfruit cholla

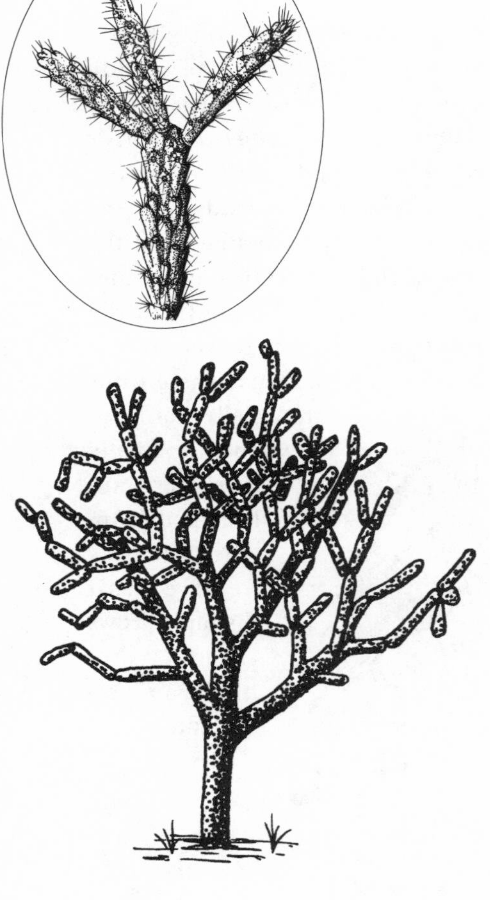

Staghorn cholla

The staghorn cholla (*Opuntia versicolor*) has a more spare, elegant appearance than its relatives. The segments are longer and don't detach as easily, and the spines are fewer and shorter. Staghorns are often purplish in color, and the late spring flowers can be anything from yellow to red; the fruits are yellow and sometimes form small chains of two or three. The plant grows to about 7 feet.

Prickly pear cactus are the low, sprawling cactuses with interconnected pear-shaped flat pads. Several species of prickly pear cactus are found in Pima County and are easy to differentiate.

Engelmann's prickly pear (*Opuntia engelmannii*) is our predominant species; it is found throughout the county in desertscrub. A pleasing light green in color, with teardrop-shaped flat pads and 1- to 2-inch-long spines, the desert prickly pear produces dozens of ruby fruits that persist well into fall if not eaten by animals or collected by humans to make jelly and candy (see August). The waxy spring flowers are yellow.

The beavertail prickly pear (*Opuntia basilaris*), so-called because of the shape of its pads, at first appears not to have spines. This is deceiving because the cactus is well-endowed with tiny barbs called glochids. A negligent brush against a beavertail will result in an hour-long session with magnifying glass and tweezers. Although the range of beavertail overlaps that of desert prickly pear, the former can tolerate drier conditions and extends into the low-elevation deserts near the Colorado River delta.

Often planted in urban yards because of its lovely purple tinge, the Santa Rita prickly pear (*O. violacea*) is indeed an indigenous cactus, but it is usually found in grasslands at higher elevations, from about 3,000 feet up to 4,500 feet. The Santa Rita is another "spineless" prickly pear. Its flowers are a bright yellow contrast to the pads.

MISTLETOES

*In winter when desert trees lose a good portion of their leaf canopies, basketball-sized clumps of desert mistletoe (*Phorandendron californicum*) are conspicuous. Do they kill the trees? is a commonly asked question. Not usually. Desert mistletoe, a nearly leafless variety with dark pink winter berries, parasitizes mesquites, palo verdes, and ironwoods (rarely, whitethorn and catclaw acacias); its stems contain chlorophyll and can photosynthesize but the plant depends on its host tree for water and minerals, which it obtains via root-like* haustoria *that bore into the branches. Mistletoe seeds, which are sticky, are carried to other trees on birds' feet or in their droppings. Common mistletoe (*P. flavescens*) has true leaves and white berries and can be seen on cottonwood, oak, and sycamore trees in desert riparian areas.*

Above, *phainopepla with a mistletoe berry*

FAUNA

Enjoying Winter Resident Birds

This month as you listen to birds in the desert, you'd be forgiven for thinking spring was just around the corner. Although we are approching the "dead of winter," many species are as active as ever in the lower elevations; some, in fact, will be courting mates late in the month. A good percentage of these birds are permanent residents, the loyalists that stick it out through both burning summers and semi-frigid winters. Whenever a touch of the winter solstice blues hit, a good antidote is to get out and watch the "natives" acting like there is no winter.

Walking through desertscrub habitat, you'll notice striking black birds that flash white wing patches as they fly from treetop to treetop, sporting a distinctive crest and calling with a low, questioning *Wurp?* These male phainopeplas will be gorging themselves on ripe mistletoe berries at this time of year—at other times they eat

COMMONLY SEEN RESIDENT BIRDS AND THEIR HABITATS*

	Desert	*Riparian*	*Oak and Pine Forests*
Red-tailed hawk	✔	✔	✔
Gambel's quail	✔	✔	
Mourning dove	✔	✔	
Greater roadrunner	✔	✔	
Anna's hummingbird	✔	✔	
Acorn woodpecker		✔	✔
Gila woodpecker	✔	✔	
Ladder-backed woodpecker	✔	✔	
Northern red-shafted flicker		✔	✔
Black phoebe		✔	
Gray-breasted jay			✔
Common raven	✔		
Bridled titmouse			✔
Verdin	✔		
Cactus wren	✔		
Black-tailed gnatcatcher	✔	✔	
Hermit thrush			✔
Northern mockingbird	✔		
Curve-billed thrasher	✔		
Phainopepla	✔	✔	
Northern cardinal	✔	✔	
Pyrrhuloxia	✔	✔	
House finch	✔	✔	
Black-throated sparrow	✔		
Yellow-eyed junco			✔

**Commonly seen resident=occurring permanently, year-round, and conspicuously; this list is very general and variations in habitat will occur season to season. Habitat listed for each bird is where it is found most conspicuously, not exclusively. Species are listed according to systematic order used in field guides. For a detailed description of habitats, see the chapter Exploring the Nature of Pima County and Southern Arizona.*

mostly insects. Females are less conspicuous and colored soft gray with darker gray wings, but crested as well.

Phainopeplas breed in the desert in early spring—from February through March—raising two or three young. Some, but not all, adults then migrate to cooler and damper areas in California, where they nest again and raise a second family. This habit gives these birds a double shot at a successful brood, in case weather or food conditions in one area prove insufficient in a given year.

Another common and active desert resident is the curve-billed thrasher, a robin-sized, dark gray bird with a pointed, curved bill and startling orange-red eyes. Its sharp *tweetWEET!* often emanates from clumps of cholla or ocotillo; its territory song is a rich mixture of warbles and trills and whistles (thrashers belong to the vocally talented mimic thrush family, as do mockingbirds). You might see the thrasher running swiftly on the ground from bush to bush, looking for the insects that share its plate with seeds and fruit.

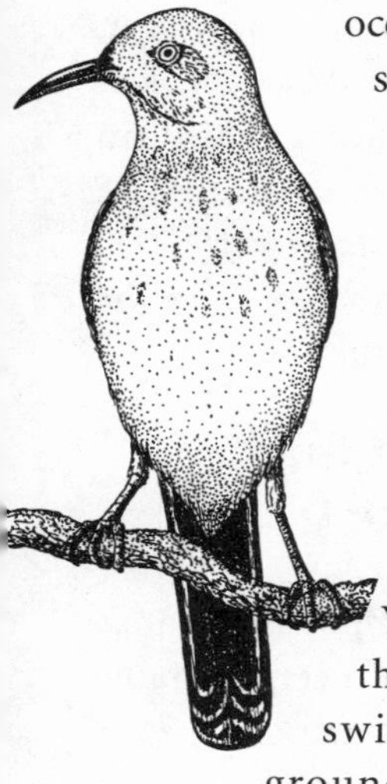

A curve-billed thrasher

One of the signature birds of the desert—in fact, it's the state bird of Arizona—is the cactus wren, the largest wren in the United States. About 8 inches in length, the cactus wren has a distinctive white stripe over each eye, a pale breast covered with lines of black dots, and a black chin. Its call is a metallic *Chrchrchrchrchr,* like a cold car engine turning over. Cactus wrens build covered nests deep within the spiny arms of chollas and are seemingly at peril of empalement every time they return home. Of course, their long legs enable them to land and hop among the spines with impunity. Not satisfied with one impregnable fortress, cactus wren pairs often build a couple of extra nests just for roosting. A cactus wren involved with foraging will often approach close to a quiet observer. They hop through low branches and along the ground, flipping over leaves and small rocks to search for invertebrate prey underneath.

People who leave their hummingbird feeders up through the winter will doubtless find them frequented by our only regular winter hummingbird, the Anna's (this makes hummer I.D. in December really easy). Male Anna's are feisty little buggers that aggressively defend their feeders and sing from

To Feed or Not to Feed?

Many people take down their hummingbird feeders in the fall, having heard that failing to do so would delay or even abort the hummers' migratory instincts, thus leading to the specter of little hummingbird popsicles littering the ground after the first freeze.

Those rumors, however, are untrue. Simply put, a little sugar water is not going to short-circuit thousands of years of evolution. Migratory cycles are shown to be triggered by many other stimuli such as day length and temperature—and backyard feeders constitute only a fraction of a hummingbird's diet.

Besides that fact, we have at least one species, the Anna's hummingbird, that now resides year-round in Pima County, although most field guides still list it as a summer migrant. Males can be heard belting out their squeaky territorial songs on positively frigid mornings and will energetically defend feeders kept full through the winter months.

nearby trees with a quirky, squeaky voice. Males have a gleaming ruby throat and head in sunlight; females are more drab but still show some ruby flecks on the throat. Anna's have only recently become permanent residents; many bird books only show them in southern Arizona in the summer. But they do breed here, and in late December will be looking for mates.

How does a bird weighing around one-tenth of an ounce live through near-freezing nights? It has been found that hummingbirds will sink into torpor and let their body temperatures drop far below normal when nighttime temperatures fall even into the 60°s. Slowing that ferocious metabolism can actually prevent a hummingbird from starving to death through the course of one frigid night. Females on eggs, however, cannot afford to let their temperature drop; they must maintain warmth for the brood. Fortunately, hummingbird nests are effective insulators that help to conserve the female's heat output.

White-Tailed and Mule Deer

December is an important month for both species of deer in southern Arizona, for it marks the start of the rut—when males begin rounding up females and defending their harems against rivals. This activity will peak in January.

The males' antlers have been growing since April (although the antlers are shed each year, they grow back larger the succeeding year). By early fall they are fully developed and the velvet—an arterially rich covering that supplies nutrients to the growing rack—dries up and is rubbed off by the animal. The antlers harden and are ready for battle by winter.

When male deer fight to establish dominance, it is rare for one to be hurt. In fact, scientists have determined that antlers have evolved so that injury to the opponent is avoided. The evolutionary wisdom of this is clear: if deer suddenly began growing antlers likely to injure or kill their opponent, the victor would gain much in the short term—but the species as a whole would suffer if half the male population was disabled or lost every mating season. So the fierce-looking jousting that one sees is very ritualized and serves only to establish dominance. The antlers are shaped so that permanent entanglement, which results in the death of both participants by exhaustion or starvation, is very uncommon as well.

When the rut is over and the deer have finished mating, usually in February, the antlers drop off and the males return to their solitary existence and will begin to grow antlers again in a couple of months. Meanwhile, gestation for the females is about 200 days; fawns are born in July and August.

Although their ranges and habitats overlap in southern Arizona, our two deer species tend to use discreet territories. In winter, particularly, mule deer prefer lower desertscrub. White-tails usually stay higher, in oak woodlands. But in spring mule deer will migrate up the hillsides into similar habitat.

Our white-tailed deer, *Odocoileus virginianus couesi,* are a subspecies of the eastern *O. virginianus.* Coues' deer, as they are called (pronunciation varies depending on which expert you ask; either "cooze" or "cows"), are much smaller than their eastern relatives: an average male will weigh only about 85 pounds, a female 65. They are active early in the morning, late in the evening, and on moonlit nights, browsing on leaves, twigs, and fruits of trees such as oak, mesquite, and acacia. During the day they bed down on hillsides (where they have a commanding overview of approaching trouble) or in thickly foliated drainages.

Mule deer are larger than white-tails—males weigh up to 200 pounds or so, females 100 to 130. Mule deer fawns are precocial at birth—they are fully furred, their eyes are open and they can follow their mothers in a few minutes. A distinctive trait of mule deer when alarmed is their habit of bouncing away with all four feet hitting the ground at the same time, called pogo-ing or, to use a really arcane mammalogy term, "stotting."

PLACES TO VISIT IN DECEMBER

Saguaro National Park

A morning walk along a desert wash in Saguaro National Park is a symphony for the eyes and ears. So many beautiful shades of green punctuated by bright flashes of reds. The woodwind sound of a breeze gently playing through the standing ribs of a long-dead saguaro, *clickety-clack, clickety-clack, clack, clack.* The melancholy, questioning *Wurp? Wurp?* of a phainopepla interrogating from a treetop. The harsh, confident *BrEEp! BrEEp! BrEEp!* of a passing Gila woodpecker. A distracted *Buzz-buzz-buzz* coming from the depths of a mesquite tree, the foraging language of a black-tailed gnatcatcher. This is the refrain of the Sonoran Desert in winter.

The Sus Picnic Area in the Tucson Mountains unit of Saguaro National Park is an excellent destination for wash-walking, for more strenuous hiking, and for picnic lunches. Running parallel to the picnic area road is a deep, wide wash with a sandy bottom. It drains the nearby foothills of the Tucson Mountains, although rare is the time water douses the earth with enough volume to fill up both the thirsty soil and the sandy washes. Its banks comprise a thicket of desert hackberry, wolfberry, catclaw, canyon ragweed, ironwood, bursage, mesquites, and foothill palo verde. Black-tailed gnatcatchers and verdins cruise for insects in the inner foliage, Gila woodpeckers and curve-billed thrashers roam their territories from tree to tree and saguaro to saguaro, and red-tailed hawks float in the sky above them all.

Just north up Who-ka-kam Road is the trailhead for the Hugh Norris Trail, which climbs 2,000 feet up to the summit of the Tucson Mountains, Wasson Peak. The 360° views around Pima County are worth the effort of the climb.

Catalina State Park

The wonderful thing about walking in the rain is the shifting of the senses. With hoods pulled up over our ears and the thrumming of droplets drowning out most sounds, hearing is dampened, as is our sight, blurred by the curtains of water. But smell is intensified, magnified in the conductive, wet air. Confidently, we know what *green* smells like: sharp, like pepper, so that the nostrils flare wide, but sweet, like honey, only not thick. So pungent is the smell of the wet desert that we can taste it in the back of our mouths. When we awake to the sound of gentle winter rain pittering on the roof, we pull on our rubber boots and head out to walk the canyon creeks of Catalina State Park, just 25 minutes north of town.

High in the western Santa Catalina Mountains, Samaniego Ridge and Pusch Ridge create a formidable-looking L-shaped wall that appears to enclose Catalina State Park. Cargodera and Romero canyons, and several other smaller, unnamed clefts, spill water into the park for most of the winter months, filling Sutherland and Cargodera washes with a foot or more of copper-colored water. You'll receive a simple hiking map when you pay the entry fee to the park. Head to the parking lot at the end of the road. From here you can take the Canyon Loop Trail, which crosses and re-crosses the creek many times and is the rationale for our rubber boots. This hike begins in low-desert riparian habitat among a bosque of mesquite trees, then progresses into a riparian canyon filled with junipers, oaks, and sycamores. The neat thing about this canyon is that although it nurtures a habitat that you might find at 5,000-foot elevation in the heart of a mountain, if you climb out of its steep banks you find that the surrounding terrain is still desertscrub and you're at 2,800 feet. Thirsty saguaros, mesquites, and palo verdes peer into the trickling oasis like poor kids standing at the playground fence where the rich kids frolic. It is one of those wonderful desert dichotomies we never take for granted.

Cabeza Prieta National Wildlife Refuge

The finest Sonoran Desert habitat in the United States is found in the more than 860,000 acres of this nearly 65-year-old refuge, which extends along the Mexican border west of Organ Pipe Cactus National Monument. Through its heart runs Devil's Highway, El Camino del Diablo, which for centuries served as a route for pioneers and prospectors traveling from the northern Mexico frontier to the lush valleys and gold fields

Tinajas *(waterholes) hold precious rainfall for drought periods*

of California. Many did not make it along this nearly waterless route, and their graves can be seen today as if their bodies were just interred. Today the road, heading across the desert from Ajo, is still a single dirt track and suitable only for four-wheel-drive vehicles. Since much of the refuge lies within the Barry M. Goldwater Air Force Gunnery Range, permission to enter must be gained and a waiver signed at the refuge headquarters in Ajo.

The refuge is home to more than 30 species of mammals—among them desert bighorn sheep and the endangered Sonoran pronghorn. Eighteen species of lizards and 18 species of snakes have been recorded, and the refuge's bird checklist comprises over 165 species.

El Camino del Diablo runs through pristine basin and range topography—miles of creosote flats rising to rich arboreal desertscrub and low, rocky mountain ranges. Scattered throughout the precipitous canyons of the ranges are waterholes, called tanks or *tinajas*, which hold precious rainfall long into the dry months. These sites are magnets for the larger mammals, and biologists frequent them to perform censuses and other studies.

DECEMBER SKIES

"Moon of the Backbone"

TRADITIONAL O'ODHAM NAME FOR DECEMBER

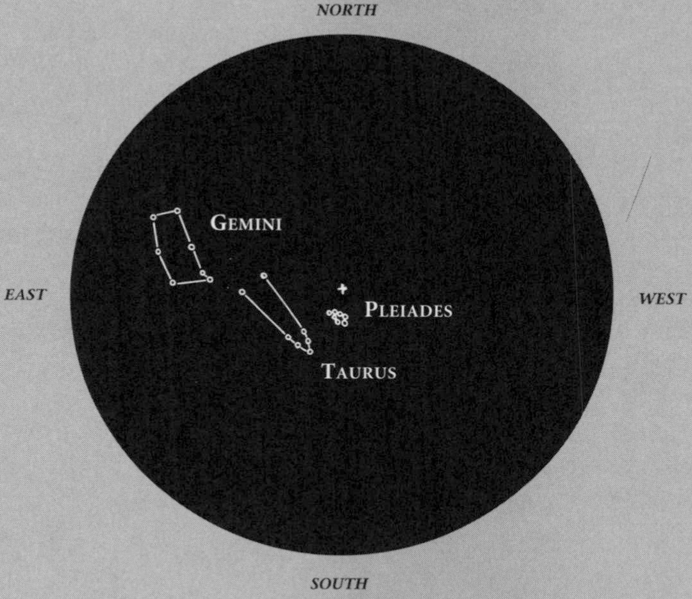

Star Chart for 32°N
Mid-month, 9 pm

FEATURE CONSTELLATION

Taurus, the bull, is an infamous mythological creature. When the great philanderer-god Zeus wanted to come down to earth to abduct human maidens, he often took the form of Taurus. The abduction of Europa, daughter of the king of Crete, is among his most famous exploits. Taurus faces Orion the Hunter in the sky, squaring off for a battle; you can see his fiery red eye, the star Aldebaran, flashing in anger.

DECEMBER AT A GLANCE

Desertscrub

❧ Mesquites (*Prosopis* spp.) and acacias (*Acacia* spp.) continue to drop their leaves.

❧ Ocotillos (*Fouquieria splendens*) will produce leaves as soon as five days after a decent rainfall in the lower, west deserts. Brittlebush (*Encelia farinosa*) and creosote (*Larrea tridentata*) will also grow a whole new wardrobe in the wetter climate.

❧ Among the canopies of mesquites, palo verdes (*Cercidium* spp.), and ironwoods, desert mistletoe (*Phorandendron californicum*) is bearing fruit, as are desert Christmas cactus (*Opuntia leptocaulis*) in the shady understories.

❧ Curve-billed thrashers and Anna's hummingbirds map out their territories with song.

❧ Glossy black phainopepla males seem to be everywhere in the desert.

Desert Grasslands

❧ Cassin's, chipping, vesper, savannah, sage, Brewer's, Lincoln's, and white-crowned sparrows add to the winter landscape.

❧ Later in the month, male mule deer begin their rut.

Oak Woodlands

❧ Tall seed stalks of some agaves, including those of shindaggers (*Agave schottii*), lie dead in the cool, damp grass or stand starkly above the dormant plants.

❧ Yellow-eyed juncos and black-chinned sparrows are among the most conspicuous birds in the evergreen oaks, manzanitas, and grasses of the oak woodlands.

❧ Small mixed-species foraging flocks of bridled titmice, verdins, and ruby-crowned kinglets are common, especially along riparian areas.

Pine-Oak Woodlands

❧ The pine-oak woodlands are quiet, as most of the conspicuous birds have moved down to lower and more temperate elevations to spend the winter.

❧ Creeks that may have been dry over the after-summer drought now are flowing.

Coniferous Forests

❧ Understories of red-osier dogwood (*Cornus stolonifera*), raspberry (*Rubus* spp.), snowberry (*Symphoricarpos* spp.), and New Mexican locust (*Robinia neomexicana*) are bare, divested of their freeze-prone leaves.

❧ Snow decorates the frozen ground in patches, or perhaps in a wet year as much as a foot already has fallen.

Special Events

❧ Annual Christmas Bird Counts, with the Audubon Society. Contact Tucson Audubon (see Appendix 6 for contact information).

In the Sky

❧ Winter solstice, December 21, is the shortest day of sunlight.

❧ The Geminid meteor shower will grace the skies around December 14.

❧ Taurus is visible high in the sky between the Pleiades and Orion. Gemini is east of Taurus.

❧ Sirius, the brightest star in the sky, is rising in the evening. Binoculars will bring out the red color of Betelgeuse, a red giant that forms the left shoulder of Orion the hunter. Compare to the blue-white of Sirius.

See the chapter Exploring the Nature of Pima County and Southern Arizona for definitions and descriptions of communities.

APPENDIXES

Southern Arizona Desert Plants Blooming Calendar

Common Birds of Southern Arizona

Mammals of Southern Arizona

Reptiles and Amphibians of Southern Arizona

Common Butterflies of Southern Arizona

Southern Arizona Nature Resources

Keeping a Field Bag and Notebook

Glossary

APPENDIX 1: SOUTHERN ARIZONA DESERT PLANTS BLOOMING CALENDAR

	JAN	FEB	MAR	APR	MAY	JUN	JUL	AUG	SEP	OCT	NOV	DEC
Pink to Red												
Beavertail cactus (*Opuntia basilaris*)			■	■	■							
Cholla, staghorn* (*Opuntia versicolor*)				■	■							
Cholla, chainfruit (*Opuntia fulgida*)						■	■	■				
Coral bean (*Erythrina flabelliformis*)					■	■						
Desert (rock) hibiscus (*Hibiscus denudatus*)			■	■	■	■	■	■	■	■		
Desert willow (*Chilopsis linearis*)				■	■	■						
Fairy duster (*Calliandra eriophylla*)			■	■						■	■	■
Fleabane (*Erigeron divergens*)		■	■	■	■	■	■	■	■	■		
Indian paintbrushes (*Castilleja spp.*)			■	■	■	■	■	■	■	■		
Ocotillo (*Fouquieria splendens*)				■	■							
Penstemon (*Penstemon parryi*)			■	■								
Senita cactus (*Lophocereus schottii*)					■	■						
Yellow												
Barrel cactus (*Ferocactus wislizenii*)							■	■	■			
Bladderpod (*Lesquerella gordonii*)		■	■	■								
Brittlebush (*Encelia farinosa*)			■	■	■							
Buffalo gourd (*Cucurbita foetidissima*)					■	■	■	■				
Creosote bush (*Larrea tridentata*)			■	■	■							
Desert dandelion (*Malacothrix glabrata*)			■	■								
Desert groundsel (*Senecio douglasi*)		■	■	■	■							

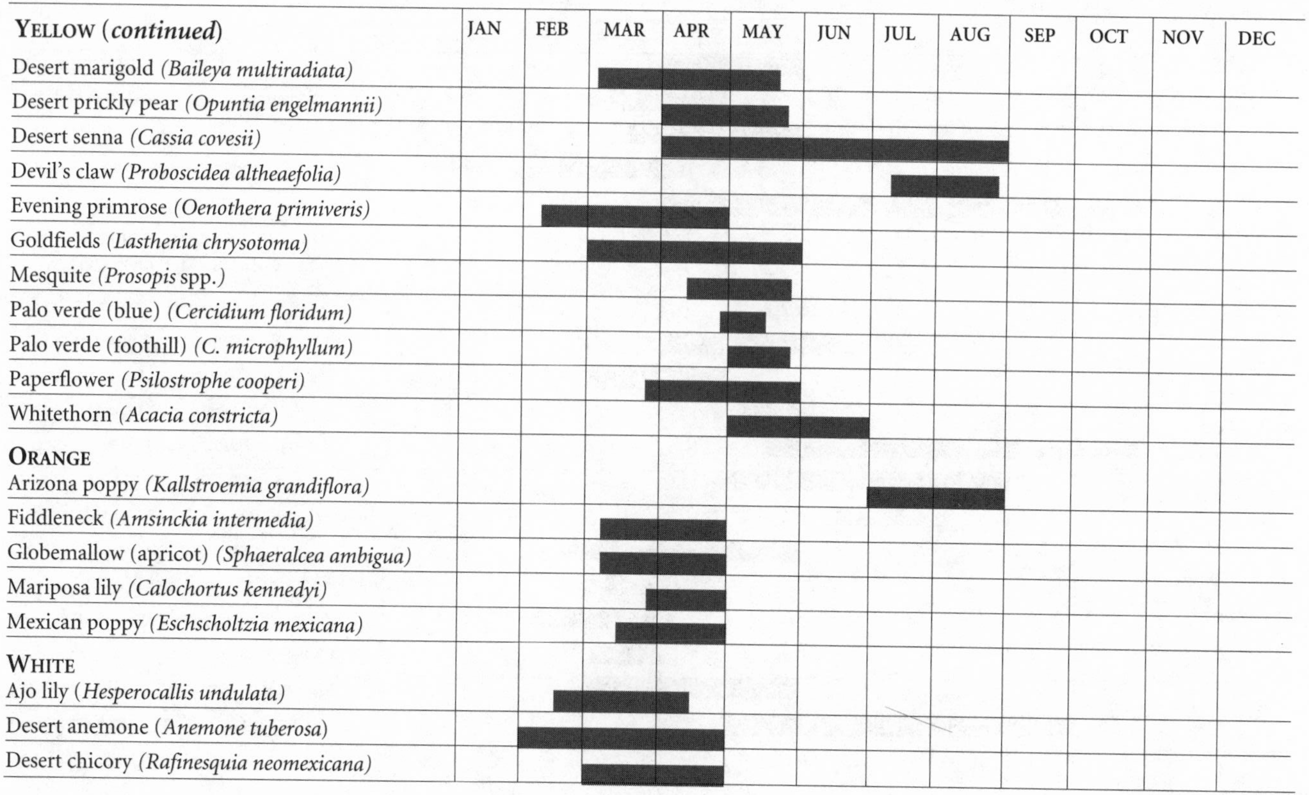

Yellow (*continued*)	JAN	FEB	MAR	APR	MAY	JUN	JUL	AUG	SEP	OCT	NOV	DEC
Desert marigold *(Baileya multiradiata)*												
Desert prickly pear *(Opuntia engelmannii)*												
Desert senna *(Cassia covesii)*												
Devil's claw *(Proboscidea altheaefolia)*												
Evening primrose *(Oenothera primiveris)*												
Goldfields *(Lasthenia chrysotoma)*												
Mesquite *(Prosopis* spp.*)*												
Palo verde (blue) *(Cercidium floridum)*												
Palo verde (foothill) *(C. microphyllum)*												
Paperflower *(Psilostrophe cooperi)*												
Whitethorn *(Acacia constricta)*												
Orange												
Arizona poppy *(Kallstroemia grandiflora)*												
Fiddleneck *(Amsinckia intermedia)*												
Globemallow (apricot) *(Sphaeralcea ambigua)*												
Mariposa lily *(Calochortus kennedyi)*												
Mexican poppy *(Eschscholtzia mexicana)*												
White												
Ajo lily *(Hesperocallis undulata)*												
Desert anemone *(Anemone tuberosa)*												
Desert chicory *(Rafinesquia neomexicana)*												

	JAN	FEB	MAR	APR	MAY	JUN	JUL	AUG	SEP	OCT	NOV	DEC
WHITE *(continued)*												
Desert cotton *(Gossypium thurberi)*					■	■	■	■	■			
Desert daisy *(Melampodium leucanthum)*			■	■	■							
Desert onion *(Allium macropetalum)*			■									
Desert mock-orange *(Crossosoma bigelovii)*		■	■									
Desert (dune) primrose *(Oenothera deltoides)*		■	■	■								
Desert star *(Monoptilon bellioides)*		■	■	■	■							
Night-blooming cereus *(Peniocereus greggii)*						■	■					
Organ pipe cactus *(Stenocereus thurberi)*					■	■	■	■				
Sacred datura *(Datura meteloides)*					■	■	■	■	■	■		
Saguaro *(Carnegeia gigantea)*					■	■						
Tackstem *(Calycoseris wrightii)*			■	■								
Yucca, banana *(Yucca baccata)*				■	■	■						
Yucca, soaptree *(Yucca elata)*					■	■						
BLUE TO VIOLET TO PURPLE												
Dichelostemma *(Dichelostemma pulchellum)*			■	■								
Desert aster (*Machaeranthera tephrodes*)				■	■	■	■	■	■	■		
Filaree *(Erodium circutarium)*		■	■	■								
Gilias (*Gilia* spp.)			■	■	■							
Hedgehog cactus *(Echinocereus engelmannii)*			■	■								
Indigobush *(Dalea parryi)*				■	■							

	JAN	FEB	MAR	APR	MAY	JUN	JUL	AUG	SEP	OCT	NOV	DEC
Blue to Violet to Purple *(continued)*												
Ironwood *(Olneya tesota)*												
Locoweed *(Astragalus nuttallianus)*												
Lupine *(Lupinus sparsiflorus)*												
Monkey flower *(Mimulus bigelovii)*												
Nama *(Nama demissam)*												
Nightshade *(Solanum elaegnifolium)*												
Owl clover *(Orthocarpus purpurascens)*												
Phacelias *(Phacelia* spp.*)*												
Pincushion cactus *(Mammillaria microcarpa)*												
Smoke tree *(Psorothamnus spinosus)*												
Verbenas *(Verbena* spp.*)*												
Verbena (sand) *(Abronia villosa)*												
Greenish, Buff, Creamy, or Non-Descript												
Acacia, catclaw *(Acacia greggii)*												
Agave, Palmer's *(Agave palmeri)*												
Cholla, teddybear *(Opuntia bigelovii)*												
Christmas cactus *(Opuntia leptocaulis)*												
Dock *(Rumex hymenosepalus)*												
Desert plantago *(Plantago insularis)*												
Sotol (desert spoon) *(Dasylirion wheeleri)*												

Greenish, Buff, Creamy, or Non-descript *(continued)*	JAN	FEB	MAR	APR	MAY	JUN	JUL	AUG	SEP	OCT	NOV	DEC
Streptanthus *(Streptanthus carinatus)*		■	■	■								

*Blooms also yellow, orange, or reddish-purple

Blooming periods are common, not absolute, times of blooming, based on William G. McGinnies's *Flowering Periods for Common Desert Plants, Southwestern Arizona* (Office of Arid Lands Studies, University of Arizona). Other sources include Theodore F. Niehaus, *Flowers of the Southwest Deserts* (Southwest Parks and Monuments Association, Tucson, 1985); Natt N. Dodge, *Southwestern and Texas Wildflowers* (Houghton Mifflin Co., Boston, 1984); and Janice Emily Bowers, *100 Desert Wildflowers* (Southwest Parks and Monuments Association, Tucson, 1989). Flowering periods are average estimates only; they will vary year-to-year. Interpretations of flower colors are arbitrary and may vary.

APPENDIX 2: COMMON BIRDS OF SOUTHERN ARIZONA

BIRD/FAMILY*	SEASON	BEST HABITAT
WATERBIRDS (GREBES, HERONS, DUCKS, CRANES)		
Pied-billed grebe	All year/best Sept–April/nests here	Lakes, ponds
Great blue heron	All year/best Sept–March/nests here	Lakes, ponds, rivers
Green-winged teal	Mid-Sept–mid-April	Lakes, ponds, rivers
Mallard	Sept–April/nests here	Lakes, ponds, rivers
Northern shoveler	Sept–April/nests here	Lakes, ponds
American wigeon	Mid-Sept–April	Lakes, ponds
Ring-necked duck	Oct–April	Lakes, ponds
Ruddy duck	All year/best Sept–April/nests here	Lakes, ponds
Killdeer	All year/nests here	Lakes, ponds, rivers
American pipit	Sept–April	Lakes, ponds, rivers
VULTURES		
Turkey vulture	March–Oct	Desertscrub to grassland
BIRDS OF PREY (HAWKS, EAGLES, FALCONS, OWLS)		
Northern harrier	Mid-Sept–April/nests here	Grasslands
Cooper's hawk	All year/best mid-Sept–April/nests here	Riparian woodlands, coniferous forests
Harris' hawk	All year/nests here	Desertscrub, esp. w/saguaros
Red-tailed hawk	All year/best in winter/nests here	All habitats, esp. desertscrub, grasslands
American kestrel	All year/best Sept-April/nests here	Desertscrub to oak woodlands
Flammulated owl	April–Aug/nests here	Pine-oak woodlands
Western screech-owl	All year/nests here	Desertscrub, riparian and oak woodlands
Whiskered screech-owl	All year/nests here	Oak woodlands up to pine-oak woodlands
Great horned owl	All year/nests here	All woodland habitats, esp. open areas
Elf owl	April–mid-Aug/nests here	Desertscrub, esp. w/saguaros
GROUND BIRDS & DOVE FAMILY (QUAIL, DOVES, PIGEONS, ROADRUNNERS)		
Gambel's quail	All year/nests here	Desertscrub, grassland
Rock dove (introduced)	All year/nests here	Urban, suburban areas
Band-tailed pigeon	May–Sept/nests here	Oak woodlands up to coniferous forests
White-winged dove	Mid-Feb–mid-Sept/nests here	Desertscrub
Mourning dove	All year/nests here	Desertscrub up to oak woodlands
Inca dove	All year/nests here	Urban, suburban areas
Greater roadrunner	All year/nests here	Desertscrub

Bird/*Family**	Season	Best Habitat
Nighthawks		
Lesser nighthawk	Mid-April–mid-Oct/nests here	Desertscrub to grasslands
Common nighthawk	June–Aug/nests here	High grasslands
Common poorwill	April–mid-Oct/nests here	Desertscrub to oak woodlands
Whip-poor-will	May–Sept/nests here	Oak woodland to coniferous forests
Hummingbirds		
Broad-billed hummingbird	March–Sept/nests here	Riparian woodlands
Magnificent hummingbird	April–mid-Oct/nests here	Riparian, pine-oak woodlands, coniferous forests
Black-chinned hummingbird	Mid-April–mid-Oct/nests here	Riparian, esp. pine-oak woodlands
Anna's hummingbird	All year/best Aug–March/ nests here	Urban, desertscrub, low riparian
Costa's hummingbird	Mid-Jan–April/nests here	Desertscrub, washes, grasslands
Broad-tailed hummingbird	Mid-April–Sept/nests here	Pine-oak woodlands to coniferous forests
Rufous hummingbird	Mid-July–mid-Sept	Mountain canyons, esp. pine-oak woodlands
Woodpeckers		
Acorn woodpecker	All year/nests here	Riparian, oak and pine-oak woodlands
Gila woodpecker	All year/nests here	Desertscrub, urban, suburban areas
Ladder-backed woodpecker	All year/nests here	Desertscrub, riparian, oak woodlands
Red-shafted flicker	All year/nests here	Riparian, oak woodlands up to coniferous forest
Gilded flicker	All year/nests here	Desertscrub, esp. w/saguaros
Flycatchers		
Western wood-pewee	May–Sept/nests here	Riparian woodlands, esp. in montane
Cordilleran flycatcher	Sept–mid-May/nests here	Riparian woodlands, esp. pine-oak, conifer
Black phoebe	All year/nests here	Riparian woodlands, all elevations
Say's phoebe	All year/nests here	Desertscrub up to oak woodlands, esp. ponds
Vermilion flycatcher	All year/best Feb–Oct/ nests here	Riparian woodlands, esp. lower elevations
Ash-throated flycatcher	April–August/nests here	Oak woodlands

BIRD/*FAMILY**	SEASON	BEST HABITAT
***FLYCATCHERS* (continued)**		
Brown-crested flycatcher	May–July	Riparian woodlands, to mid-elevations
Cassin's kingbird	Mid-March–Sept/nests here	High grasslands, riparian woodlands
Western kingbird	Mid-March–mid-Oct/nests here	Desertscrub to oak woodlands
SWIFTS AND SWALLOWS		
White-throated swift	April–Sept/nests here	Canyons, rocky areas
Purple martin	Mid-May–Sept/nests here	Desertscrub, esp. w/saguaros
Violet-green swallow	Mid-Feb–Oct/nests here	Oak woodlands to coniferous forests
Cliff swallow	March–August/nests here	Desertscrub to grasslands, esp. structures
Barn swallow	Mid-March–mid-Oct/nests here	Desertscrub to grasslands
JAYS AND RAVENS		
Steller's jay	All year/nests here	Pine-oak woodland to coniferous forests
Gray-breasted jay	All year/nests here	Oak woodlands
Common raven	All year/nests here	Desertscrub to coniferous forests
SMALL WOODLAND BIRDS (CHICKADEES, VERDINS, WARBLERS, VIREOS, GNATCATCHERS, ETC.)		
Mountain chickadee	All year/nests here	Coniferous forests
Bridled titmouse	All year/nests here	Riparian, oak woodlands
Verdin	All year/nests here	Desertscrub, riparian
Bushtit	All year/nests here	Oak, pine-oak woodlands, esp. riparian
White-breasted nuthatch	All year/nests here	Pine-oak woodland to coniferous forests
Pygmy nuthatch	All year/nests here	Coniferous forests
Brown creeper	All year/nests here	Pine-oak woodland to coniferous forests
Ruby-crowned kinglet	All year/best Oct–April/nests here	Oak to pine-oak woodlands
Black-tailed gnatcatcher	All year/nests here	Desertscrub, esp. washes
Bell's vireo	Mid-March–mid-Sept/nests here	Desertscrub to oak woodland, riparian
Solitary vireo	Mid-April–Sept/nests here	Oak, pine-oak woodlands, riparian
Hutton's vireo	All year/best mid-March–mid-Oct/nests	Oak, pine-oak woodlands

Bird/*Family**	Season	Best Habitat
Small Woodland Birds (continued)		
Warbling vireo	April–Sept/nests here	Riparian, esp. pine-oak woodlands
Virginia's warbler	Mid-April–August/nests here	Oak woodlands, esp. dense brush
Lucy's warbler	March–August/nests here	Desertscrub riparian
Yellow warbler	April–Sept/nests here	Riparian woodlands, esp. mid-elevation
Yellow-rumped warbler	All year/nests here	Coniferous forests
Black-throated gray warbler	April–mid-Oct/nests here	Oak to pine-oak woodlands
Grace's warbler	April–Sept/nests here	Pine-oak woodlands, coniferous forest
Common yellowthroat	All year/best April–Oct/nests here	Low-elevation moist areas (riparian, fields)
Red-faced warbler	Mid-April–Aug/nests here	Pine-oak woodlands, coniferous forest
Painted redstart	April–mid-Sept/nests here	Pine-oak woodlands, esp. riparian
Yellow-breasted chat	Mid-April–Sept/nests here	Low-elevation riparian woodlands
Olive warbler	April–Sept/nests here	Coniferous forest, esp. ponderosa pine
Wrens		
Cactus wren	All year/nests here	Desertscrub, esp. w/cholla cactus
Rock wren	All year/nests here	Desertscrub to coniferous forest, esp. rocky
Canyon wren	All year/nests here	Desertscrub to coniferous forest—canyons
Bewick's wren	All year/nests here	Riparian woodland, esp. oak woodlands
House wren	All year/best Sept–April/ nests here	Riparian woodland, up to coniferous forest
Thrushes (Robins, Mockingbirds, Thrashers)		
Western bluebird	All year/best Oct–March/ nests here	Oak, pine-oak woodlands
Hermit thrush	All year/nests here	Riparian, oak woodland to coniferous forest
American robin	All year/nests here	Oak woodland to coniferous forests

BIRD/*FAMILY**	SEASON	BEST HABITAT
THRUSHES (continued)		
Northern mockingbird	All year/nests here	Desertscrub to grasslands, esp. urban areas
Bendire's thrasher	All year/nests here	Desertscrub
Curve-billed thrasher	All year/nests here	Desertscrub, esp. w/cholla cactus
Crissal thrasher	All year/nests here	Desertscrub, riparian, oak woodland
SILKY FLYCATCHERS		
Phainopepla	All year/nests here	Desertscrub, esp. w/trees, mistletoe
SHRIKES		
Loggerhead shrike	All year/best Oct–March/ nests here	Desertscrub to oak woodlands, open areas
FARMLAND/URBAN BIRDS (STARLINGS, GRACKLES, BLACKBIRDS, COWBIRDS)		
European starling	All year/nests here	Desertscrub to grasslands, esp. farmland
Red-winged blackbird	All year/nests here	Marshes, farmlands near riparian
Yellow-headed blackbird	Mid-Aug–mid-May/nests here	Marshes, farmlands, feedlots
Brewer's blackbird	Oct–mid-April	Marshes, farmlands, feedlots, urban areas
Great-tailed grackle	All year/nests here	Farmlands, feedlots, urban areas
Bronzed cowbird	Mid-May–July/breeds here	Desertscrub to oak woodlands, also feedlots
Brown-headed cowbird	All year/breeds here	Riparian and oak woodlands, also feedlots
TANAGERS		
Hepatic tanager	Mid-April–mid-Sept/nests here	Oak woodlands to coniferous forest
Summer tanager	Mid-April–mid-Sept/nests here	Low-elevation riparian wood-lands
Western tanager	May–Sept/nests here	Coniferous forests
MEADOWLARKS, LARKS, ORIOLES		
Horned lark	All year/nests here	Grasslands, farmlands
Eastern meadowlark	All year/nests here	Grasslands, farmlands

Bird/*Family**	Season	Best Habitat
Meadowlarks, Larks, Orioles (continued)		
Western meadowlark	Oct–mid-April/nests here	Grasslands, farmlands
Hooded oriole	April–mid-Sept/nests here	Riparian woodlands, up to oak woodlands
Bullock's northern oriole	April–Aug/nests here	Riparian woodlands, up to oak woodlands
Scott's oriole	April–mid-Aug/nests here	Grasslands to pine-oak woodlands
Seed Eaters (Cardinals, Grosbeaks, Sparrows, Finches)		
Northern cardinal	All year/nests here	Desertscrub, esp. riparian, urban areas
Pyrrhuloxia	All year/nests here	Desertscrub, esp. w/dense mesquites
Black-headed grosbeak	April–Sept/nests here	Oak woodlands to coniferous forest
Blue grosbeak	June–Sept/nests here	Desertscrub to grassland, esp. mesquites
Varied bunting	June–Aug/nests here	Desertscrub, esp. riparian
Green-tailed towhee	Mid-Sept–April	Desertscrub to oak woodlands, brushy areas
Rufous-sided towhee	All year/nests here	Oak woodlands to coniferous forests
Canyon towhee	All year/nests here	Desertscrub to oak woodlands, rocky areas
Abert's towhee	All year/nests here	Low-elevation riparian woodlands
Botteri's sparrow	July–mid-Sept/nests here	Grasslands, esp. native w/mesquites
Cassin's sparrow	All year, best July–Sept/nests here	Grasslands, esp. w/mesquites
Rufous-crowned sparrow	All year/nests here	Desertscrub to oak woodlands
Chipping sparrow	All year/best Sept–April/nests here	Grasslands to oak woodlands, esp. brushy
Brewer's sparrow	Sept–April	Desertscrub to grasslands, esp. open areas
Vesper sparrow	Oct–mid-April	Desertscrub to grasslands, esp. open areas
Lark sparrow	All year/nests here	Desertscrub to grasslands
Black-throated sparrow	All year/nests here	Desertscrub, grasslands
Lark bunting	Aug–mid-May	Desertscrub to grasslands, esp. open areas
Savannah sparrow	Sept–April	Grasslands, also agricultural fields

BIRD/*FAMILY**	SEASON	BEST HABITAT
SEED EATERS (continued)		
Grasshopper sparrow	All year/nests here	Grasslands, esp. native, also agricultural
Song sparrow	All year/nests here	Riparian woodlands, to mid-elevations
Lincoln's sparrow	Mid-Sept–April	Desertscrub brushy areas, also urban areas
White-crowned sparrow	Oct–April	Desertscrub to oak woodlands, brushy areas
Dark-eyed junco	Nov–March	Oak woodlands to coniferous forests
Yellow-eyed junco	All year/nests here	Oak woodlands to coniferous forests
Chestnut-collared longspur	Oct–March	Grasslands
House finch	All year/nests here	Desertscrub to pine-oak woodlands, urban
Lesser goldfinch	All year/nests here	Riparian woodlands, up to oak woodlands
House sparrow (introduced)	All year/nests here	Any human-inhabited areas

*With apologies to systematists, we have rearranged the bird groupings somewhat to make an easier-to-use guide for beginning birders or for non-birders who are just curious about certain birds. N.B. In the season listings above, a listing such as "April–Sept" means the beginning of April through the end of September. Also, the months refer to the times these birds are expected and most common; the birds may be present but uncommon other times or nature will always surprise us, so use this list as a guideline only. Refer to *Davis and Russell's Finding Birds in Southeast Arizona* (Tucson Audubon Society, Tucson, 1995) for the most detailed listings of all recorded birds of our area, their habitats, and flight schedules.

APPENDIX 3: MAMMALS OF SOUTHERN ARIZONA

OPOSSUMS (ORDER MARSUPIALIA)

Virginia opossum *(Didelphis virginiana)*

SHREWS (ORDER INSECTIVORA)

Gray shrew (*Notiosorex crawfordi*)
Arizona shrew (*Sorex arizonae*)
Dusky shrew (*Sorex monticolus*)

BATS (ORDER CHIROPTERA)

Peter's ghost-faced bat (*Mormoops megalophyll*)
California leaf-nosed bat (*Macrotis californicus*)
Long-tongued bat (*Choeronycteris mexicana*)
Long-nosed bat (*Leptonycteris curasoae*)
California myotis (*Myotis californicus*)
Yuma myotis (*Myotis yumanensis*)
Cave myotis (*Myotis velifer*)
Southwestern myotis (*Myotis anriculus*)
Fringed myotis (*Myotis thysanodes*)
Silver-haired bat (*Lasionycteris noctivagans*)
Western pipistrelle (*Pipistrellus hesperus*)
Big brown bat (*Eptesicus fuscus*)
Red bat (*Lasiurus blossevillii*)
Hoary bat (*Lasiurus cinereus*)
Southern yellow bat (*Lasiurus xanthinus*)
Spotted bat (*Euderma maculatum*)
Townsend's big-eared bat (*Plecotus townsendii*)
Pallid bat (*Antrozous pallidus*)
Brazilian free-tailed bat (*Tadarida brasiliensis*)
Pocketed free-tailed bat (*Nyctinomops femorosacca*)
Big free-tailed bat (*Nyctinomops macrotis*)
Underwood's mastiff bat (*Eumops underwoodi*)
Western mastiff bat (*Eumops perotis*)

HARES AND RABBITS (ORDER LAGOMORPHA)

Desert cottontail (*Sylvilagus audubonii*)
Eastern cottontail *(Sylvilagus floridanus)*
Black-tailed jackrabbit *(Lepus californicus)*
Antelope jackrabbit (*Lepus alleni*)

RODENTS (ORDER RODENTIA)

Harris' antelope squirrel (*Ammospermophilus harrisii*)
Rock squirrel (*Spermophilus variegatus*)
Round-tailed ground squirrel (*Spermophilus tereticaudus*)
Abert's squirrel (*Sciurus aberti*)
Arizona gray squirrel (*Sciurus arizonensis*)
Cliff chipmunk (*Eutamias dorsalis*)
Botta's pocket gopher (*Thomomys bottae*)
Southern pocket gopher (*Thomomys umbrinus*)
Silky pocket mouse (*Perognathus flavus*)
Arizona pocket mouse (*Perognathus amplus*)
Apache pocket mouse (*Perognathus apache*)
Desert pocket mouse (*Chaetodipus penicillatus*)
Bailey's pocket mouse (*Chaetodipus baileyi*)
Rock pocket mouse (*Chaetodipus intermedius*)
Hispid pocket mouse (*Chaetodipus hispidus*)
Merriam's kangaroo rat (*Dipodomys merriami*)
Banner-tailed kangaroo rat (*Dipodomys spectabilis*)
Desert kangaroo rat (*Dipodomys deserti*)
Ord's kangaroo rat (*Dipodomys ordi*)
Western harvest mouse (*Reithrodontomys megalotis*)
Plains harvest mouse (*Reithrodontomys montanus*)
Fulvous harvest mouse (*Reithrodontomys fulvescens*)
Deer mouse (*Peromyscus maniculatus*)
Cactus mouse (*Peromyscus eremicus*)
Mesquite mouse (*Peromyscus merriami*)
Brush mouse (*Peromyscus boylei*)
White-footed mouse (*Peromyscus leucopus*)
Southern grasshopper mouse (*Onychomys torridus*)
White-throated woodrat (*Neotoma albigula*)
Arizona cotton rat (*Sigmodon arizonae*)
Porcupine (*Erethizon dorsatum*)

CARNIVORES (ORDER CARNIVORA)

Coyote (*Canis latrans*)
Kit fox (*Vulpes macrotis*)
Gray fox (*Urocyon cinereoargenteus*)
Black bear (*Ursus americanus*)
Ringtail (*Bassariscus astutus*)
Raccoon (*Procyon lotor*)
Coati (*Nasua nasua*)
Badger (*Taxidea taxus*)
Spotted skunk (*Spilogale gracilis*)
Striped skunk (*Mephitis mephitis*)
Hooded skunk (*Mephitis macroura*)
Hog-nosed skunk (*Conepatus mesoleucus*)
Mountain lion (*Felis concolor*)
Bobcat (*Felis rufus*)
Jaguar (*Felis onca*)

HOOVED ANIMALS (ORDER ARTIODACTYLA)

Javelina (*Tayassu tajacu*)
Mule deer (*Odocoileus hemionus*)
White-tailed deer (*Odocoileus virginianus*)
Pronghorn (*Antilocapra americana*)
Desert bighorn sheep (*Ovis canadensis deserti*)

*This list is not intended to be a complete catalog of southern Arizona's mammals. Adapted from *Mammals of the Southwestern United States and Northwestern Mexico* by E. Lendell Cockrum and Yar Petryszyn (Treasure Chest Publications, Tucson, 1992). For a complete treatment of mammals of Arizona, see Donald F. Hoffmeister, *Mammals of Arizona* (University of Arizona Press, Tucson, 1986).

APPENDIX 4: REPTILES & AMPHIBIANS OF SOUTHERN ARIZONA

FROGS AND TOADS

Pelobatidae (Spadefoot Toads)
- Couch's spadefoot toad (*Scaphiopus couchii*)
- Southern spadefoot toad (*Scaphiopus multiplicatus*)
- Plains spadefoot toad (*Scaphiopus bombifrons*)

Leptodactylidae (Neotropical Frogs)
- Barking frog (*Hylactophryne augusti*)

Bufonidae (True Toads)
- Sonoran desert toad (*Bufo alvarius*)
- Woodhouse toad (*Bufo woodhouseii*)
- Great Plains toad (*Bufo cognatus*)
- Green toad (*Bufo debilis*)
- Sonoran green toad (*Bufo retiformis*)
- Red-spotted toad (*Bufo punctatus*)

Hylidae (Treefrogs & Allies)
- Canyon treefrog (*Hyla arenicolor*)
- Mountain treefrog (*Hyla eximia*)
- Northern casque-headed frog (*Pternohyla fodiens*)

Microhylidae (Narrow-mouthed Toads and Allies)
- Plains narrow-mouthed toad (*Gastrophryne olivacea*)

Ranidae (True Frogs)
- Lowland leopard frog (*Rana yavapaiensis*)
- Chiricahua leopard frog (*Rana chiricahuensis*)
- Ramsey Canyon leopard frog (*Rana subaquauocalis*)
- Plains leopard frog (*Rana blairi*)
- Rio Grande leopard frog (introduced) (*Rana berlandieri*)
- Bullfrog (introduced) (*Rana catesbeiana*)

TURTLES

Kinosternidae (Musk and Mud Turtles)
- Sonoran mud turtle (*Kinosternon sonoriense*)
- Yellow mud turtle (*Kinosternon flavescens*)

Emydidae (Freshwater and Marsh Turtles)
- Western box turtle (*Terrapene ornata*)
- Sliders (introduced) (*Trachemys scripta*)

Testudinidae (Land Tortoises)
- Desert tortoise (*Xerobates agassizi*)

LIZARDS

Helodermatidae (Beaded Lizards)
- Gila monster (*Heloderma suspectum*)

Gekkonidae (Geckos)
- Western banded gecko (*Coleonyx variegatus*)
- Mediterranean gecko (introduced) (*Hemidactylus turcicus*)

Iguanidae (Iguanid Lizards)
- Desert iguana (*Dipsosaurus dorsalis*)
- Common collared lizard (*Crotaphytus collaris*)
- Leopard lizard (*Gambelia wislizenii*)
- Common chuckawalla (*Sauromalus obesus*)
- Greater earless lizard (*Cophosaurus texanus*)
- Lesser earless lizard (*Holbrookia maculata*)
- Zebra-tailed lizard (*Callisaurus draconoides*)
- Bunch-grass lizard (*Sceloporus scalaris*)
- Mountain (Yarrow's) spiny lizard (*Sceloporus jarrovii*)
- Eastern fence lizard (*Sceloporus undulatus*)
- Desert spiny lizard (*Sceloporus magister*)

LIZARDS **(continued)**

Clark's spiny lizard (*Sceloporus clarkii*)
Long-tailed brush lizard (*Urosaurus graciosus*)
Tree lizard (*Urosaurus ornatus*)
Side-blotched lizard (*Uta stansburiana*)
Regal horned lizard (*Phrynosoma solare*)
Desert horned lizard (*Phrynosoma platyrhinos*)

Scincidae (Skinks)
Mountain skink (*Eumeces tetragrammus*)
Great Plains skink (*Eumeces obsoletus*)

Teidae (Whiptail Lizards & Allies)
Western whiptail lizard (*Cnemidophorus tigris*)
Sonoran spotted whiptail lizard (*Cnemidophorus sonorae*)
Gila spotted whiptail lizard (*Cnemidophorus flagellicaudus*)
Desert grassland whiptail lizard (*Cnemidophorus uniparens*)
Canyon spotted whiptail lizard (*Cnemidophorus burti*)
Little striped whiptail lizard (*Cnemidophorous inornatus*)
Chihuahuan spotted whiptail lizard (*Cnemidophorus exsanguis*)

Anguidae (Alligator Lizards and Allies)
Madrean alligator lizard (*Elgaria kingi*)

Xantusiidae (Night Lizards)
Night lizard (*Xantusia vigilis*)

SNAKES

Leptotyphlopidae (Blind Snakes)
Western blind snake (*Leptotyphlops humilis*)
Texas blind snake (*Leptotyphlops dulcis*)
Boidae (Boas)
Rosy boa (*Lichanura trivirgata*)
Colubridae (Colubrid Snakes)
Black-necked garter snake (*Thamnophis cyrtopsis*)
Mexican garter snake (*Thamnophis eques*)
Checkered garter snake (*Thamnophis marcianus*)
Mexican hognose snake (*Heterdon nasicus*)
Sonoran whipsnake (*Masticophis bilineatus*)
Coachwhip (*Masticophis flagellum*)
Desert patch-nosed snake (*Salvadora hexalepis*)
Mountain patch-nosed snake (*Salvadora grahamiae*)
Green rat snake (*Senticolis triaspis*)
Regal ringneck snake (*Diadophis punctatus*)
Gopher (bull) snake (*Pituophis melanoleucus*)
Glossy snake (*Arizona elegans*)
Long-nosed snake (*Rhinocheilus lecontei*)
Common (desert) kingsnake (*Lampropeltis getula*)
Sonoran mountain kingsnake (*Lampropeltis pyromelana*)
Saddled leaf-nosed snake (*Phyllorhynchus browni*)
Spotted leaf-nosed snake (*Phyllorhynchus decurtatus*)
Sonoran (thornscrub) hook-nosed snake (*Gyalopion quadrangulare*)
Chihuahuan hook-nosed snake (*Gyalopion canum*)
Western ground snake (*Sonora semiannulata*)
Western shovel-nosed snake (*Chionactis occipitalis*)
Sonoran shovel-nosed snake (*Chionactis palarostris*)
Banded burrowing (sand) snake (*Chilomeniscus cinctus*)
Vine snake (*Oxybelis aeneus*)
Sonoran lyre snake (*Trimorphodon bisculatus*)
Night snake (*Hypsiglena torquata*)
Southwestern black-headed snake (*Tantilla hobartsmithi*)

SNAKES ***(continued)***

Plains black-headed snake (*Tantilla nigriceps*)
Chihuahuan black-headed snake (*Tantilla wilcoxi*)
Mexican (Yaqui) black-headed snake (*Tantilla yaquia*)

Elapidae (Coralsnakes, Cobras, Allies)
Western coralsnake (*Micruroides euryxanthus*)

Viperidae (Rattlesnakes, Moccasins, Old World Vipers)
Massasauga (*Sistrurus catenatus*)
Western diamondback rattlesnake (*Crotalus atrox*)
Ridge-nosed rattlesnake (*Crotalus willardi*)
Rock rattlesnake (*Crotalus lepidus*)
Twin-spotted rattlesnake (*Crotalus pricei*)
Black-tailed rattlesnake (*Crotalus molossus*)
Mojave rattlesnake (*Crotalus scutulatus*)
Arizona black rattlesnake (*Crotalus viridis cerberus*)
Speckled rattlesnake (*Crotalus mitchellii*)
Tiger rattlesnake (*Crotalus tigris*)
Sidewinder rattlesnake (*Crotalus cerastes*)

This list is not intended to be a complete catalog of the reptiles and amphibians of southern Arizona. Adapted from Robert C. Stebbins, *A Field Guide to Western Reptiles and Amphibians* (Houghton Mifflin Company, Boston, 1985); Charles H. Lowe, editor, *The Vertebrates of Arizona* (University of Arizona Press, Tucson, 1964); and Howard E. Lawler, curator of reptiles and amphibians, Arizona–Sonora Desert Museum, personal communication.

APPENDIX 5: COMMON BUTTERFLIES OF SOUTHERN ARIZONA

COMMON NAME & SPECIES NAME	DESCRIPTION & COMMENTS	COMMON NECTAR PLANTS	SEASON (MOST COMMON)
COMMON BLUE *Celestrina argiolus*	Small; light blue w/dark gray margins; desertscrub to forests. Most common spring, and in hilly terrain.	Not widely known; probably *Calliandra*, *Baccharis* spp., *Ceonothus* spp., etc.	All Year (Spring)
ISOLA BLUE *Hermiargus isola*	Small; lilac-blue w/brown margins; low desertscrub to high forests, very widespread. Common in warm months.	*Baccharis* spp. & fairy duster (*Calliandra eriophylla*)	All year (Spring–Summer)
PYGMY BLUE *Brephidium exile*	Small (15 mm); copper w/blue sheen; desertscrub to woodlands, especially disturbed areas. Most common in summer. Our smallest butterfly.	*Baccharis, Bidens,* & *Acacia* spp., tumbleweed (*Saisola kali*)	All year (Summer)
COMMON GRAY HAIRSTREAK *Strymon melinus*	Small; dark gray w/orange-red eyespots; "hairs" on hind-wings; desertscrub to forests, also cities. Fall; hairstreaks rub wings together.	*Baccharis, Lantana, Verbena* spp.	All year (Fall)
GREAT BLUE HAIRSTREAK *Atlides halesus*	Medium; irridescent blue; hairs on hind-wings; males favor hilltop trees in p.m.; desertscrub to woodlands. Common spring/late summer in canyons.	*Baccharis, Chrysothamnus* & *Senecio* spp.	Feb through Nov
BUCKEYE *Junonia coenia*	Medium; brown/gray w/3 eyespots per side; flap-flap-glide flight; desert-scrub to pine/oak woodland. Most common April through August.	*Verbena, Lantana, Senecio,* & *Baccharis* spp.	All year (Spring–Summer)
TEXAS CRESENTSPOT *Anthanassa texana*	Small; brownish w/light & orange spots; desertscrub to mountain canyons; cities, moist areas, riparian areas. Most common April through September.	*Verbena,* desert marigold (*Baileya multiradiata*)	All year (Spring–Fall)

COMMON NAME & SPECIES NAME	DESCRIPTION & COMMENTS	COMMON NECTAR PLANTS	SEASON (MOST COMMON)
AMERICAN PAINTED LADY *Vanessa virginiensis*	Medium; reddish orange complex patterns w/2 eyespots on underwing; desertscrub to forests. Most common late summer, early fall.	*Cirsium, Bidens, Baccharis* & *Chrysothamnus* spp.	All year (Summer–Fall)
VARIEGATED FRITILLARY *Euptoieta claudia*	Medium; dull orange, checkered, w/black dots on outer wings; grasslands; perches w/wings apart. Common in fall; often only butterfly on warm winter days.	*Baccharis, Senecio,* & *Chrysothamnus* spp.	All year (Fall)
RED ADMIRAL *Vanessa atalanta*	Medium; red wing stripes, brown background; desertscrub to oak woodlands. Seen in ones & twos during winter by creeks.	*Baccharis* spp; *Chrysothamnus sauseosus*	All year (Winter)
LANCINIA CHECKERSPOT *Chlosyne lacinia*	Medium; brownish with lighter hind wing stripes; citified, desertscrub to forests; males like hilltops. Most common late summer & fall.	*Baccharis* & *Bidens* spp.	Feb through Oct
LEILIA HACKBERRY *Asterocampa leilia*	Medium; copper w/brown forewing-tips & white/black spots; along washes w/desert hackberry shrubs. Desertscrub washes. Broods through season.	Sap and rotting fruit, but will visit some nectar (*Baccharis sarathroides*)	Mar through Nov
MOUNTAIN HACKBERRY *Asterocampa celtis*	Medium; copper w/black-tipped forewings; along watercourses w/hackberry trees (mountain canyons). Late spring and fall broods.	Sap and rotting fruit	May through Oct
GULF FRITILLARY *Agraulis vanillae*	Medium; bright orange w/silvery spots; desertscrub and cities (gardens). Common April through October.	*Lantana, Verbena, Zinnia, Bidens* spp.	All year (Spring–Fall)

COMMON NAME & SPECIES NAME	DESCRIPTION & COMMENTS	COMMON NECTAR PLANTS	SEASON (MOST COMMON)
FATAL METALMARK *Calephelis nemesis*	Small; gray brown w/dark band on each side; weak flier; riparian areas from desertscrub to woodlands. Most common early spring through late fall.	*Lantana, Verbena, Senecio Baccharis* spp.	All year (Spring–Fall)
PALMER'S METALMARK *Apodemia palmerii*	Small; gray-brown w/red & white spots; rapid, erratic flight; desertscrub & grassland. Most common late summer. Heat tolerant.	*Lantana, Verbena* spp. & mesquites (*Prosopis* spp.)	April through Oct
MORMON METALMARK *Apodemia mormo*	Small; reddish-copper/brown/white checkered; oak woodlands to forests. Variable colors among several subspecies.	*Baccharis* & *Eriogonum* spp.	May–June & Aug–Oct
QUEEN *Danaus gilippus*	Large; chocolate brown w/light spots; desertscrub and foothill canyons, up to about 6,500 ft. Common in summer. Roosts in grasses.	*Asclepias, Zinnia* & *Baccharis* spp.; *Chrysothamnus nauseosus*	All year (Summer)
MONARCH *Danaus plexippus*	Large; orange with black webbing; lazy-appearing cruising flight; desertscrub to forests. Most common during late summer migration.	*Asclepias, Zinnia* & *Baccharis* spp. *Chrysothamnus nauseosus*	All year (Late Summer)
CHECKERED SKIPPER *Pyrgus albescens*	Small; dull gray w/white checkers; low, rapid flight; lands on ground often; desertscrub to forests. Favors gray & white strata.	Clovers (*Tribolium* spp.), variety of nectar	All year (Spring–Summer)

COMMON NAME & SPECIES NAME	DESCRIPTION & COMMENTS	COMMON NECTAR PLANTS	SEASON (MOST COMMON)
ORANGE SKIPPERLING *Copaeodes aurantiacus*	Small; bright orange; in a.m., bask in sun w/forewings together, hindwings horizontal; canyons. Common April through October; favors heat.	*Lantana, Verbena, Baccharis* spp., etc.	All year (Spring–Fall)
FUNEREAL DUSKYWING *Erynnis funeralis*	Small; dark gray-brown w/pointed forewings; males favor streambeds and high banks; all habitats. Widespread. Most common in summer.	Nightshades (*Solanum* spp.), *Baccharis* spp., etc.	All year (Summer)
FIERY SKIPPER *Hylephila phyleus*	Small; bright copper w/flame-like darker spray; desertscrub to woodland canyons. Numbers increase as grasses flourish w/rain.	Nightshades (*Solanum* spp.), *Verbena*, and cultivated alfalfa	All year (Summer)
EUFALA SKIPPER *Lerodea eufala*	Small; brown w/white specks on fore-wings; rapid flier; desertscrub to lower woodlands. Look for in gardens, farm fields. Frost sensitive.	*Lantana, Verbena,* & *Bidens* spp.	April through Nov
SNOUT BUTTERFLY *Libytheana bachmanii*	Medium; brown w/orange & white squares; angular wings; long snout; desertscrub to woodlands. Mass late-summer migrations.	*Baccharis, Chrysothamnus* spp.	All year (Late summer)
PIPEVINE SWALLOWTAIL *Battus philenor*	Medium; glossy black; holds wings still when watering; common. Spring through fall most common.	Variety of flowers, including *Lonicera* spp., *Asclepias* spp., *Ipomoea* spp.	All year (Spring–Fall)

COMMON NAME & SPECIES NAME	DESCRIPTION & COMMENTS	COMMON NECTAR PLANTS	SEASON (MOST COMMON)
GIANT SWALLOWTAIL *Papilio cresphontes*	Large; black and yellow, yellow abdomen; common in southern Arizona. Broods all seasons.	Butterfly bush (*Buddleia* spp.) Orange, citrus blossoms	Mar through Oct
TWO-TAILED SWALLOWTAIL *Papilio multicaudatus*	Large; mostly yellow w/black margins; two "tails"; oak woodlands to forests, occ. desertscrub. Conspicuous, flashy.	Variety of flowers, esp. thistles (*Cirsium* spp.)	Mar through Oct
BLACK SWALLOWTAIL *Papilio polyxenes*	Medium; black w/double row of orange spots on top of hindwing. Males common on hilltops. Early spring & mid-summer broods.	Milkweed (*Asclepias* spp.)	Mar through Oct
SARA ORANGE TIP *Anthocharis sara*	Small; white with orange forewing tips; mostly canyons and hillsides, desertscrub to oak woodland. Single, early brood.	Probably early blooming plants such as *Erigeron, Crossosoma* spp.	Feb through Mar
SLEEPY ORANGE *Eurema nicippe*	Medium/large; orange with bold black margins; males more bright; desertscrub to coniferous forests. May be found all year; summer & fall commonly.	Turpentine bush (*Ericameria laricifolia*), *Lobelia* spp.	May through Nov
SOUTHERN DOGFACE *Colias cesonia*	Medium/large; yellow with black (poodle-like face on wings); very common; desertscrub to pine forests. Common "puddle partier" during heat of the day.	Desert broom (*Baccharis sarathroides*) and others	All year (Fall)
MEXICAN SULPHUR *Eurema mexicanum*	Small/medium; pale cream, yellow & brown; abundant from desertscrub to coniferous forests. Active even in winter in lower canyons, deserts.	Turpentine bush (*Ericameria laricifolia*)	All year (Fall)

COMMON NAME & SPECIES NAME	DESCRIPTION & COMMENTS	COMMON NECTAR PLANTS	SEASON (MOST COMMON)
Cabbage Butterfly *Pieris rapae*	Medium; white w/dusky tips, spots; slow in flight; easy to approach; common along creeks, gardens. Introduced from Europe.	Turpentine bush (*Ericameria laricifolia*)	All year *(Fall)*
Checkered White *Pieris protodice*	Medium; white with dusky checkers; males frequent hilltops; hardy in hot, dry times; desertscrub to forests. In low deserts, may be seen any time of year.	*Lobelia cardinalis*, *Lepidum* sp., and *Chrysothamnus* sp.	Mar through Oct
Cloudless Sulphur *Phoebis sennae*	Large; males bright sulphur yellow; females w/black tips, spots; most common at lower elevations. Moves north with summer rains; attracted to red.	Honeysuckle (*Lonicera* spp.) and others	July through Sept
Sonoran Satyr *Cyllopsis henshawi*	Medium; rust brown w/grayish-purple cast; bounding flight; oak woodlands. Single brood centers around first of June.	Sap and rotting fruit	May through July
Nabokov's Satyr *Cyllopsis pyracmon*	Small; dull brown w/dark spots; oak woodlands; bouncy flight; most often found in shady areas. Males are slightly smaller.	Sap and rotting fruit	Aug through Oct

Descriptions & Comments: Sizes are approximations only, in relation to other butterflies; colors are for dorsal (top) of butterflies, can vary widely with individuals, and are given only for relative comparisons; ranges are variable as well and are listed here as broad guidelines.
Common Nectar Plants: These are known common food sources for adults, but there are many others for each species.
Season: These are common flight periods for adults.
Observation Tips: Butterflies fly throughout the day. In fall and winter, they need plenty of time to warm up, so start looking around noon. Certain blooming plants can be especially good butterfly "stations"; common ones are *Baccharis* plants in September/October (seep willow, desert broom), and plants in the milkweed family (*Asclepias* spp. and others) throughout spring and summer. During times of drought, station yourself near a mud puddle or pond edge. Use binoculars and stay quiet and still.
Source: This table is not intended to be a complete catalog of the butterflies of southern Arizona; it is a list of common butterflies for Pima County, and thus for much of southern Arizona. Sources for this table are Carol Cochran, editor, *The Docent Notebook: An Information and Resource Manual for Arizona–Sonora Desert Museum Docents* (Arizona–Sonora Desert Museum, Tucson, 1993); and Richard A. Bailowitz and James P. Brock, *Butterflies of Southeastern Arizona* (Sonoran Arthropod Studies, Tucson, 1991), which includes a complete checklist of Southern Arizona butterflies.

APPENDIX 6: SOUTHERN ARIZONA NATURE RESOURCES

Listings designated with an asterisk are not local but are excellent sources of information.

CONSERVATION AND EDUCATION

Arthropods
Sonoran Arthropod Studies
PO Box 5624
Tucson AZ 85703
(520) 883-3945
www.sasionline.org

Bats
*Bat Conservation International**
PO Box 162603
Austin TX 78716
(512) 327-9721
www.batcon.org

Birds
Tucson Audubon Society
300 E. University, #120
Tucson AZ 85705
(520) 629-0510

*Cornell Laboratory of Ornithology**
159 Sapsucker Woods Road
Ithaca NY 14850
(607) 254-BIRD

Butterflies
Sonoran Arthropod Studies
See "Arthropods" above.

Southeast Arizona Butterfly Association
P.O. Box 1012
Hereford, AZ 85615
http://www.naba.org/chapters/nabasa/home.html

Plants
Arizona Native Plant Society
PO Box 41206, Sun Station
Tucson AZ 85717

*Ironwood Alliance Task Force**
c/o Conservation International
1015 18th Street, NW, Suite 1000
Washington DC 20036
(202) 429-5660

Native Seeds/SEARCH
526 N. 4th Ave.
Tucson AZ 85705
(520) 622-5561
www.nativeseeds.org

Tohono Chul Park
7366 N. Paseo del Norte
Tucson AZ 85704
(520) 742-6455

Tucson Botanical Gardens
2150 N. Alvernon Way
Tucson AZ 85716
(520) 326-9686

Reptiles ("Herps")
Tucson Herpetological Society
PO Box 31531
Tucson AZ 85751
(520) 885-2555

Wolves
Preserve Arizona's Wolves (PAWS)
1413 E. Dobbins Road
Phoenix AZ 85040

Ecosystems
Arizona–Sonora Desert Museum
2021 N. Kinney Road
Tucson AZ 85743
(520) 883-3022

Arizona Nature Conservancy
1510 E. Ft. Lowell
Tucson AZ 85719
(520) 622-3861
www.nature.org

Friends of Buenos Aires
[Cooperating nonprofit of Buenos Aires National Wildlife Refuge in Altar Valley]
P.O. Box 109
Sasabe, AZ 85633
(520) 823-4251

Friends of Madera Canyon
[Cooperating nonprofit of Coronado National Forest's Madera Canyon]
P.O. Box 1203
Green Valley AZ 85622

Friends of San Pedro River
[Cooperating nonprofit of the BLM's San Pedro National Riparian Conservation Area]
1763 Paseo San Luis
Sierra Vista AZ 85635-4611
(520) 459-2555

Sky Island Alliance
[Nonprofit alliance for conservation of southern Arizona's sky island mountain ranges]
P.O. Box 41165
Tucson AZ 85717
(520) 624-7080
www.skyislandalliance.org

Tucson Audubon Society
See "Birds" listing above.

LAND AGENCIES (including nongovernment)

Arizona Nature Conservancy
738 N. 5th Ave.
Tucson AZ 85705
(520) 622-3861

Coronado National Forest
Federal Building
300 W. Congress
Tucson AZ 85701
(520) 670-4552

Bureau of Land Management, Tucson Resource Area
12661 E. Broadway
Tucson AZ 85748
(520) 722-4289

National Park Service

Organ Pipe Cactus National Monument
National Park Service Southern Arizona Group
202 E. Earl, Suite 115
Phoenix AZ 85012
(520) 387-6849 (monument headquarters)

Saguaro National Park
Old Spanish Trail, Route 8, Box 695
Tucson AZ 85730
(520) 296-8576 (Rincon Mountains Unit)
(520) 883-6366 (Tucson Mountains Unit)

U.S. Fish & Wildlife Service

Buenos Aires NWR
P.O. Box 109
Sasabe AZ 85633
(520) 823-4251

Cabeza Prieta NWR
1611 N. 2nd Avenue
Ajo AZ 85321
(520) 387-6483

Pima County Parks and Recreation

Agua Caliente Park, Ciénega Creek, and *Tucson Mountain Park*
3500 W. River Road
Tucson AZ 85713
(520) 877-6000

State Parks

Catalina State Park
11570 N. Oracle Road
Tucson AZ 85737
(520) 628-5798

Tribal Lands

Tohono O'odham Nation
P.O. Box 3001
Sells AZ 85634
(520) 383-3808 or 383-2366

MAPS
(Available at map and outdoor shops)

Santa Catalina Mountains, Rincon Mountains, and *Santa Rita Mountains* by Rainbow Expeditions

Coronado National Forest: Nogales and *Sierra Vista Ranger Districts, Catalina Ranger District* by U.S.D.A. Forest Service

Arizona Atlas & Gazetteer by DeLorme Mapping.

SUPPLIES
Naturalist Equipment (Binoculars, hand lenses, journals, etc.)
Audubon Nature Shop
See "Birds" listing above: Tucson Audubon Society

The Nature Company
4500 N. Oracle Road (Tucson Mall)
Tucson AZ 85705
(520) 292-0870

The Summit Hut
5045 E. Speedway
Tucson AZ 85712
(520) 325-1554

Wild Bird Store
See "Publications," below

PUBLICATIONS
General Southwest Nature and Recreation
Arizona Wildlife Views
2221 W. Greenway Road
Phoenix AZ 85023
Published by Arizona Game & Fish
By subscription (less than $10/year)

sonorensis
2021 N. Kinney Road
Tucson AZ 85743
(520) 883-3022
Published by the Arizona–Sonora Desert Museum
Included with membership

Technical Southwest Nature
Journal of the Southwest
1052 N. Highland Avenue
Tucson AZ 85721
(520) 621-2484
Published by the University of Arizona Southwest Center (interdisciplinary regional study)
By subscription (less than $20/year)

Topical Southwest Nature
Desert Plants
2120 E. Allen Road
Tucson AZ 85719
(520) 318-7046
By subscription (about $20/year)

Wild Bird Store Newsletter
3522 E. Grant Road
Tucson AZ 85716
(800) 396-BIRD
(520) 322-9466
Published by The Wild Bird Store
By subscription (less than $10/year)

FIELD GUIDES
Arthropods
Bailowitz, Richard A., and Brock, James P. *Butterflies of Southeastern Arizona.* Tucson: Sonoran Arthropod Studies, 1991.
Pyle, Robert Michael. *National Audubon Society Field Guide to North American Butterflies.* New York: Alfred A. Knopf, 1994.
Werner, Floyd, and Olson, Carl. *Learning About and Living with Insects of the Southwest.* Tucson: Fisher Books, 1994.

Birds

Ehrlich, Paul R., Dobkin, David S., and Wheye, Darryl. *The Birder's Handbook.* New York: Simon and Schuster, 1988.

National Geographic Society. *Field Guide to the Birds of North America.* National Geographic Society, 1987, revised edition.

Sibley, David Allen. *National Audubon Society: The Sibley Guide to Birds.* New York: Alfred A. Knopf, 2000.

Taylor, Richard Cachor. *A Birder's Guide to Southeastern Arizona.* Colorado Springs: American Birding Association, 1995, revised edition.

Tucson Audubon Society. *Davis and Russell's Finding Birds in Southeast Arizona.* Tucson: Tucson Audubon Society, 1995.

Mammals

Burt, William H. *A Field Guide to the Mammals of America North of Mexico.* Boston: Houghton Mifflin Company, Peterson Field Guides 1976.

Cockrum, E. Lendell, and Petryszyn, Yar. *Mammals of the Southwestern United States and Northwestern Mexico.* Tucson: Treasure Chest Books, 1992.

Halfpenny, James. *A Field Guide to Mammal Tracking in North America.* Boulder: Johnson Books, 1986, second edition.

Hanson, Roseann, and Hanson, Jonathan. *Basic Essentials: Animal Tracks.* Guilford, Conn.: Globe Pequot Press, 2001.

Plants

Arnberger, Leslie P. *Flowers of the Southwest Mountains.* Tucson: Southwest Parks and Monuments Association, 1982.

Bowers, Janice Emily. *100 Desert Wildflowers of the Southwest.* Tucson: Southwest Parks and Monuments Association, 1989.

———. *100 Roadside Wildflowers of Southwest Woodlands.* Tucson: Southwest Parks and Monuments Association, 1987.

———. *Shrubs and Trees of the Southwest Deserts.* Tucson: Southwest Parks and Monuments Association, 1993.

Dodge, Natt N. *Flowers of the Southwest Deserts.* Tucson: Southwest Parks and Monuments Association, 1985.

Elmore, Francis H. *Shrubs and Trees of the Southwest Uplands.* Tucson: Southwest Parks and Monuments Association, 1976.

Niehaus, Theodore F. *Southwestern and Texas Wildflowers.* Boston: Houghton Mifflin Company, Peterson Field Guides, 1984.

Petrides, George A., and Petrides, Olivia. *Western Trees.* Boston: Houghton Mifflin Company, Peterson Field Guides, 1992.

Reptiles and Amphibians

Hanson, Jonathan, and Hanson, Roseann Beggy. *50 Common Reptiles and Amphibians of the Southwest.* Tucson, Ariz.: Southwest Parks and Monuments Assoc.,1997.

Lowe, Charles H., Schwalbe, Cecil R., and Johnson, Terry B. *Venomous Reptiles of Arizona.* Phoenix: Arizona Game and Fish Department, 1986.

Stebbins, Robert C. *Western Reptiles and Amphibians.*, 2d ed. Boston: Houghton Mifflin Company, 1985.

Other

Kerry, Bob. *Scenic Tucson.* Tucson: Backcountry Books of Arizona, 1994.

SUGGESTED READING LIST

Alcock, John. *Sonoran Desert Spring.* Tucson: University of Arizona Press, 1994.

———. *Sonoran Desert Summer.* Tucson: University of Arizona Press, 1990.

Brown, David E., editor. *Biotic Communities: Southwestern United States and Northwestern Mexico.* Salt Lake City: University of Utah Press, 1995.

Dykinga, Jack W., and Bowden, Charles. *The Sonoran Desert.* New York: Harry N. Abrams, 1992.

Hanson, Roseann. *The San Pedro River.* Tucson: University of Arizona Press, 2001.

Hornaday, William T. *Camp-Fires on Desert and Lava.* Tucson: University of Arizona Press, 1983.

Krutch, Joseph Wood. *The Desert Year.* New York: Viking Press, 1951.

Murphy, Alexandra. *Graced by Pines: The Ponderosa Pine in the American West.* Missoula: Mountain Press, 1994.

Nabhan, Gary Paul. *Desert Legends: Re-Storying the Sonoran Borderlands.* New York: Henry Holt and Company, 1994.

———. *Counting Sheep: 20 Ways of Seeing Desert Bighorn.* Tucson: University of Arizona Press, 1993.

———. *Gathering the Desert.* Tucson: University of Arizona Press, 1989.

———. *The Desert Smells Like Rain.* Tucson: University of Arizona Press, 1982.

Phillips, Steven, and Patricia Wentworth Comus, editors. *A Natural History of the Sonoran Desert.* Tucson: Arizona-Sonora Desert Museum; Berkeley: University of California Press, 2000.

Pyle, Robert Michael. *Handbook for Butterfly Watchers.* Boston: Houghton Mifflin Company, 1992.

Shaw, Harley. *Soul Among Lions: The Cougar as Peaceful Adversary.* Boulder: Johnson Books, 1989.

Voices from the Pimería Alta. Nogales: Pimería Alta Historical Society, 1991.

Wilbur-Cruce, Eva Antonia. *A Beautiful, Cruel Country.* Tucson: University of Arizona Press, 1987.

Zwinger, Ann Haymond. *The Mysterious Lands.* New York: Truman Talley Books/Plume, 1989.

APPENDIX 7: KEEPING A FIELD BAG AND NOTEBOOK

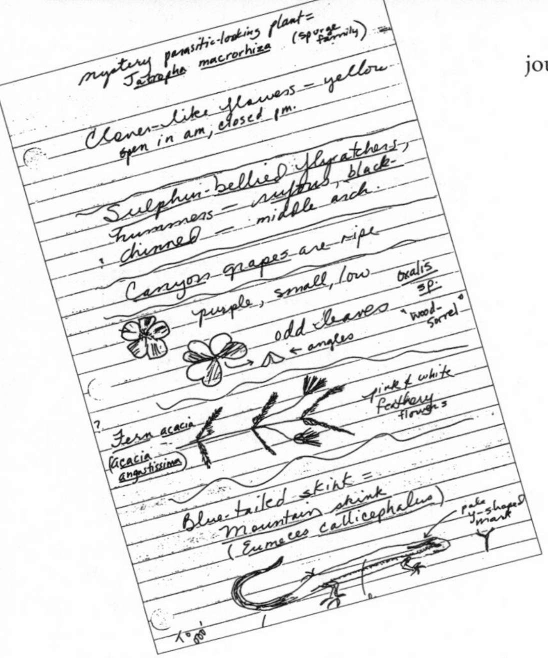

Words are powerful. The moment an ephemeral thought or observation is captured and applied to physical existence, that thought or idea or fact takes on another dimension. It has weight, can be used, passed on, accessed.

A field notebook or nature journal can greatly enhance your nature explorations. By keeping a regular journal, especially if you attend to it daily or nearly daily, you reinforce your memory of plant or animal names and their natural cycles (sometimes referred to as phenology), and you tie yourself firmly to place, be it your backyard or a whole mountain range. If you keep your journals labeled and accessible, you can refer to them and remind yourself of events, such as when you last saw a particular bird or flower or what the weather was like in a place during a specific month the previous year.

Try these ideas for field notebooks or journals:

- For free-form journals, blank books from bookstores or nature supply shops (see Appendix 6) make excellent journals. They come ruled or unruled.
- Sketches add a lot to a journal—because you really study the object in order to commit its image to paper. For a good sketching journal, try artists' acid-free paper sketching books available at good art supply stores (they usually have black covers and come in a variety of sizes). Don't be afraid to try sketching. Practice will make your drawings recognizable if not perfect.
- Use permanent, nonfading ink; look for these pens at art supply stores or some office supply stores.
- For a more serious field notebook, a three-ring binder that takes a decent-sized paper like 9 1/2 x 6 inches is very useful. You can carry small amounts of paper with you on a clipboard or a thin binder. You can archive them in thicker binders, labeled by date.
- For each entry, always record the full date, time, and place (as specific as possible so you will recognize it exactly years later). Some people also include the names of others in their party as well as weather details. Develop your own "form" for each entry; consistency will make it easier to access information in the future.
- Form a habit of making a journal entry per day. Naturalist and author Terry Tempest Williams said she lists the names of all the birds she

sees every day; naturalist Peter Friederici keeps a list of his "backyard birds" as well as a daily nature journal/field notebook. Even if you just record the weather, it's a worthwhile entry.

A field bag can be another nature experience enhancer. Once we got our "bag" together, we wondered how we did without it.

Over the years we tried many containers to transport our nature watching tools and books to field camps. At first a small metal ammo box from a surplus store held a few field guides, paper and pencils, and snake bags, but we soon outgrew it. A wooden box was considered, then abandoned because it was awkward to carry and heavy as well. We finally settled on a lightweight but durable canvas photographer's bag (by Domke), with five outside pockets. Here's what we currently have in it, ready to go at a moment's notice:

- 17 field guides (the titles change by season or current interests) for cactuses, trees, shrubs, grasses, flowers, reptiles and amphibians, regional birds, bird nests, hawks, mammals, mammal tracks, butterflies, and stars.
- 5-inch Planisphere for latitude 32°N. (A Planisphere is a simple, round star map, which can be "dialed" to match the desired date.)
- Pocket-sized species lists for birds of southern Arizona; raptors of Arizona; birds of the Santa Catalinas; birds of Patagonia–Sonoita Creek Sanctuary; birds of the Chiricahuas; plants, birds, reptiles, and mammals of the Grand Canyon; birds of the San Pedro River; mammals, reptiles and amphibians, and plants of Organ Pipe Cactus National Monument.
- Large hand lens and small pocket loupe, 25X magnification.
- Pentax mini-microscope in case.
- Small plant press.
- Taylor thermometer in field case.
- Two snake bags with ties (white pillow cases).
- Pens, pencils, pad of paper.

These items stay in the bag all the time. We are careful to put any book or tool back when we use them at home, so that when we do leave for field work, we don't have to worry that anything is missing.

We each also have our own personal "kits" for carrying nature tools on walks and hikes. Binoculars with anti-swing straps (like the BinoBuddy system) are invaluable, and small fanny packs that hold bird and plant guides, field notebook and pens, lunch and water bottles are usually more than adequate and keep the field guides at our fingertips. A compass, small magnifier, and ruler may also find their way into the fanny packs. A Swiss Army knife or a multi-tool like a Leatherman is mandatory. One trick we've learned is to keep our field notebooks handy to make observations while we're moving; if we tell ourselves "we'll jot it down at the next water break," we'll forget or our memory may not serve well enough. That's why we've gotten away from carrying large day packs unless we're out all day away from camp or the truck.

Once you compile a field kit you will immediately start adapting it. Indeed, it is an ever-evolving item that will grow with you as your knowledge of the world around you grows.

accipiter: Hawks of the forest; they have long, slender tails and short wings for maneuvering around the trees.

altricial: Describes a baby animal that is totally helpless when hatched/born, making it dependent on the parents for survival (opposite of **precocial**).

amphibian: A vertebrate animal with moist, smooth skin, such as frogs, toads, and salamanders, the larval stage of which is aquatic (with gills) but the adult stage terrestrial (with lungs).

annual: In plants, those that complete their life cycle, from germination to seed production to death, within one year. Also referred to as **ephemeral**.

arroyo: Spanish word for creek or gutter; equivalent in Southwest of a **wash** or sandy, dry creekbed.

bosque: Spanish word for "forest" or "grove"; often applied to mesquite groves.

buteo: Hawk with a broad tail and wings, often seen soaring in open country.

chaparral: A plant community comprising dense, low-growing, largely evergreen shrubs with thick, leathery leaves (such as manzanita); it is usually found between grasslands and mixed woodlands.

chubasco: Spanish word for brief, violent storms.

ciénega: Spanish word for natural spring.

composite: Describes plants with flowers that look like single flowers but are actually many individual, tiny flowers that together give the illusion of one big flower, such as sunflowers (the two flower types are rays, which look like petals, and disks, which are tiny and form the center of the "flower").

cotyledon: The first leaf (usually as a pair) that a seed sends out from its embryo.

crepuscular: Describing animals that are active primarily at dawn or dusk (see also **nocturnal** and **diurnal**).

deciduous: Describing a plant that is leafless part of the year.

desert rat: A person who is compelled to spend most of their free time exploring the deserts of the world, even or perhaps especially in summer.

dioecious: Plants that have male and female sexual parts (flowers) on separate "male" and "female" plants.

diurnal: Describing animals that are active primarily during daylight.

encinal: Spanish word used to describe a plant community comprising mostly evergreen oaks (*encino*=oak).

ephemeral: See **annual.**

herpetology: The study of reptiles and amphibians, which are known as herpetofauna.

legume: Any plant in the pea family (often with bacteria-containing nodules growing on the roots that fix nitrogen from the atmosphere); examples are mesquite trees and acacia shrubs.

monoecious: Plants that have both male and female sexual parts on individual plants, usually contained in each flower but sometimes in "male" flowers and "female" flowers.

monsoon: This word describes a seasonal wind of the Indian Ocean that blows from the southeast. Used here in southern Arizona, it describes our summer rainy season, which often blows up from the southeast.

niche: The "position," or role, an organism occupies in its community, especially related to food consumption.

nocturnal: Describing animals that are active primarily at night.

omnivore, omnivorous: An animal that feeds on both animal and plant material.

ornithology: The study of birds.

perennial: In plants, those that persist throughout the year (opposite of **annual**).

ornithophilous: Literally means "bird-loving" and is applied most often to plants whose blossoms are colored and shaped (usually long and red) to attract hummingbirds. When hummingbirds sip the nectar of ornithophilous plants, they also pollinate them.

playa: Spanish word for a shallow lake or sometimes dry lakebed, usually with no outlet.

precocial: Describing a baby animal that is alert and fully developed at birth/hatch and is able to virtually fend for itself immediately.

riparian: From Latin, meaning of or pertaining to the bank of a watercourse. More specifically, it describes a community of plants dependent on a perennial or intermittent watercourse such as a lake, river, or arroyo.

scarify: A processs by which the seed of a plant is chipped or cracked, usually by vigorous tumbling in running water; many seeds have thick outer shells that must be penetrated in order for the seed to germinate.

semelparity: Describing a plant that uses all of its energy to produce one set of flowers and seeds and then dies.

symbiosis: The process by which two unrelated organisms "live together" but to varying degrees of benefit. Types of symbiosis are parasitism, mutualism, and commensalism.

transpiration: Evaporation of water from leaves and other plant parts.

wash: Sandy, dry creekbed; also called an arroyo in Spanish.

xerophyte: Something, especially plants, adapted specifically to live in arid conditions ("lover of dryness").

Sources

Exploring the Nature of Southern Arizona

Historical and geographic definitions of deserts: Ruth Kirk, *Desert: The American Southwest* (Houghton Mifflin Co., Boston, 1973).

Desert and mountain habitat variations in temperature and rainfall: Charles H. Lowe, editor, *The Vertebrates of Arizona, with Major Section on Arizona Habitats* (University of Arizona Press, Tucson, 1980).

Climb up the Rincon Mountains and views of Apachería: Gary Paul Nabhan, *Saguaro: A View of Saguaro National Monument and the Tucson Basin* (Southwest Parks and Monuments Association, Tucson, 1986).

Sonoran Desert climate: Lowe, *The Vertebrates of Arizona.* David Lazaroff, *Sabino Canyon* (University of Arizona Press, Tucson, 1994).

Southern Arizona biotic communities: Lowe, *The Vertebrates of Arizona,* for descriptions of specific habitat types by flora and for typical vertebrate representatives. Examples of habitat types along the Catalina Highway were adapted from the Arizona–Sonora Desert Museum's "A Guide to the Mt. Lemmon Highway," *sonorensis,* Summer 1994.

Arizona wildlife and plant species numbers: mammals, Lowe, *The Vertebrates of Arizona*; birds, G. Monson and A. R. Phillips, *Annotated Checklist of the Birds of Arizona* (University of Arizona Press, Tucson, 1981); reptiles and amphibians, Lowe, *The Vertebrates of Arizona*; plants, Thomas H. Kearney and Robert H. Peebles, *Arizona Flora* (University of California Press, Berkeley, 1960).

Wildlife viewing tips: Adapted from Gerry Perry, "Wildlife Through the Looking Glass," *Arizona Wildlife Views,* February, 1995.

January

Seed scarification: Carol Cochran, editor, *The Docent Notebook: An Information and Resource Manual for Arizona–Sonora Desert Museum Docents* (Arizona–Sonora Desert Museum, Tucson, 1993). Most successful seed scarification and germination occurs after summer thunderstorms; seeds that germinate after winter flash floods would successfully develop into seedlings only if the climate remains mild.

Creosote bushes (*Larrea tridentata*) at Yucca Flats: Gary Paul Nabhan, *Gathering the Desert* (University of Arizona Press, Tucson, 1986).

MIMICRY IN THE FAMILY *MIMIDAE*: John K. Terres, *The National Audubon Society Encyclopedia of Birds* (Alfred A. Knopf, New York, 1980). National Geographic Society, *Field Guide to the Birds of North America* (National Geographic Society, Washington, D.C., 1987).

HARRIS' HAWK (*PARABUTEO JAMAICENSIS*) POLYANDRY: John Alcock, *Sonoran Desert Summer* (University of Arizona Press, Tucson, 1990). J. C. Bednarz, "Cooperative hunting in Harris' hawks," *Science* 239 (1988): 1525–1527.

BINOCULAR ASTRONOMY: Patric Moore, *Exploring the Night Sky with Binoculars* (Cambridge University Press, Cambridge, 1986). Philip Harrington, *Touring the Universe Through Binoculars* (John Wiley and Sons, New York, 1990).

MOUNTAIN SPINY LIZARD (*SCELOPORUS JARROVII*) ANTIFREEZE: Robert C. Stebbins, *A Field Guide to Western Reptiles and Amphibians*, Peterson Field Guides (Houghton Mifflin, Boston, 1985).

AFRICANIZED HONEY BEE SAFETY TIPS: Dale Turner, "Hiking with Killer Bees," *Desert Skies*, Fall-Winter 1993.

February

COSTA'S HUMMINGBIRD (*CALYPTE COSTAE*) SEASONAL RANGES: G. Monson and A. R. Phillips, *Annotated Checklist of the Birds of Arizona* (University of Arizona Press, Tucson, 1981). M. L. Avery and C. van Riper III, "Postbreeding territoriality and foraging behavior in Costa's hummingbirds (*Calypte costae*)," *The Southwestern Naturalist*, 38(4) (1993): 374–377. Studies have been inconclusive as to whether Costa's breed a second time in their summer California ranges.

ABERT'S SQUIRRELS AND PONDEROSA PINE TREES: M. A. Snyder, "Interactions between Abert's squirrel and ponderosa pine: The relationship between selective herbivory and host plant fitness," *American Naturalist*, 141(6) (1993): 866–879.

CACTUSES AND FREEZING TEMPERATURES: Gary Paul Nabhan, *Saguaro* (Southwest Parks and Monuments Association, Tucson, 1986). Frederick J. Santana, "The biology of immature *Diptera* associated with bacterial decay in the giant saguaro cactus," University of Arizona, doctoral dissertation.

GILA WOODPECKER (*MELANERPES UROPYGIALIS*) NESTING AND ECOLOGY: Richard D. Krizman,"The saguaro tree-hole environment in southern Arizona," University of Arizona, master's thesis, 1964.

ARIZONA BLACK BEAR (*Ursus americanus*) ECOLOGY: Al LeCount, 1994, retired Arizona Game and Fish biologist, personal communication. LeCount pioneered radio-tracking surveys on northern Arizona bears and found some dens that extended 20 feet into the mountainside. State black bear numbers were confirmed by John Phelps, a biologist with the Arizona Game and Fish Department, personal communication, 1995.

SAND BLAZING STARS (*MENTZELIA INVOLUCRATA*) AND GHOST FLOWERS (*MOHAVEA CONFERTIFLORA*): Robert J. Little, Jr., "Floral mimicry between two desert annuals, *Mohavea confertiflora* and *Mentzelia involucrata*," Claremont Graduate School, doctoral dissertation, 1980.

CRYPTOBIOTIC SOIL, DESERT VARNISH AND PAVEMENT: J. B. Adams, F. Palmer, J. T. Staley, "Rock weathering in deserts: mobilization and concentration of ferric iron by microorganisms," *Geomicrobiology*, 10(2) (1992): 99–114. Ann Haymond Zwinger, *The Mysterious Lands* (Truman Talley Books/ Plume, New York, 1990). J. Belnap, K. T. Harper, S. D. Warren, "Surface disturbance of cryptobiotic soil crusts," *Arid Soil Research and Rehabilitation*, 8(1) (1994): 1–8.

DESERT PUPFISH (*CYPRINODON MACULARIUS*): Boyd E. Kynard, "Preliminary study of the desert pupfish and their habitat at Quitobaquito Springs, Arizona," Cooperative National Park Resources Studies Unit, Arizona, Technical Report 1, University of Arizona, 1976.

SAGUARO ECOLOGY AND GRANDDADDY SAGUARO: Roseann Beggy Hanson and Jonathan Hanson, *Discovering the Sonoran Desert* (Arizona–Sonora Desert Museum, Tucson, 1996). Notes on Granddaddy were from personal communication with Saguaro National Park biological technician Tim Jones in 1993.

March

CARPENTER BEES (*XYLOCOPA* SPP.): *Xylocopa californica* is more common in the desert, where nest sites of yucca and agave bloom stalks occur; both sexes are black. *X. varipuncta* is larger than *X. californica*, and the females are black while the males are golden-orange with green eyes. *X. varipuncta* prefers chinaberry and mulberry trees. Floyd Werner and Carl Olson, *Insects of the Southwest* (Fisher Books, Tucson, 1994).

DESERT FLOWER ECOLOGY AND BLOOMING SCHEDULE: William G. McGinnies, *Flowering Periods for Common Desert Plants* (University of Arizona, College of Agriculture, Office of Arid Lands Studies, n.d.).

A ROSE BY ANY OTHER NAME: Natt N. Dodge, *Flowers of the Southwest Deserts* (Southwest Parks and Monuments Association, Tucson, 1985).

LUCY'S WARBLER (*VERMIVORA LUCIAE*): P. R. Ehrlich, D. S. Dobkin, and

D. Wheye, *The Birder's Handbook: A Field Guide to the Natural History of North American Birds* (Simon and Schuster, New York, 1988). The other cavity nesting warbler is the prothonotary warbler.

DESERT CANIDS: COYOTES, GRAY FOXES, KIT FOXES: E. Raymond Hall, *The Mammals of North America* (John Wiley and Sons, New York, 1981). William H. Burt and Richard P. Grossenheider, *A Field Guide to the Mammals,* Peterson Field Guide Series (Houghton Mifflin Company, Boston, 1976). E. Lendell Cockrum and Yar Petryszyn, *Mammals of the Southwestern United States and Northwestern Mexico* (Treasure Chest Publications, Tucson, 1992).

DESERT OWLS: John K. Terres, *The National Audubon Society Encyclopedia of Birds* (Alfred A. Knopf, New York, 1980). Ehrlich, Dobkin, and Wheye, *The Birder's Handbook.* National Geographic Society, *Field Guide to the Birds of North America* (National Geographic Society, Washington, D.C., 1987).

DESERT PINES: Janice Emily Bowers, *Shrubs and Trees of the Southwest Deserts* (Southwest Parks and Monuments Association, Tucson, 1994).

DESERT TORTOISES (*XEROBATES AGASSIZII*): Terry B. Johnson, "Desert Tortoise," *Arizona Wildlife Views,* April, 1986. Jeffrey M. Howland, "Desert Tortoise," *Arizona Wildlife Views,* March, 1993.

COYOTE LORE AMONG THE TOHONO O'ODHAM: Gary Paul Nabhan, *The Desert Smells Like Rain: A Naturalist in Papago Indian Country* (North Point Press, San Francisco, 1982).

April

MESQUITE BUDDING AND GAMBEL'S QUAIL: According to Carol Cochran, editor, *The Docent Notebook: An Information and Resource Manual for Arizona–Sonora Desert Docents* (Arizona–Sonora Desert Museum, Tucson, 1993), high vitamin-A content in mesquite buds, on which Gambel's quail feast in the spring, triggers the large flocks to break up and commence pairing and breeding.

MESQUITES LEAVES AND THE FROSTLESS SEASON: William G. McGinnies, *Flowering Periods for Common Desert Plants* (University of Arizona, College of Agriculture, Office of Arid Lands Studies, n.d.).

SAND FOOD (*AMMOBROMA SONORAE*) AND THE HIA C-ED O'ODHAM: Gary Paul Nabhan, *Gathering the Desert* (University of Arizona Press, Tucson, 1985). Sandfood, and possibly broomrape, have become rare, some researchers think, because the plants depend on regular harvesting for seed dispersal. The Hia C-ed O'odham, who are nearly gone, may have been the plants' main seed dispersal agents.

SYCAMORE TREES (*PLATANUS WRIGHTII*): George A. Petrides and Olivia Petrides, *Western Trees,* Peterson Field Guides (Houghton Mifflin, Boston, 1992). Ruth Kirk, *Desert: The American Southwest* (Houghton Mifflin, Boston, 1973). Francis H. Elmore, *Shrubs and Trees of the Southwest Uplands* (Southwest Parks and Monuments Association, Tucson, 1976). Janice Emily Bowers, *Shrubs and Trees of the Southwest Deserts* (Southwest Parks and Monuments Association, Tucson, 1993).

THORNS: See above references on sycamore trees; and Mark Dimmitt, curator of botany, Arizona–Sonora Desert Museum, personal communication, 1995.

MIGRATION: John K. Terres, *The National Audubon Society Encyclopedia of Birds* (Alfred A. Knopf, New York, 1980). Paul Ehrlich, David S. Dobkin, and Darryl Wheye, *The Birder's Handbook* (Simon and Schuster, New York, 1988). National Geographic Society, *Field Guide to the Birds of North America* (National Geographic Society, Washington, D.C., 1987). Data on loss of riparian habitat from the Arizona Riparian Council and Arizona Nature Conservancy.

PROCYONIDS: E. Raymond Hall, *The Mammals of North America* (John Wiley and Sons, New York, 1981). William H. Burt and Richard P. Grossenheider, *A Field Guide to the Mammals,* Peterson Field Guides (Houghton Mifflin Company, Boston, 1976). E. Lendell Cockrum and Yar Petryszyn, *Mammals of the Southwestern United States and Northwestern Mexico* (Treasure Chest Publications, Tucson, 1992). Terry A. Vaughan, *Mammalogy* (Saunders College, Philadelphia, 1978). Donald F. Hoffmeister, *Mammals of Arizona* (University of Arizona, Tucson, 1986).

TRICHOMONIASIS: J. W. Davis, R. C. Anderson, L. Karstad, and D. O. Trainer, editors, *Infectious and Parasitic Diseases of Wild Birds* (Iowa State University Press, Ames, 1971).

ENDANGERED DESERT LEGUMES: Gary Paul Nabhan and John L. Carr, editors, *Ironwood: An Ecological and Cultural Keystone of the Sonoran Desert* (Conservation International, Occasional Papers in Conservation Biology, Paper No. 1, April 1994). Mark Dimmitt, Arizona–Sonora Desert Museum, personal communication, 1995.

HISTORY AND LORE OF BABOQUIVARI: Gary Paul Nabhan, *The Desert Smells Like Rain: A Naturalist in Papago Indian Country* (North Point Press, San Francisco, 1982). John Annerino, *Adventuring in Arizona: The Sierra Club Travel Guide to the Grand Canyon State* (Sierra Club Books, San Francisco, 1991). Source of Douglas quote is Annerino.

May

SONORAN DESERT SUCCULENTS AND NIGHTTIME POLLINATORS: Gary Paul Nabhan, "A Midsummer Night's Pollination," *sonorensis*, Spring 1995. Judith L. Bronstein, "Yuccas and Yucca Moths," *sonorensis*, Spring 1995. Theodore Fleming, "Nocturnal Partners: Columnar Cacti and Nectar-Feeding Bats," *sonorensis*, Spring 1995. Alexander B. Klots, *The World of Butterflies and Moths* (George G. Harrap, London, 1958). Donald J. Borror and Richard E. White, *A Field Guide to the Insects* (Houghton Mifflin, Boston, 1970). E. Lendell Cockrum and Yar Petryszyn, *Mammals of the Southwestern United States and Northwestern Mexico* (Treasure Chest Publications, Tucson, 1992).

RATTLESNAKE ECOLOGY: Carl H. Ernst, *Venomous Reptiles of North America* (Smithsonian Institution Press, Washington, D.C., 1992). Laurence M. Klauber, *Rattlesnakes: Their Habits, Life Histories and Influence on Mankind* (University of California Press, Berkeley, 1972). A marvelous book on one of the Native American folktales involving the rattlesnake is *Soft Child: How Rattlesnake Got Its Fangs* by Joe Hayes and illustrated by Kay Sather (Harbinger House, Tucson, 1993).

HUMMINGBIRDS AND ORNITHOPHILOUS FLOWERS: David Lazaroff, *The Secret Lives of Hummingbirds* (Arizona–Sonora Desert Museum Press, Tucson, 1995). Janice Emily Bowers, *100 Roadside Wildflowers* (Southwest Parks and Monuments Association, Tucson, 1987).

BRING ON THE DROUGHT (CAM PLANTS): Carol Cochran, editor, *The Docent Notebook: An Information and Resource Manual for Arizona–Sonora Desert Museum Docents* (Arizona–Sonora Desert Museum, Tucson, 1993).

June

PINE TREES AND CONES: The cones we identify with pine trees are the mature woody female cones that contain many small seeds; for most pines it takes about two years for the seeds to mature from fertilization to viable fruits. Most pine seeds are small and winged, and dispersed by wind. George A. Petrides and Olivia Petrides, *Western Trees*, Peterson Field Guides (Houghton Mifflin, New York, 1992).

MESQUITES AND JOJOBA: Petrides and Petrides, *Western Trees.* Janice Emily Bowers, *Shrubs and Trees of the Southwest Deserts* (Southwest Parks and Monuments Association, Tucson, 1993). Carol Cochran, editor, *The Docent Handbook: An Information and Resource Manual for Arizona–Sonora Desert Museum Docents* (Arizona–Sonora Desert Museum, Tucson, 1993).

Personal notes, 1994 Mesquite Conference, "Mesquite: Regarding a Resource: Ecological and Socio-Economic Values of Mesquite Trees and their By-Products," Cascabel Community Center, sponsored by the Redington Natural Resource Conservation District.

HEAT ADAPTATIONS: Ruth Kirk, *Desert: The American Southwest* (Houghton Mifflin, Boston, 1973). Knut Schmidt-Nielsen, *Desert Animals: Psychological Problems of Heat and Water* (Dover Publications, New York, 1979).

BIGHORN SHEEP: Gary Paul Nabhan, editor, *Counting Sheep: 20 Ways of Seeing Desert Bighorn* (University of Arizona Press, Tucson, 1993). Gale Monson and Lowell Sumner, editors, *The Desert Bighorn: Its Life History, Ecology, and Management* (University of Arizona Press, Tucson, Arizona, 1980).

SUMMER LIZARDS: Robert C. Stebbins, *A Field Guide to Western Reptiles and Amphibians*, Peterson Field Guides (Houghton Mifflin, Boston, 1985).

BLACK AND WHITE OF DESERT DRESSING: John Alcock, *Sonoran Desert Summer* (University of Arizona Press, Tucson, 1990).

CICADAS: Donald J. Borror and Richard E. White, *A Field Guide to the Insects*, Peterson Field Guide Series (Houghton Mifflin Company, Boston, 1970). *The Sonoran Desert Year Calendar and Guide* (Tucson Audubon Society, Tucson, 1993).

PEREGRINE FALCON RECOVERY: Arizona Game and Fish Department press release, June 1995.

July

NECTAR-FEEDING BATS AND MIGRATION: Theodore H. Fleming, "Nocturnal Partners: Columnar Cacti and Nectar-Feeding Bats," *sonorensis*, Spring, 1995. About a dozen species of bats are found in the Sonoran Desert. The nectar-feeding lesser long-nosed bat (*Leptonycteris curasoae*) is a tropical species that spends its winters in south-central Mexico; females move north into northern Mexico and southern Arizona to give birth and feed on the nectar and pollen of saguaros, organ pipes, and cardón cactuses in the spring. In mid- and late-summer they start to move south again, following the blooms of agave plants. The long-tongued bat (*Choeronycteris mexicana*) has similar life habits.

SECOND SPRING: Carol Cochran, editor, *The Docent Notebook: An Information and Resource Manual for Arizona–Sonora Desert Museum Docents* (Arizona–Sonora Desert Museum, Tucson, 1993).

ANCIENT CONIFERS: David E. Brown, editor, *Biotic Communities of the Southwest United States and Mexico* (University of Utah Press, Salt Lake City, 1994;

Desert Plants Special Issue, Vol. 4, Nos. 1–4, 1982). Cochran, *The Docent Notebook.* Stephen Whitney, *Western Forests,* National Audubon Society Nature Guides (Alfred A. Knopf, New York, 1985). *A Correlated History of Earth* (Pan Terra, Afton, Minn., 1994). Robert A. Wallace, Jack L. King, Gerald P. Sanders, *Biology: The Science of Life* (Goodyear Publishing Co., Santa Monica, Calif., 1981).

DESERT TOADS: Ruth Kirk, *Desert: The American Southwest* (Houghton Mifflin, Boston, 1973). Cochran, *The Docent Notebook.* Robert C. Stebbins, *A Field Guide to Western Reptiles and Amphibians,* Peterson Field Guide Series (Houghton Mifflin, Boston, 1985). John S. Thompson, "The Lonely Raven" on *A Powerful Spell* (home cassette recording, 1992). Excerpt reprinted with permission.

SUMMER NESTERS: Paul Ehrlich, David S. Dobkin, Darryl Wheye, *The Birder's Handbook: A Field Guide to the Natural History of North American Birds* (Simon and Schuster, New York, 1988).

VOLATILE OILS OF CREOSOTE BUSHES: Gary Paul Nabhan, *Gathering the Desert* (University of Arizona Press, Tucson, 1986). For a full treatment of the chemistry and ecology of creosote bushes, see Tom J. Mabry, J. H. Hunziker, and D. R. Difeo, Jr., editors, *Creosote Bush: Biology and Chemistry of* Larrea *in New World Deserts* (Dowden, Hutchinson and Ross, Stroudsberg, Pa., 1977). Creosote is widely classified as *Larrea tridentata;* botanist Richard S. Felger considers the creosote of this area to be *Larrea divaricata* ssp. *tridentata,* a subspecies of the South American creosote.

LIGHTNING SAFETY STATISTICS AND TIPS: Rich Dulaney, "Lightning Safety Tips," *sonorensis,* Summer, 1993.

August

LADYBUG BEETLES: Floyd Werner and Carl Olson, *Insects of the Southwest* (Fisher Books, Tucson, 1994).

WHIPTAIL LIZARD REPRODUCTION: Jonathan M. Hanson, "Land of the Amazons," *Desert Skies,* Summer 1992.

JACKRABBITS AS COMPASSES: Knut Schmidt-Nielsen, *Desert Animals: Physiological Problems of Heat and Water* (Dover Publications, New York, 1979).

DESERT FLYING ANTS: Diana Wheeler, "Desert Ants and the Monsoon," *sonorensis,* Summer 1993.

BUG REPELLENT DANGERS: Tejal Parikh, M.D., and Kevin Carmichael, M.D., "Bug Juice Dangers," *Desert Skies,* Fall 1995.

GILA MONSTERS: David E. Brown, Neil B. Carmony, *Gila Monster: Facts and*

Folklore of America's Aztec Lizard (High-Lonesome Books, Silver City, N.M., 1991). Carl H. Ernst, *Venomous Reptiles of North America* (Smithsonian Institution Press, Washington, D.C., 1992).

TARANTULAS: Carol Cochran, editor, *The Docent Notebook: An Information and Resource Manual for Arizona–Sonora Desert Museum Docents* (Arizona–Sonora Desert Museum, Tucson, 1993).

PONDEROSA PINE "BUTTERSCOTCH" AROMA: Alexandra Murphy, *Graced by Pines* (Mountain Press, Missoula, Mont., 1994). On warm summer days, the jigsaw-puzzle bark of ponderosa pine trees (*Pinus ponderosa*) smells unmistakably like butterscotch or vanilla. The smell comes from terpenes, types of volatile oils, in the tree's sap, or resin. The amount of terpenes released increases with ambient temperature.

September

SEED DISPERSAL: Gary Paul Nabhan, *Gathering the Desert* (University of Arizona Press, Tucson, 1985). Francis H. Elmore, *Shrubs and Trees of the Southwest Uplands* (Southwest Parks and Monuments Association, Tucson, 1976).

ASPENS: Jonathan M. Hanson, "Giants Among Us," *Desert Skies*, Fall-Winter 1993. George A. Petrides and Olivia Petrides, *Western Trees*, Peterson Field Guides (Houghton Mifflin, Boston, 1992).

BATS: Donald F. Hoffmeister, *Mammals of Arizona* (University of Arizona Press, Tucson, 1986). E. Lendell Cockrum and Yar Petryszyn, *Mammals of the Southwestern United States and Northwestern Mexico* (Treasure Chest Publications, Tucson, 1992). Jonathan Hanson, "Beautiful Bats," *Desert Skies*, Winter, 1991. Ronnie Sidner, personal communication, October, 1995.

BIRD MIGRATION SCHEDULE: *Davis and Russell's Finding Birds in Southeast Arizona* (Tucson Audubon Society, Tucson, 1995).

ETHNOBOTANY OF AGAVES AND YUCCAS: Carol Cochran, editor, *The Docent Notebook: An Information and Resource Manual for Arizona–Sonora Desert Museum Docents* (Arizona–Sonora Desert Museum, Tucson, 1993). Thomas H. Kearney, Robert H. Peebles, and collaborators, *Arizona Flora* (University of California Press, Berkeley, 1960).

October

BOUNTY OF THE WILD: Gary Paul Nabhan, personal communication, 1993. There is a great little book published by the Arizona–Sonora Desert Museum called *Wild Foods of the Sonoran Desert* by Kevin Dahl of Tucson's

Native Seeds/SEARCH. It contains more information about the study area discussed in this chapter as well as about many more of the wild and domesticated southwestern food crops.

BIG CATS: Donald F. Hoffmeister, *Mammals of Arizona* (University of Arizona Press, Tucson, 1986). E. Lendell Cockrum and Yar Petryszyn, *Mammals of the Southwestern United States and Northwestern Mexico* (Treasure Chest Publications, Tucson, 1992).

BIRD CLANS: Paul Ehrlich, David S. Dobkin, Darryl Wheye, *The Birder's Handbook: A Field Guide to the Natural History of North American Birds* (Simon and Schuster, New York, 1988). "Oak Trees and Acorn Woodpeckers," *sonorensis,* Summer 1994.

CACTUS WRENS: Anders H. Anderson and Anne Anderson, *The Cactus Wren* (University of Arizona Press, Tucson, 1973).

PINACATE BEETLES: Floyd Werner and Carl Olson, *Learning About and Living with Insects of the Southwest* (Fisher Books, Tucson, 1994).

TUCSON MOUNTAINS GEOLOGY: The information from this essay came from Dave Thayer, curator of geology at the Arizona–Sonora Desert Museum. The last paragraph is taken from Roseann Beggy Hanson and Jonathan Hanson, *Discovering the Sonoran Desert* (Arizona–Sonora Desert Museum, Tucson, 1996).

COCHINEAL DYES: Werner and Olson, *Learning About and Living with Insects of the Southwest.*

November

MERRIAM'S KANGAROO RATS (*DYPODOMYS MERRIAMI*) WINTER BROODS: E. Lendell Cockrum and Yar Petryszyn, *Mammals of the Southwestern United States and Northern Mexico* (Treasure Chest Publications, Tucson, 1992).

DESERT BROOM (*BACCHARIS SAROTHROIDES*) ECOLOGY: Carol Cochran, editor, *The Docent Notebook: An Information and Resource Manual for Arizona–Sonora Desert Museum Docents* (Arizona–Sonora Desert Museum, Tucson, 1993). Janice E. Bowers, *Shrubs and Trees of the Southwest Deserts* (Southwest Parks and Monuments Association, Tucson, 1994).

REPTILES AND WINTER HIBERNATION: Robert C. Stebbins, *A Field Guide to Western Reptiles and Amphibians,* Peterson Field Guides (Houghton Mifflin, Boston, 1985).

OTHER HIBERNATORS: Donald F. Hoffmeister, *Mammals of Arizona* (University of Arizona Press, Tucson, 1986). Cockrum and Petryszyn, *Mammals of the Southwestern United States and Northwestern Mexico.*

NORTHERN HARRIER (*CIRCUS CYANEUS*) ECOLOGY: Arthur C. Bent, *Life Histories of North American Birds of Prey,* Part 1 (Dover Publications, New York, 1961).

RAPTOR EYESIGHT: John K. Terres, *The National Audubon Society Encyclopedia of Birds* (Alfred A. Knopf, New York, 1980).

WASP GALLS: James Zimmerman, retired curator of insects, New Mexico State University, personal communication, 1993.

BUFFEL GRASS (*CENCHRUS CILIARIS*): "Non-native Grass Is Called a Threat to Desert," *Arizona Daily Star,* August 21, 1994.

December

SEMELPARITY: R. E. Ricklefs, *Ecology* (Chiron Press, New York, 1979).

WILDFLOWER GERMINATION: Gary Paul Nabhan, *The Desert Smells Like Rain: A Naturalist in Papago Indian Country* (North Point Press, San Francisco, 1982). Carol Cochran, editor, *The Docent Notebook: An Information and Resource Manual for Arizona–Sonora Desert Museum Docents* (Arizona–Sonora Desert Museum, Tucson, 1993).

CACTUS ECOLOGY: Cochran, *The Docent Notebook.*

RESIDENT DESERT BIRD ECOLOGY: *Davis and Russell's Finding Birds in Southeast Arizona* (Tucson Audubon Society, Tucson, 1995). Cochran, *The Docent Notebook.*

MULE DEER AND WHITE-TAILED DEER ECOLOGY: Donald F. Hoffmeister, *Mammals of Arizona* (University of Arizona Press, Tucson, 1986). E. Lendell Cockrum and Yar Petryszyn, *Mammals of the Southwestern United States and Northwestern Mexico* (Treasure Chest Publications, Tucson, 1992).

HUMMINGBIRD FEEDER MYTHS: Peter Siminski, curator of mammalogy and ornithology, Arizona–Sonora Desert Museum, personal communication, 1993.

DESERT MISTLETOE (*PHORANDENDRON CALIFORNICUM*) ECOLOGY: Cochran, *The Docent Notebook.*

Index